MOUNTAIN WILDLIFE

MOUNTAIN WILDLIFE

Richard Perry

Stackpole Books

Published by
STACKPOLE BOOKS
Cameron and Kelker Streets
P.O. Box 1831
Harrisburg, Pa. 17105

Printed in Great Britain by arrangement with Croom Helm

ISBN 0-8117-1004-1
Library of Congress Catalog Number 80-9062

CONTENTS

ACKNOWLEDGEMENTS

Grateful acknowledgements to all those unwitting authors on whose works I have drawn freely, and in particular to Peter Matthiessen and his publishers, Chatto and Windus, for permission to quote from *The Snow Leopard*, and to his other publishers, Andre Deutsch, for similar permission in respect of *The Cloud Forest;* to Guinness Superlatives for permission to quote from their *Guide to Mountain Animals;* Ronald Kaulback and his publishers, Hodder and Stoughton, for permission to quote from *Salween;* Charles Stonor and his publishers, Hollis and Carter, for permission to quote from *The Sherpa and the Snowman;* and to Carl B. Koford and the Duke University Press of Durham N. C. for permission to quote from his 'Ecological Monograph on the Vicuna'. Also, once again, I am immensely indebted to the Reference Department of the Northumberland County Central Library.

Richard Perry
Northumberland

ILLUSTRATIONS: ACKNOWLEDGEMENTS

1, 2 and 3. Dr Alan Beaumont; 4. Robert J. Erwin, The Natural History Photographic Agency; 5. Dr Alan Beaumont; 6. Edgar T. Jones, Aquila Photographics; 7. Phillippa Scott, The Natural History Photographic Agency; 8. Dr Alan Beaumont; 9. E. K. Thompson, Aquila Photographics; 10. Dr Alan Beaumont; 11 and 12. Eric Hosking; 13. Edgar T. Jones, Aquila Photographics; 14. Dr Alan Beaumont; 15. Pamela Harrison, The Royal Society for the Protection of Birds; 16. Edgar T. Jones, Aquila Photographics; 17 and 18. Eric Hosking; 19. Dr Alan Beaumont.

TO MY WIFE

Chapter One

THE UPLANDS OF BRITAIN

It will be logical to begin at the bottom, as it were, with the lowest hills that are generally regarded as mountains: those in the British regions of Snowdonia, Cumbria and the Scottish Highlands, though there is virtually no true alpine fauna in either Snowdonia or Cumbria. Hunters must have traversed these uplands for centuries, particularly those of the Highlands when the red deer went up to the high tops in June to graze the new grasses and sedges; but there is no record of a naturalist exploring any of Britain's hills until nearly a hundred years after Gesner's botanising in the Alps. However in 1639 Thomas Johnson, botanist and apothecary, betook himself, together with an interpreter and two companions to 'our British Alps', and with the essential aid of a farmboy as guide, since 'the whole mass of the mountain was veiled in cloud', climbed Y Wyddfa, the highest peak of Snowdon, on August 3; but his prosaic account of this ascent is ambiguous, and he may actually have climed Glyder Fawr. He describes how:

> Leaving our horses and outer garments, we began to climb the mountain. The ascent at first is difficult, but after a bit a broad open space is found, but equally sloping, great precipices on the left, and a difficult climb on the right. Having climbed three miles, we at last gained the highest ridge of the mountain, which was shrouded in thick cloud. Here the way was very narrow, and climbers are horror-stricken by the rough, rocky precipices on either hand, and the Stygian marshes, both on this side and that, the greatest of which is called the 'Abode of the Devil' by the inhabitants. But when we got to such a point on the ridge that we could not proceed any further, we sat down in the midst of the clouds, and first of all we arranged in order the plants we had, at our peril, collected among the rocks and precipices, and then we ate the food we had brought with us.

Subsequently, Johnson also climbed Carnedd-Llewelyn; but though his party reached the ridge, which was enveloped in dense cloud, their guide refused to take them to the precipices, where the rarer plants were inaccessible to sheep and cattle:

> Our rustic guide feared the eagles nesting there, for they are accustomed to swoop crosswise on swift pinions before the faces of the cattle feeding on the precipices, and by suddenly frightening them, make them fall down the rocks and become their prey.

There were two other ascents of Snowdon during the seventeenth century, including one by Edward Lloyd, who achieved immortality by spotting the delicate waxy white petals of the mountain spiderwort in its only British station, although it has a wide range over the Alps and the Himalaya. Thomas Pennant, who climbed all the principal peaks of Snowdonia in the 1780s, was more descriptive than Johnson in his account of a sunrise from Y Wyddfa:

> I took much pains to see this prospect to advantage: sat up at a farm on the west till about twelve, and walked up the whole way. The night was remarkably fine and starry: towards morn, the stars faded away, and left a short interval of darkness, which was soon dispersed by the dawn of day. The body of the sun appeared most distinct, with the rotundity of the moon, before it rose high enough to render its beams too brilliant for our sight. The sea which bounded the western part was gilt by its beams, first in slender streaks, at length glowed with redness. The prospect was disclosed to us like the gradual drawing up of a curtain in a theatre. We saw more and more till the heat became so powerful, as to attract the mists from the various lakes, which in a slight degree obscured the prospect. The shadow of the mountain was flung many miles, and showed its bicapitated form; the *Wyddfa* making one, *Crib y Distill* the other head.

Although botanists were exploring the northern hills of Britain from the middle of the seventeenth century onwards it was not until the last quarter of the eighteenth century that one, George Don, traversed the highest Highland hills, including the Cairngorms, Ben Lawers and Ben Nevis. It was at that time too that a celebrated sportsman, Colonel Thomas Thornton, introduced us to the wild life of the high tops when in August 1786 he made two ascents of a 3,500-foot hill in the western Cairngorms, killing a dotterel and three and a-half brace of ptarmigan with his tiercels; and subsequently saw a snow bunting on a hill in Lochaber while stalking ptarmigan. No ornithologist or zoologist worked the Cairngorms until well on into the nintheenth century, though in 1847 J. H. Balfour, Professor of

Botany at Edinburgh University, in company with seven of his students, climbed all the highest peaks in the Cairngorms between August 9 and 16.

Naturally, these early botanists and sportsmen restricted their mountain expeditions to the summer months, and it was not until 1865 that any of them could give us an account of winter conditions on Britain's highest massif, the Cairngorms, when on December 7 the notorious zoologist and bird collector, Edward T. Booth, set out at 3.00 a.m. or 4.00 a.m. to shoot ptarmigan. He described this venture in his *Rough Notes:*

It was well on towards midday before we reached the top of the hill, and on approaching the summit, it was evident that all the surrounding ranges were enveloped in mist. . . The surface of the snow being hard and frozen, we were able to advance at some speed. . . On reaching a large patch of broken stones. . . the croak of a Ptarmigan was heard, and. . . I soon made out a white head over some large blocks of stone. . . During a slight break in the clouds. . . a drive was attempted. . . some birds were heard croaking a hundred yards or so in front of the line. On making towards the sound, intently examining the outline of the snow to obtain an early view of the pack, a large sheet of ice was overlooked and, my feet slipping, away I went downhill. Luckily there was a drift of newly-fallen snow (soft as a feather bed) about twenty feet below, and into this I pitched quite easily. . . Had it not been for the snow, I must have gone over a hundred feet to the bottom of a steep gulley. . .

It was nearly dusk, and time to be leaving the hill; so the keeper called the men together. As two of them. . . had not been seen for over an hour, I fired several shots without, however, the slightest result. . . We then started downhill, finding no little difficulty in picking our way owing to the uncertain light and extent of the tracts of frozen snow. . . After proceeding about a couple of hundred yards, a faint cry some distance to the north was audible, during one of our halts. After answering, and waiting for a few minutes, the men came up. Both were nearly beat. . . the poor fellows had been. . . cutting their way as best they could through a frozen snow-drift, till at last it was discovered impossible to proceed further, and on turning back they found. . . that some fresh snow had fallen over their tracks. . . It was lucky the shouts were heard, as . . . they were utterly incapable of reaching shelter. . . A heavy fall of snow commencing as we at last took leave of the mountain-top, it is unlikely that any tidings would have been learned concerning their fate till the snows had melted from the hills the following summer.

Chapter Two

THE HIGHLANDS OF SCOTLAND

The Cairngorms incorporate the most extensive mass of ground over 2500 feet in Britain and form the only large area of montane tundra supporting an arctic-alpine fauna and flora. Immense stony plateaus and ridges are cushioned with greyish-green fringe-moss. Vast undulating sweeps of alpine grass are pocked with wind-bared peat-hags and here and there by small lochans or lumbered with chaotic jumbles of rock outcrops and piles of boulders. Above 3,000 feet acres of shifting, ankle-deep, granite gravel are almost devoid of vegetation, except for islets of desiccated bent and sedge and small clumps of moss-campion. At 4,000 feet the waste of greyish-white gravel disappears beneath a scree of flat granite slabs, packed so closely, one overlaying another, that the way to the ultimate peaks lies from rocking slab to slab.

Glacial lochs lie 2,000 feet deep in the massif, which is riven by gloomy canyons that sunder one mountain from another; colossal punchbowl corries have been scooped out of the mountainsides, which are scarred by livid red screes, while the great corries within the massif are seamed with black burns and flood channels littered with broken scree and granite blocks and walled in by fantastically weathered black and dark-green crags and by 500-foot stacks, sphinxes and 'cheese-rings'. For much of the year these are heavily buttressed with snow, as are the lips of the corries whose crumbling edges support friezes of snow cornices many yards in breadth. A few semi-permanent snow beds, unmelted for years or decades, lie in the highest corries.

The flora and fauna on the high tops of all the Highland hills are more typical of those on an arctic tundra than on a European alp and have to adapt not only to almost incessant, mainly strong winds, but to a high rainfall in the West and to a heavy snowfall and low temperatures in the East. While the observatory on Ben Nevis, more than 4,400 feet above sea-level, was manned from 1883 to 1902 the annual rainfall averaged 161 inches, with a maximum of 242 inches in 1898. There are no long-term records of annual snowfall on the Cairngorms, but this would be much heavier than the average accumulation of 12 to 14 feet on the summit of Ben Nevis and winter temperatures would fall 10 or 15 degrees lower than the minimum reading of 0° F recorded at the observatory. Over a period of thirteen years on Ben Nevis there were on average 261 days a year with gales exceeding 50 mph; and on a July day, when the temperature was 80° F in the glens, Seton Gordon witnessed a striking illustration of wind strength on the Cairngorms when he was on the 4,000-foot plateau of the Wells of Dee below the summit of Braeriach. A half-grown ptarmigan rose ahead of him, it flew perhaps a hundred yards with difficulty: 'Then the gale hurled it to the ground, where it rolled over and over, and lay stunned until I was almost upon it. At another time I saw a small ptarmigan blown to the ground with such violence that it rebounded a distance of three or four feet and did not rise again.'

It is usually late in the winter before there is prolonged snowfall on the Cairngorms and in some years there may be almost no snow on them in December, though in others the high tops may be continuously under snow from early October until mid-May. In May 1923 there was unbroken snow cover throughout the month, sheep were being dug out of drifts on the Monadhliath on June 10, and it was early July, when an iceberg was floating on a lochan at 3,600 feet, before the snow began to disappear from the Wells of Dee. Yet, nine days after the snow had melted, green blades of grass were sprouting and there were flower-buds on the moss-campion — so rapidly can an alpine flora burgeon.

In the early morning and again in the evening after blizzards the long remote white ranges of the Cairngorms rise against an ink-blue vault of unfathomable depths of colour, heavy with snow to come. But during the day their iced domes glisten in the sunshine and the smooth, dead-white sweep of their contours are sharply outlined against an alpine-blue heaven. Such may be the snow's depth that not an outcrop of rock nor vent of spring, not a trace of blackness mars the immaculate whiteness of their mantle. Yet even under such conditions there is life on the high tops. Watching through binoculars from the glen nine miles distant I can see companies of red stags marching along the dazzling white crests, some to couch down in clumps in the sun which is hot up there, others to plunge down through the deep snow to feed on the bilberry in the pine forest.

I have climbed to above 3,500 feet in every winter month in order to discover what animals inhabit the highest mountains in Britain at that season. If the snow cover is bare enough in places to permit sprays of crowberry, fingers of fir-club moss and bright red tufts of bent and sedge to protrude, then there will still be the odd red grouse, a few ptarmigan and flocks of a score or two of snow buntings on the 3,000 feet 'mosses', and perhaps the tracks of a blue mountain hare or of a fox crossing a high plateau. Although foxes do not occupy breeding earths higher than 2,500 feet in Britain, individuals roam over the highest tops during the winter, presumably to hunt for grouse or ptarmigan, hares or voles, and occasionally trot up to the summit of Ben Nevis, where they characteristically investigated the flat roof of the observatory. However, they are infrequent visitors to the high tops of the Highlands, in contrast to the red hill-foxes in the Himalaya, which hunt as high as 18,500 feet even during the winter months, and whose tracks, and also those of hares, have been seen on glaciers at an altitude of 21,500 feet.

Stoats are also only occasional visitants to Highland summits, though their tracks are sometimes to be seen in the snow on Cairngorm ridges and they were trapped in midwinter at the Ben Nevis observatory. Environmentally, there is perhaps little difference between a 4,000-foot summit in Scotland and that 14,000-foot pass between the mountains of Burma and Tibet where Ronald Kaulback observed that a pair of stoats were as fascinated by the sound of flint and steel jingling in the small bags carried by his coolies as British stoats are by a gamekeeper squeaking on the back of his hand.

The most remarkable inhabitants of the highest mountains in Britain, and apparently permanently resident on them except in very severe winters with prolonged snowfall and low temperatures, are shrews. Both common and pygmy shrews have been seen running over the snow from one patch of vegetation to the next at a height of 3,500 feet on the Cairngorms, and shrews were frequently caught by the observatory cat on Ben Nevis at various seasons of the year; but in fact these diminutive predators, preying mainly on small invertebrates, range as far north as the shores of the arctic and eastwards to the Yenisey and Lake Baikal, while the pygmy shrew also inhabits the Himalaya and the mountains of central Asia. In Pakistan the latter have been trapped at a height of 11,800 feet on rocky slopes where snow lies for eight months of the year, during which period they must survive on a diet of arthropods, woodlice and beetles. In southern Europe the pygmy shrew is said to be restricted to a montane habitat, whereas the blackish-grey alpine shrew — which is larger on average than the common shrew, with a tail nearly twice as long — lives mainly in the upper and dwarf-tree zones of coniferous forest between 3,000 and 6,000 feet.

Individual pygmy and common shrews may occupy the same habitat, but competition for food may be solved by the fact that the former are reported to pass most of their time underground, while the latter are mainly above ground. That both should have populated such an extensive range throughout Europe and Asia is extraordinary, since they are solitary animals with each individual occupying its own system of underground and surface runs, and are exceptionally aggressive at all times except during the mating season, even though this aggressiveness tends to be resolved by 'squeaking matches' rather than by actual combat. Moreover, in order to remain alive they must hunt for prey day and night, involving ten or twelve periods of intense activity every 24 hours; and since they do not hibernate this incessant lifelong activity, with heart beating 1,200 times a minute, must be maintained throughout the adverse conditions of a mountain winter. Furthermore, their natural increase in numbers is limited not only by the heavy predation to which they are subjected and to which the pygmy shrew, living mainly above ground, must be especially vulnerable, but also by the fact that the majority do not breed until the year following birth, and die in the autumn of that year. As a counter-balance to this mortality the female is able to produce three or four litters of six or seven young apiece during the course of the summer and if a population is at a low ebb this may be increased by females breeding in their first year.

Short-tailed field voles, though typically grassland dwellers, especially in young forestry plantations, also range far above the tree limit in Britain, providing that there is rock or scree to replace long vegetation as cover. In the Cairngorms there are local colonies in the mat grass at 3,000 feet and a few as high as 4,000 feet in hollows dominated by this grass. Although the range of these voles extends as far south as the Pyrenees and the Alps, they are largely replaced in the Alps by the snow or alpine voles, which are almost twice as big, with grey or pure white tails half the length of their bodies, white feet and larger ears than the field voles; for as in the arctic, so under alpine conditions, small mammals tend to be bigger and also to have longer fur than lowland individuals. Snow voles, being the highest resident mammals in the Alps, are seldom found below 5,000 feet; and though some frequent the upper forests of larch, stone pine, dwarf pine and rhododendron, the majority live above the tree-line on sunny slopes of rock and grass, or on moraines among the glaciers up to 13,000 feet, visiting the highest peaks. They feed on grasses, herbs, roots and bilberry shoots, and inhabit shallow though complex burrow systems to which there are several entrances. The burrows contain nest-chambers for the one or two litters of from two to seven young and also food storage vaults, though these voles do not in fact hibernate during the winter but tunnel under the snow from one edible plant to another, and also filch provisions, including meat, from mountain-refuge camps.

There are isolated populations of snow voles in most of the high mountain ranges in Europe, and voles may be found worldwide on the upper slopes of mountains. Père David's voles, for instance, are apparently resident in the Himalaya as high as 18,500 feet. During the summer they are active night and day in their surface runways, harvesting the stems and leaves of herbaceous plants and drying them in the sun before storing them for winter use, though like the snow voles, they do not hibernate but tunnel under the snow in search of food on the slopes and banks of the alpine grassland.

Water voles, mainly of the black variety, sometimes make their way up the streams to heights of almost 3,500 feet on the Cairngorms in those localities where water runs underground below a thick roof of soil and turf. Nor, despite the creature's typical association with lowland woods, should one be surprised by the capture of a field mouse on the summit of Cairn Gorm at over 4,000 feet, for it was probably this species that was trapped on several occasions in the Ben Nevis observatory, and its specific range extends across Eurasia to the Himalaya and the Mongolian Altai mountains. One might add that C.K. Howard-Bury, who took part in a reconnaissance of Everest from the Tibetan approaches in 1921, recorded a small black rat gnawing at the food-boxes in a camp at 20,000 feet.

Small mammals and birds are the most successful vertebrates at high altitudes because they can regulate their body temperature for warmth and also avoid climatic extremes, either by sheltering underground or by migrating. Most mammals above the timber-line are herbivores, with rodents the commonest, and by burrowing, hibernating or storing food several species of mice are able to exist at high altitudes. Although there are earthworms, black in colour, at 13,000 feet in Kashmir and up to the snow-line in the Andes, they are replaced as cultivators and aerators in excessively cold habitats by these small burrowing mammals. Their high-altitude environment is very cold, but at a depth of only six inches below the ground the night temperatures are higher than those above ground, and as L.W. Swan has suggested in a study of the ecology of the high Himalaya, if nocturnal mammals slept in the sun they might well be too warm. On the same mountainside, therefore, diurnal insects may be living in a tropical environment side by side with nocturnal mammals searching for food in an arctic world of sub-freezing temperatures. Individual differences in behaviour and the ability to move from one place to another, make it possible for the various members of an alpine community to occupy a wide variety of environments.

On those occasions when the Cairngorms have been completely mantled by heavy snow whose frozen crust glints with a faintly bluish ice-shine, one looks out from a 3,500-foot summit over interminable snowy ranges and peaks rising above the pall of freezing fog filling the strath below. The high plateaus, mosses and ridges are devoid of any visible life, for since all vegetation lies buried beneath the white blanket of snow, the blue hares and ptarmigan have been obliged to move down to the lower corries where rank old heather is tall enough to protrude above the snow; and presumably in such conditions even the shews must scurry down to the pinewoods and birch groves.

In Britain the majority of blue hares live on well-burned grouse moors between 1,000 and 2,500 feet, subsisting on the young heather; and at lower levels where blue and brown hares are found together, they may interbreed to produce infertile offspring. In normal winter weather the winds ensure that sufficient heather is exposed on the moors, and on this the blue hares feed at night mainly, returning uphill after sunrise. According to J.E.C. Flux they pass most of the hours of daylight resting in their forms with their forefeet tucked under, palms uppermost against the chest and the hind toes projecting in front of the body; their ears are laid back and their eyes half closed, though I doubt whether anyone has ever found a wild hare actually asleep. Leaving their forms about dusk, the hares at first feed intermittently, breaking off from time to time to skip about and chase one another and, if it is a fine night, to roll and dust themselves in the gravel. Although they are capable of digging down to vegetation through several inches of snow, or removing the snow from it by striking rapidly with their forefeet, they are more likely, when there is heavy snow-cover, to feed on vegetation exposed on ridges and do so intensively during the day instead of night — and before rain. During a blizzard groups of as many as forty will move to the lee side of a ridge just below the skyline, and sit with their backs to the wind, or shelter in snow scrapes, usually shallow but in many cases from three to six feet long. Among those hares permanently resident at lower levels on moors around the 1,700-foot contour, Flux found that many of these 'burrows' were regularly used as shelters, for their walls were covered with moss and a coating of white winter fur, and were kept open during the winter via tunnels through the snow. Later in the year the leverets would run into the burrows at the slightest sign of danger, though only until they reached adult size.

Since ptarmigan are also almost exclusively vegetarian, feeding on heather tips, the stems and leaves of bilberry, the leaves and shoots of crowberry, and especially on the blue-green leaves of dwarf willow — together with quantities of berries in the autumn — they are affected by a heavy snowfall in very much the same way as the hares, though heather becomes their main source of food only when deep overall snow has forced them to descend from the high tops to those moors that are the summer habitat of the red grouse. In such conditions no ptarmigan remain on the tops above 3,500 feet, and if these conditions are prolonged the entire mountain population migrates to the moors below 2,500 feet. There, small coveys, or occasionally packs of as many as 450, feed predominantly on heather for days or weeks at a time on snow-free ridges and sheltered slopes or wherever the constant winds have drifted the snow off the vegetation. During this period they roost in hollows or holes in the snow, in which there is no danger of them being buried because they select exposed places where any snow that falls drifts quickly away. Even in winters of exceptionally heavy snowfall the frequent gales not only keep some areas clear of snow but also blow the snow off the tips of vegetation in other places, ensuring a continuous provision of snow-free heather shoots, and their water supply is provided by the snow, which they frequently eat. Although ptarmigan will often scratch through a couple of inches of powdery snow in order to lay bare the heather, they will not do so when the snow has a frozen crust and is hard-packed, nor will they burrow under the snow in order to feed, since both they and grouse rely almost entirely on the short tips of the heather.

Ptarmigan and grouse often feed close together in the hard-weather zone, but do not intermingle. Since the latter occasionally nest above 3,000 feet in those places where the heather is taller than normal at that altitude and also forage at above 3,500 feet, they must be included in any account of mountain life. Their dense plumage and thickly feathered legs and claws point to their boreal origins, and they are in fact a local race of the willow grouse, which have a circumpolar range and sub-arctic distribution. In the Cairngorm region most grouse live on the high moors, which experience the hardest frosts and heaviest snowfall in Britain; but so long as an adequate supply of bushy heather protrudes through the snow the grouse can survive, because they are provided with exceptionally long caeca or blind guts in which bacteria probably break down the woody parts (the lignin and cellulose) into an additional source of food. The fact that they renew their long, hard toenails every year also enables them to scratch through the snow to the heather and to scrape out holes in which to roost and shelter, insulated by the snow from the wind. According to Adam Watson, they are only able to excavate shallow surface hollows in wet spring snow or snow with a crust of ice, but in dry powder-snow can dig down twelve inches and then horizontally inwards for another twelve inches.

Though some pairs of ptarmigan nest as low as 2,000 feet and exceptionally 1750 feet on exposed ridges or screes, providing that mats of crowberry or bilberry are growing among the rocks, the majority do so on the tops as high as 4,150 feet in those places where patches of dwarf willow grow among boulders and gravel. None nest on the 'deserts' of the highest summits, visiting them only infrequently, and on the extensive swards of alpine grassland they do so only where heather or willow grows on 'islands' of scree, gravel or stony moraine. There is a higher density of breeding ptarmigan on the Cairngorms — their stronghold in Britain — than any recorded in the arctic, because, as Watson has pointed out, the relatively low rainfall and well-drained ground favour the growth of the arctic-alpine heaths that are their main food, rather than the mosses and grasses typical of the wetter western hills; and the breeding stock is densest in areas of scree or boulders — hence the bird's North American name of rock ptarmigan — even though there is less heath to the acre on such ground than on boulder-free stretches of heather. The rocks and screes provide not only conspicuous perches for courting cocks, but cover from other aggressive ptarmigan and also from predators such as golden eagles and the foxes that take both sitting birds and eggs.

Although the ptarmigan return to their breeding places on the high tops during the first prolonged settled periods of milder weather in March or April, it may be late in May before the snow has melted sufficiently for them to lay eggs. Similarly, although the 3,500-foot ridges of the Cairngorms may still present immaculately white bulwarks of snow at the beginning of March, when nine-tenths of the ground above 3,000 feet may in fact still be under snow, it is nevertheless at this season that the earliest of the migrant summer-resident mountain birds, the golden plover, return from their wintering grounds on more southerly fields and marshes to visit prospective breeding places as high as 3,250 feet in the peat-hags, the alpine mosses and deer pastures and gentler mountain slopes. Under such conditions these plover must presumably spend only an hour or two a day on the tops before flying down to the moors to feed, though there is no actual evidence that this is the case. Moreover, since there is a considerable area of well-drained heather devoid of suitable nesting bogs, intervening between those plover that breed on the tops and those that do so on the moors below, one may be justified in describing them as separate races, particularly as the majority of the former wear a plumage intermediate between that of the typical southern race and that of the black-faced race of northern Europe. There are probably more breeding pairs of golden plover on the high tops of the Cairngorms than on the moors below, which is also the case with another summer-resident wading bird, the dunlin. In the central Highlands dunlin are indeed virtually restricted to the mountains, on which some nest above 3,500 feet, though in other parts of Britain they may do so on coastal salt marshes.

Early in April, when the blue alpine-foxtail grasses are already barbed with yellow anthers and queen bumble bees are zooming over the mosses on their mysterious errands, heroic meadow pipits are rising and parachuting down is song everywhere to stony ridges and mosses. These extraordinary little birds — more typical of north-country moors and south-country commons, with a range reaching into furthest Asia — have been able to extend their colonisation of the moors to that of the mountain tops. There they nest in tussocks or heather, as high as 4,000 feet, and hunt for insects two or three hundred feet higher than this on the last remaining summer snowfields, where in August there may be as many as 150 on a single patch of snow. In some parts of the Cairngorms they are more numerous than the ptarmigan and if there is no early autumn snow may linger on the tops until October.

The altitudinal range and habits of another small passerine, the wheatear — returning to the high tops somewhat later than the pipits and leaving them towards the end of August — are very similar; but though they have the advantage over the pipits in being provided with an inexhaustible supply of nesting holes under stones, they are not as numerous as them, with no more than twenty to be seen chasing insects on a snowfield.

At the end of April, when the moss-campion's cushions of tiny leaves are beginning to show green, the first of the few snow buntings — Britain's rarest mountain bird — return to nest just above the highest pipits and wheatears in crevices among the slabs on some steep scree of tumbled boulders below one of the sizeable lingering snowfields high on the side of a corrie. The long strip of scree, some 3,000 square yards in extent, reaches down into the green grass of the corrie; its granite slabs and boulders are weathered yellow-green with whorls of map-lichen and stained purple-black, bottle-green or dark-brown with cushion-moss. A vari-coloured swath of lurid mosses, bedding the spring trickling down the scree from the snowfield, harbours a plentiful supply of craneflies for the nestling buntings. Like the wheatears and pipits, the buntings also catch insects on the snowfields and on hot days run over the snow with heads half buried, throwing up a furrow like a miniature snowplough. What are the origins of these few Cairngorm snow buntings, which even in their most successful year never exceed a dozen birds? Do they derive from the flocks of wintering birds? Some of the latter are still frequenting the high tops in April, and may be attracted by climatic and environmental conditions — which above 3,000 feet resemble those near sea-level in the arctic habitat of the snow bunting — to remain and establish nesting territories. They include typical individuals of two races: one of which normally nests in Scandinavia and Greenland, the other in Iceland, and individuals of both races may be nesting in the Cairngorms in the same summer.

That other true mountain bird in the Cairngorms, the dotterel, also returns to the high tops about the same time as the snow buntings and breeds in small colonies in a favourable year. However, dotterel may at one time have nested below 1,500 feet on the fells of Lakeland and most of their world population breed on the stony hills, with a vegetation of short grass, lichens and mosses, that form the tundras of the USSR. Dotterel, like ptarmigan and snow bunting, are an arctic or subarctic species rather than an alpine one and may originally have been a tundra species now in process of extending their range into the mountains in such regions as the Austrian Alps, where they nest on long, flat ridges of alpine pasture at an altitude of between 6,600 and 7,600 feet, and the Abruzzi in Italy where, as in the Mongolian Altai, they nest on plateaus well above 9,500 feet; but it must be admitted that their most recent extension of range includes the unlikely habitat of agricultural land reclaimed by the Dutch polders!

These then with the addition of dunlin and a few common sandpipers are the regular breeding birds in the arctic-alpine zone of Highland mountains, for while pairs of golden eagles and peregrine falcons sometimes build eyries at 3,000 feet in the Cairngorms, and regularly hunt for ptarmigan over the tops, both usually nest on crags or in trees in the glens below 2,000 feet.

Ravens, which visit the Cairngorms tops rather infrequently, nest at lower elevations in the Highlands than in Snowdonia and the Lake District. That they nest in the mountains of Snowdonia may, however, be the consequence of persecution in the valleys, where they formerly nested in trees, as they still do in south-west England. Over their immense global range from North America to Siberia and from North Africa to Greenland ravens are equally at home in arctic barrens, deserts, steppes and mountains.

Summer is long in coming to the Cairngorms and may last only from May, when nevertheless there may be falls of several inches of snow, until early August; and it is the latter half of May before their bleakness is softened in damper places by the greenery of golden saxifrage and the yellow blooms of marsh marigold, and in drier, grittier places by lady's-mantle and the grey-green, lavender-like needles of dwarf cudweed. Although the red deer begin to move up from the moors to the high tops at this time, it is mid-June before a smooth green sward of grass and sedge on the mossess at 3,000 feet attracts herds several hundred strong. Their arrival coincides with the flowering of the alpine plants, with here and there a pink carpet on a green cushion of moss-campion and the pale pink stars of creeping azalea emerging from their scarlet buds. At this season hover-flies and spiders are to be seen on the naked slabs of the highest peaks. The latter, living under the stones and venturing out only in fine weather, can exist at much higher altitudes than web-making spiders exposed to extremes of temperature.

Early in July the white star-flowers of the exquisite star-saxifrage thrust up six or nine inches from their leathery rosettes of red, green or brown leaves. With colonies on the summits of Ben Nevis and Ben MacDhui they are the highest flowering plants in Britain. But the pride of the Cairngorms is the moss-campion which, by driving down a relatively immense tap-root, flourishes between 3,000 and 4,000 feet on bare scalds of gravel among the less densely piled boulders and also on flats and slopes of loose gravel. Wherever the alpine grasses, sedges and fringe-moss peter out, there the gravel is colonised by scattered particles, clumps and small islands of moss-campion and a cushion only nine inches in diameter may have a tap-root more than twelve inches long. Early in July the green cushions of leaves are overlaid by masses of thyme-like flowerlets, varying in colour from palest-pink to the deepest china-pink of centaury; but so ephemeral is this mountain beauty that by the middle of July one must search far and wide for a cushion still bearing flowers. It is fortunate that the moss-campion flourishes on the highest slopes and plateaus, for while the deer gorge on it greedily at lower elevations only a few hinds and yearlings go up as high as 4,000 feet, and it has taken perhaps twenty years to come into full flower.

The moss-campion, together with the creeping azalea, the cyphel and no doubt the crowberry, are the food plants of the caterpillars of the mountain burnet moth — one of the four or five moths restricted on the mainland of Britain to the highest Highland summits. Most alpine moths fly only in sunshine, though the netted mountain moth, which frequents many of the Highland summits north of Perthshire and whose caterpillars feed on the highest dwarf birch, red bilberry and bearberry, is on the wing as early as April or May despite the possibility of total snow cover above 3,000 feet. Colonies of burnet moths, flying only in the July sunshine to suck nectar from the flowers with their long tubular tongues, are very abundant locally on the alpine meadows of Europe, but if the temperature falls they very quickly become torpid. However, their warning colouration of five or six large red spots on the black of their fore-wings, advertising the presence of small amounts of prussic acid in their bodies, protects them from the attacks of birds. In its only British stations on the eastern Cairngorms the mature burnet's life on the wing extends to no more than two or three weeks, but, as in the case of some other alpine moths, this short season of activity coincides with its caterpillars hibernating for as many as four successive winters before pupating.

There are no true alpine butterflies in Britain, for although the small mountain ringlet has a wide range over the mountains of Europe, its colonies in the English Lake District may be established as low as 700 feet and are not located higher than grassy rills at 2,000 feet, while its main habitat in Scotland lies between 1,500 and 2,500 feet, with only a few individuals visiting the high tops. In Europe, however, several allied races occur as high as 8,000 feet, and one, the jet-black glacier alpine, only near the snow-line in the Alps. Strangely enough, the butterfly most often encountered on the very highest mountains in Britain, including Ben Nevis, is the small tortoiseshell, one of the most widely distributed species in the British Isles.

The mountain ringlet is, like the mountain moths, usually on the wing only in sunshine, flying close to the ground in June and July. Like the majority of mountain insects, which tend to range in colouring from reddish-brown to black, it is dark coloured, since dark surfaces absorb heat more efficiently than light-coloured ones. Its hairy body also conserves heat by trapping a layer of air, though the hairs are short and bristly, permitting the sun's rays to penetrate to its body. As in the case of the burnet moth, so the ringlet's life-cycle is prolonged by the fact that its caterpillars (green with a darker green and white stripe) feed for two or possibly three years on mat-grass, sheep's fescue and annual meadow grass in damp places before pupating among the grass stems.

Chapter Three

THE EUROPEAN MOUNTAINS

The tundra-like summits of British mountains can offer far fewer butter-flies than the alpine meadows of Europe: 200 species in the 600-mile arc of the Alps from the Riviera to Switzerland, northern Italy and the borders of Yugoslavia. Several live only above 7,000 feet, with their caterpillars feeding on various heaths and shrubs, and range up to the snow-line. The most typical mountain butterfly — with numerous species ranging across Eurasia to the Himalaya and also present in North America — is the gorgeous apollo, whose hairy white body and wings are set off by two large blood-red eye-spots encircled with black on each hind wing, and large black spots on the forewings. The thirty or so species and subspecies of European apollos, though located mainly between 2,500 and 6,000 feet, are to be found as high as 8,000 feet and, like other mountain butterflies, fly over the alpine meadows, gay with scabious and centaury, only in bright sunshine and from June to September. Since their wings are proportionately larger than those of other butterflies, with some very large females having a four-inch wing-span, it has been suggested that this feature benefits them by exposing a greater wing area to the heat of the sun; but it also enables them to fly in a manner unusual among butterflies, for instead of fluttering they soar on air-currents with wings stiffly out-stretched. In the Himalaya, because of the strong winds, apollos fly infrequently and for only short distances, and when settled, spread their wings and press them against the ground. Even in Britain the female of species like the black mountain moth have apparently adapted to a windy habitat by being wingless and running over the stony ground instead of flying.

The apollo caterpillars, which are also hairy but black with steel-blue warts and rows of red dots, are 'armed' on the nape with a scare device in the form of a fleshy orange-red fork that can be thrust out. Hatching in May or June, they feed during the heat of the day on orpine and sempervivum; but, again, growth is slow, and it is the following summer before they spin cocoons in which to pupate on the ground, where the pupae will presum-ably be less exposed to frost than if attached to the stem or leaf of a plant, as is the case with most butterfly pupae. At generally rather higher altitudes in the Alps the caterpillars (black with lemon-yellow spots) of the lesser apollo, in addition to feeding on sempervivum also do so on the yellow mountain saxifrage that grows on the wet rocks and gravel of mountain streams, with the result that they have been reported as passing much of their life virtually underwater.

There are more true alpine species of birds on the mainland of Europe than in the British Isles, though, unhappily, what has been termed the unholy trinity of industrialisation, urbanisation and centralisation is destroying both the mountain ecology and the pastoral economy of many European mountains, particularly the Alps. In an article in *Wildlife*, Robert Allen reminds us that the mosaic of mountain, forest, meadow and village so characteristic of the Alps, is in fact the product of an economic system which is now collapsing, because the small farms at the heart of this system offer a way of life that attracts fewer and fewer people. Large areas of arable land, which used to yield rye and corn, have been given over to pasture, and still larger areas of pasture, now abandoned, have been invaded by woody plants, which will eventually revert to scrub, though forest still covers a quarter of the Alps. There are far fewer cattle in the alpine meadows and there is not so much hay or straw in the alp barns. Snow finches nested in interstices under the eaves of the barns and such birds as rock partridges found shelter in them during the long hard winters; but the partridge population on the sunny slopes of glass and rock between forest and snowline has been greatly reduced since the 1960s.

However, the Alps and other European mountains are still the habitat of some finches and rock partridges, together with citril finches, alpine accentors, wallcreepers, rock thrushes and hazelhens; the citril finch, which together with the rock partridge is exclusively European, nests near the upper limits of spruce and larch forest on the edge of alpine meadows in which it feeds on plant seeds in addition to those provided by the conifer cones. Only during severe winter weather does it descend to sheltered valleys below 5,000 feet.

One species which has perhaps benefited in some small degree from the tourist invasion of the mountains is the beautiful rock thrush with its slate-blue head, chestnut breast and broad white patch in the centre of its dark back; for, like the black redstarts, these thrushes have taken to nesting in the chalets of the new ski-resorts 6,000 feet up in the Pyrenees and Alps, whereas their normal nesting sites are in crevices among the boulders in crags in wild ravines and valleys, or on open hillsides up to the tree limit at 9,000 feet, or higher still in that country whose bleakness is softened only by a few dwarf bushes and an occasional stunted and weatherbeaten pine tree. However, some breed at much lower altitudes in vineyard country, providing that this habitat includes outcrops of rock or crag faces in which to nest, and they range over much of Eurasia from Iberia (where they nest on the high sierras between 4,000 and 7,500 feet) to the Altai mountains.

In May and June, according to R.P. Bille, the rock thrush soars and sings the livelong day above the snowfields, which are broken up by large dark green clumps of juniper and small pink patches of dwarf azalea; primulas and gentians grow among the rocks encrusted with black and gold lichens. While singing its exquisite flute-like melody the rock thrush seems to hover in one place high in the sky — its triangular wings, through which the sun shines, motionless, its tail fanned — though in fact rising imperceptibly on a current of air. 'Like a small flame the unfamiliar shape continues its ascent'; then drops like a stone to join its plain, brown mate among the rocks and strike a pose, displaying its flaming tints of orange and opal, before soaring again to pour out its lovely wild song.

Although snow finches are also known as mountain finches and frequent boulder-strewn slopes, moraines and snow ridges above 6,000 feet in the mountains of Europe, the Himalaya and the Altai, it is the alpine accentors — those very large dunnocks — that share with the rose finches and wallcreepers the distinction of being the highest breeding songbirds on Earth, for while in Europe the accentors nest from 4,000 feet up to the snow-line and often near glaciers, in the Himalaya and Tibet they regularly do so in crevices among the rocks at heights of between 16,000 and 17,000 feet. They have indeed been recorded nesting actually above the snow-line at 18,500 feet and feeding on insects on the snow, which in the Himalaya recedes from 8,000 or 9,000 feet in the winter to between 15,000 and 18,000 feet in the summer. The adult accentors also winter at great heights, but the immature birds are reported to move down in severe weather to the forested foothills, where they can feed on berries and seeds: powerful muscles in the gizzard enabling them to cope with the hardest seeds.

Various races of rose finches span Eurasia from Finland in the west to eastern Siberia and throughout the mountain ranges of central Asia to as far east as Nepal and Tibet, where they nest in sandy scrub near water. In the Himalaya they are the commonest birds on the *kharkas* or summer shielings, where they search for seeds and insects disturbed by the cattle and yaks just below the snowfields, and nest in shrubs on the open mountain sides from 10,000 feet to above the snow-line. Their loud though monotonous songs are a feature of summer in the barren wastes of the Himalaya and Tibet, though only a small proportion of them are full adult males with crimson heads, breasts and shoulders:

Rose Finches, Snow Finches, Red-mantled Finches, Crimson-winged

Finches — lovely birds all of them, birds that I would go across half a world to see [wrote Douglas Carruthers in his Karakoram diary]. Dawn was the time to enjoy them. I used to leave my tent at the first glimmer of light and make the stiff climb to the snow before the sun touched the topmost peaks... The very edge of the melting snow-fields seemed to be a favourite feeding-place, ground which had only recently been exposed to yesterday's sun, the soil still sodden, and as yet not showing any growth of alpine plants — immediately the sun touched it the birds came. Birds such as Snow Finches, Rose Finches that looked like drops of blood when caught by the rays of the sun; Horned Larks, smart in their buff, black and white.

One of the most exclusively alpine birds, almost restricted during the breeding season to high rock faces of mountain gorges and precipitous cliffs throughout Eurasia from Spain to the Himalaya and the Gobian Altai, where it usually inhabits the ridges of mountain valleys, 'creeping with folded wings over the rocks, like some grey mouse, investigating fissures and slits', or sometimes hopping on the ground among the stones, is the wallcreeper. Its exquisite, harmonious plumage of soft grey and crimson — la rose vivante — has caught the eye of almost every traveller and mountaineer. For though nowhere common, it turns up in the most unexpected places. An early Everest climber, Tom Longstaff, recalls how, on a 13,700-foot peak in the Caucasus, a crimson and plum-coloured wallcreeper — gem-like amid the austerity of the scene — clung with half-open wings and fanned tail to the topmost rocks of the summit: 'It sang a tenuous song of happy repetition as it crept mouse-like across the slabs... An old friend of the Alps and afterwards of the Himalaya, yet this was the only time I have heard the wild beauty of its song.'

Longstaff was also visited by wallcreepers at a camp beside a glacier at 15,500 feet in Kumaon and subsequently saw four clinging like brilliantly coloured bats to the cliff face of a river gorge in the Karakoram, where at the end of July one year another explorer, Richard Meinertzhagen, watched a family of four at over 21,000 feet. They have also been observed flitting like giant butterflies across a rock face in Nepal, fluttering over temple buildings in the Tibetan Himalaya, and climbing up the rock walls of a Tibetan fort, whose slaty colour matched their mantles.

In the Himalaya wallcreepers nest up to 18,000 feet in deep crevices on rocky slopes between grass and snow and usually near a stream or waterfall. In the Alps, though hunting for insects as high as 14,000 feet, they normally nest between 7,000 feet and just below the snow-line in steep, overhanging walls of rock, often located near a glacier. Exceptionally, however, they may nest as low as 2,000 or 3,000 feet in mountain villages such as Les Baux, only a few hundred feet up in the Alpille of Provence, or in chateaus like that at Chillon, jutting into Lake Geneva. In the winter the majority descend to lower altitudes in all parts of their range, though to an approximately similar habitat on a lesser scale of small cliffs, steep-cut banks, walls or rocky outcrops that provide the accustomed vertical surfaces. In such circumstances wallcreepers may be observed on the old walls of Arles in Provence or even in the centre of such cities as Montreux. More than eighty years ago W.H. St Quinton watched a pair collecting nesting material within forty yards of a mountain track above Zermatt:

> One was busily engaged in filling its beak with what appeared to be light-coloured moths and spiders' nests and pursuing its irregular course up and along the precipitous rocks, shifting its position with jerky leaps, more frequently in a horizontal direction, flirting its wings and tail and showing the lovely rose-coloured shoulders in a way which, with its general plumage of quaker-grey, irresistibly suggested comparison with an enormous crimson-underwing moth. Soon its mate was also espied on the cliff-face engaged in the same occupation, and both birds were eventually watched into a crevice about six or eight inches wide at the outside, sheltered by a projecting roof of fallen rock which overhung a rushing torrent.

Since most insects seek crevices shaded from the sun, the wallcreeper's hunting grounds are mainly on north or east-facing rock faces. With the aid of long, sharp claws it is able to use rock crevices as a treecreeper does cracks in trees, climbing obliquely, progressing up the vertical slabs of stupendous cliffs with short butterfly-like spurts of flight. Alternatively, it may proceed head-first down the rock wall, probing the narrowest cracks with its curved beak for spiders and insects. It crosses the smoothest slab with ease and clings to the most precipitous and even overhanging surface, while opening and shutting its wings rapidly with downward flicks of the outermost wing-feathers. When it suddenly flutters off the cliff in an attempt to capture an insect, the spreading of its broad wings reveals their beautiful carmine-red, speckled with pearls, and two large white mirrors: 'Seen from above, this sudden burst of fire, against the greyness of the rocks, creates an extraordinary effect... The wallcreeper suddenly closes its fan and again merges with the rocks... looking like a piece of moving lichen, as it starts its ceaseless climbing again.' The curiously butterfly-like effect of this action has given it the name of 'butterfly bird' — le papillon des rochers — in countries as far removed as Switzerland and Tibet. Unlike the treecreeper, the wallcreeper has perforce to embark on long flights in passing from cliff to cliff, and it then oddly resembles a diminutive hoopoe with that same hovering, hesitant action, those same round spotted wings, the same long curved beak.

Chapter Four

CHOUGHS AND
LAMMERGEIERS

The wallcreepers may share their vertiginous cliffs with rock nuthatches, crag martins, rock doves and alpine choughs. Choughs, like ravens, have a remarkable altitudinal range throughout Eurasia. I have watched the red-legged choughs at the Atlantic edge of Europe, sailing along the Kerry cliffs, opposing the Blaskets, with their notably long, finger-spaced primaries upswept, inspecting crevices in the cliffs in which to nest or perhaps cache surplus food. Occasionally they would close their broad wings and sink earthwards — as ravens do. Other pairs or individuals probed the cowpats on the sodden croftings energetically for worms and insects with their sharply curved, dark-red beaks, better adapted than those of rooks or crows for turning up large lumps of dung and specialised, like those of hoopoes, for flicking over stones for insects or digging for ants in short turf. But a few miles inland others were circling, with high-pitched *kee-yah* cries, above the 2,000-foot summit of a pass.

At the present time 80-85 per cent of the 700-800 pairs of choughs and perhaps 400 non-breeding birds remaining in the British Isles are based in Ireland, but although they have never nested in the highest mountains in Britain and may not have done so in Snowdonia until quarrying began, they are nevertheless typical alpine birds, associating in flocks of 20 or 30 and exceptionally 200 in the Pyrenees, the western Alps and southern European mountains. They are also common in the highlands of Ethiopia, though 1,500 miles from the next nearest chough community, and large flocks frequent the Atlas mountains at an altitude of 7,000 or 8,000 feet, while in the Himalaya their slightly larger relatives nest higher than any other bird, since they have been recorded doing so at 21,000 feet. When Howard-Bury was reconnoitring Everest he was visited daily at camps at 17,000 and 20,000 feet by both the common and yellow-billed alpine choughs, the latter being widely distributed throughout Tibet; and the members of a 1952 Everest expedition have described how a solitary chough flew around their camps every day: 'We often followed him with our eyes, for he was the only living things in that oppressive immensity. He too seemed fond of our European diet.' Subsequent Everest climbers have been followed by choughs to camps at over 26,000 feet and have had their tents entered by them in search of scraps. One chough — variously reported as common or alpine, but probably the latter — has also been seen to take off into flight after a long downhill run at 27,000 feet.

It is a far reach climatically and environmentally from the moist softness of the Kerry seaboard to the extreme cold and heat of the barren Himalayan heights, yet it is easier to accept the presence of a chough near the summit of Everest than that of a hoopoe — typical inhabitant of sun-drenched Provence — at 26,000 feet on that mountain or, even more bizarre, at 21,000 feet on a Tibetan glacier, though hoopoes do in fact nest far up in the Himalayan foothills and are summer residents in Tibet as high as 15,000 feet, arriving early in April and remaining until late in November. The habitat of most Asian colonies of common choughs varies from around 5,000 feet in the winter to between 8,000 and 16,000 feet in the spring and summer, when they nest in the walls of houses in the high mountain villages and in fissures and holes in inaccessible cliffs of the lofty crags and peaks that surround the steep open pastures above the forest. They are usually to be found at the nomadic herdsmen's sheep and yak *chaupans* in the mountains and, as on the Kerry croftings, so on the camping grounds in Kashmir, for example, flocks of choughs — usually twenty or thirty strong, though as many as a hundred — sidle about the grassy meadows among the grazing sheep and pack-animals, digging up grubs and earth-worms; but though tame and fearless, they rarely feed on the ground among the village houses as the alpine choughs do. They are most characteristic on the wing, disporting high in the sky, especially at midday when an entire flock may be floating on motionless wings in graceful circles, before disintegrating as individuals begin to nose-dive, tumble and corkscrew in a series of spectacular aerobatics. Their favourite 'sport' involves planing slowly down a narrow valley, supported on the strong up-draught, and, once at the bottom, whisking up again quickly — to await their turn for the next descent.

Nevertheless, the true mountain chough is the alpine chough, with its short, only slightly curved, pale-yellow beak, orange or coral-red legs — deep red in some individuals — and longer tail, for in no part of their range from Spain, the Alps and the mountains of south-east Europe to eastern Tibet, are alpine choughs to be found away from mountains, and their lowest breeding station lies between 2,000 and 3,000 feet in the Balkans. One hesitates to suggest that they are more tolerant of cold than the common choughs, though it is perhaps significant that the decrease of the latter in many parts of Britain coincided with a cycle of cold winters between 1820 and 1880. In the Alps the alpine choughs assemble in large flocks of up to 1,000 at winter ski-resorts and in mountain villages, and sometimes nest in chalets, cable-railway huts, ruins, tunnels and stables, though normally, like the common choughs, in inaccessible caves and holes in the crags. They are much the more numerous of the two and are increasing locally, whereas the common chough has been decreasing nearly everywhere during the past twenty years. Their increase could be caused by their augmenting their winter food supply with man's scraps, for while their staple food during the spring and summer months comprises spiders, beetles, worms and snails on the alp pastures and also wind-blown insects on the high snow slopes, supplemented in the autumn by such fruit as juniper berries and rose-hips, in winter, when deep snow restricts them to the valley bottoms, they take scraps from the balconies of chalets, pick at the litter in the streets and frequent hotels and restaurant picnic tables for anything edible, including carrion.

During the winter these alpine choughs leave their communal roosts on inaccessible rock faces above the tree-line an hour or so after dawn, and towards three o'clock in the afternoon, after six or eight hours' foraging, assemble in large flocks above the roofs of the villages, to soar in ever-ascending circles, lifted almost vertically upwards on thermals, until they have reached a great height — as a prelude to returning to their roost on some craggy outcrop; for they too perform fantastic aerobatics, more frequently indeed than the common choughs. Bille has recalled how a loud strident cry, breaking the silence, would draw his attention to a flock of some thirty black birds gliding just above the slopes, seeking a rising current of air, and soon they would begin to soar in slow spirals above the grey background of larch woods and inky abyss. Their wings and spread tails resembled glistening fragments of metal in the blinding light, as they circled and wheeled around each other without any movement of their wings, until, when only small black twisting specks, they almost disappeared in the clouds. Then suddenly the black shapes would dive obliquely towards the earth, with wings pressed closely to their bodies, hurtling like a hail of pebbles from a height of some 13,000 feet to the fields in the depths of the valley in a few seconds, to alight gracefully on a crag with an effortless upward zoom.

Charles Stonor, when searching for the Yeti at an altitude of some 15,000 feet on the Nepal approaches to Everest, watched a flock of about 1,000 alpine choughs engaged in what he designated a spring courtship flight. Spread in a great dark cloud like a drifting plume of smoke or a swarm of gigantic bees, every member of the flock, whether solitary or in a small group, was dipping and diving, planing and weaving in and out of the cloud of its fellows; then all would swarm together and be reunited as a rounded whole or in a straggling streamer. When they began to spiral in wide circles even the Sherpas stopped to watch, as they soared silently up and beyond the sight of the naked eye at a height of between 25,000 and 30,000 feet.

The common choughs do not usually nest in large colonies, as the alpine does, nor at such high altitudes; nor do they associate in such large flocks. For their part, the alpine choughs in Nepal neither nest nor roost in monastery buildings as the common choughs do, though filching sticks for their nests from the roofs of the village houses. But by and large, the habits of the two species appear to be identical, and in Asia they often associate in mixed flocks of several hundred to plunder grain from the ears of ripe corn, or to forage with ravens and snow pigeons on the fallow winter cornfields, or in the early winter to feed on the orange berries of the sea-buckthorn, which grows on the banks of mountain streams in such localities as the Gilgit valley in the extreme north of Kashmir, where both species of choughs are very numerous. In Nepal too both associate casually, pouring down the valleys with their swift powerful flight in loose flocks to and from their nesting cliffs, to bustle about the village fields; though the alpine choughs are often to be seen searching for parasites on the backs of ibex or wild sheep grazing on the snow-blotched slopes high above the villages.

The mutual requirements of the two species have been summed up by Derek Godwin as comprising rocky walls or crags with caves, holes or fissures; and open ground, whether stony or pasture, that is not overgrown with rank or high vegetation or blanketed by snow in the winter. Snow-free ground may be reached by daily flights or local migrations to lower elevations, or found on clear slopes and rock faces at high elevations. But since their behaviour and structure indicate a close affinity it is difficult to understand why two species of choughs should have evolved with differently coloured and shaped beaks, differently coloured legs, and notably different call-notes and alarm calls, for the penetrating trilling whistle of the alpine chough is quite distinct from the jackdaw-like call of the common chough, and makes it as conspicuous as its black plumage does against the white surroundings of alpine winter resorts, where so many sounds are silenced by the deep snow.

In addition to acting as jackals to climbers, the mountain choughs also keep a sharp look-out for lammergeiers, as the latter glide at 80 mph in sweeping searches for carcasses of yaks or sheep left by wolves or bears on the hillsides and in the valleys below. Any carcass has probably been picked clean by the griffon vultures except for the marrow in the bones, which the lammergeiers can carry to a height of 100 or 300 feet and drop on to the rocks below to splinter. Scavengers like other vultures, lammergeiers are nevertheless renowned for this bone-breaking behaviour. They may drop the same bone as many as four times and habitually make use of the same dropping places or ossuaries, even though each drop may entail another flight of several miles in order to gain sufficient height for the long glide to the ossuary. A lammergeier usually approaches the latter down wind with the bone gripped in its blunt talons and, if a large one, alighed head to tail in the manner of an osprey carrying a fish. When over the ossuary it frequently dives or dips in flight, presumably to increase velocity, before releasing the bone and watching it fall. Then it immediately turns into the wind and alights a few seconds later with a quick fanning of its great wings.

Riding the air-currents like a mountain albatross, the huge lammergeier, with long narrow-angled wings spanning eight and a half or nine feet and diamond-shaped tail, is the perfect glider and, as Melvin Bolton commented when observing lammergeiers in Ethiopia, a specialist totally committed to a life of mountains, thermals and open space, precluded, with such a wing-span, from ever hopping nimbly about trees.

'Watch one for half-an-hour — for half a day', wrote Abel Chapman more than fifty years ago, 'yet never will you discern a sign of force exerted by those 3-yard pinions. With slightly reflexed wings he sinks 1,000 feet; then, shifting course, rises 2,000, 3,000 feet till lost to sight over some appalling skyline. You have seen the long cuneate tail deflected ever so slightly... but the wide lavender wings remain rigid...'

Another naturalist in Ethiopia, Clive Nicol, has described how the lammergeiers would 'climb' the great cliff faces in the early morning without flapping to gain height, then plane for most of the day, gliding about the cliffs or around buttresses, never more than a few yards from the rocks, their wings emitting a faint sinister howling sound as they planed along: 'The great birds seemed to approach with stealth and from behind, always from behind... As the faint howl grew I would turn and there it would be, sailing past in the void ten yards away, so close that its yellow red-rimmed eye stared plainly into mine.'

Although the lammergeiers' vast range extends from Spain and Morocco in the west to the mountain ranges of central Asia, Tibet and China, they are most numerous in the highlands of Ethiopia and Tibet, where they are often to be seen on the plains and in gorges at comparatively low altitudes. Even in the Himalaya their eyries in niches or caves in the crags or on overhung ledges are not found above 14,000 feet. Nevertheless, according to the books of the lamas, their nests are the necklaces of the five pinnacles of Kangchenjunga and from time to time, no doubt, one has settled on the summit of Everest and gazed with its fierce eyes over the grey-brown vales of Tibet that roll away in wave after wave to hills, faint outlines of snowy peaks, and more grey hills, 15,000 or 16,000-feet high and seemingly isolated from all other parts of the Earth. Such a perch would form a suitably impressive station for a lammergeier with its predatory cream and black head, aquiline rather than vulturine, despite the curious tufts of black bristles, protruding on either side of the beak, from which it takes its other name — the bearded vulture.

The circulatory breathing apparatus of these high-altitude birds must be of unparalleled efficiency, when one considers that a lammergeier has been observed flying at over 30,000 feet, and that a golden eagle plunges vertically through the rarified Himalayan air at a velocity of between 150 and 200 mph in a hunting stoop; but birds of prey, ravens and choughs are not the only birds to look down on the highest peaks on Earth. Bar-headed geese, migrating between the lakes in the hot plains of northern India, where they winter, and the high lakes of Tibet on which they breed, complete their spring migration in what is apparently a single non-stop flight, in the course of which they pass high over the Himalaya. One gaggle was seen to fly over the east spur of Dhaulagiri at about 26,000 feet, the distant honking of another flock was heard as they migrated, unseen against the stars, over the 28,790 feet peak of Makalu, and a third gaggle was watched flying in echelon directly over the summit of Everest. Ruddy shelducks, honking musically, and with golden plumage glinting in the sun, also migrate through the Himalayan passes in March and April to breeding lakes as high as 16,000 feet in Tibet; a pair of wagtails have been seen migrating over the snowfields towards Makalu at a height of more than 21,000 feet; a dying corncrake has been found on the snow at 17,600 feet just below a Kimaon pass in the middle of August, and a quail at 18,500 feet and a starling at 18,000 feet in the Karakoram, where swifts have been encountered hawking insects at 18,800 feet.

Those other vultures, the griffons, have much the same palearctic range as the lammergeier and are also very commonly distributed throughout the Himalaya and Tibet, where the breeding colonies of as many as fifty pairs of the Himalayan griffon vulture are located as high as 14,000 feet. They are not, however, as exclusively restricted to the mountains as the lammergeier — though soaring to 20,000 feet in the Himalaya — and, unlike the latter, are gregarious, both nesting and roosting colonially in caverns or rock piles or on ledges, or exceptionally in cork trees in sheltered Spanish valleys, and also feeding communally on the carcases of dead animals, mainly domestic stock. To these they are attracted by sight and there is no evidence that they are able to scent carrion. Significant flight evolutions by one griffon are perceived by other distant soarers within a radius of fifty miles or so, with the result that a hundred or more may be attracted to a carcase from a wide area, zooming in on it at speeds in excess of 100 mph, in contrast to their normal cruising speed of 40 mph, and planing down to it with partly closed wings and an audible rush of air. Abel Chapman has described how in Andalusia the griffons would leave their roost on bright sunny mornings as soon as the day began to warm up, or as soon as the air currents were strong enough for them to become airborne. Then, in infinite convolutions, opposing, concentric and elliptic, they would pass and repass along the 315 feet high crags of Arcos for half an hour or more, rising higher at each repeated circuit, before diverging in various directions in search of carrion. On the other hand all for no apparent reason might return to their roost: 'Amidst the ponderous throng, fairly-like forms thread a sinuous way... Lesser kestrels — tiny hawks so elegant and so chastely hued that the sunlight seems to shine through their gossamer figures.'

On winter mornings when a film of mist spread over the land below, the griffons would make no attempt to leave the roost before ten or eleven o'clock and when it was wet or foggy would remain huddled up on their roosting ledges all day, or until the sun came out, when they would sit about the rock-strewn hillside drying their feathers, with colossal wings, spanning eight or nine feet, outspread in the manner of cormorants. Even in fine weather the griffons probably spend sixteen of every twenty-four hours at their roosts, though during the remaining eight hours they may cover 200 or 300 miles while soaring at great heights. From such flights they return between three and five o'clock in the afternoon — the precise hour depends upon visibility — and the skies above the roost become punctuated with soaring forms. At first mere specks, they gradually increase in size until one realises that they have the typical oblong shapes of vultures with square tails, and heads and necks tucked into white ruffs. Some continue wheeling around with set pinions in ever-descending circles, others spiral down in series of half-circles. To quote Chapman again:

Often, amidst the soaring throng, a single vulture — perhaps two or three — suddenly shifts course, heads up into the wind, then dropping great bushy legs, and with extended neck and reflexed pinions... nose-dives diagonally earthwards. The angle of descent may be 30 or 40 degrees from the perpendicular, and such its velocity that one hears afar the rush of wind through rigid up-tilted primaries. The dive may be prolonged over 1,000 feet or more; then those huge wind-sails extend once more, a horizontal attitude is regained and, with a 'hurricane header', the vulture vanishes within its eyrey.

All the earliest griffons to return in the evening home to the caverns in the crags — from which hordes of rock pigeons stream out in alarm — with the result that late-comers, unable to squeeze into them, are obliged to perch on some projecting buttress or on the long open ledges that stratified limestone affords, or sheer off to other crags.

Chapter Five

MARMOTS

The steep path zigzags up to the high alp pastures, over which it undulates for five miles or more as it climbs gradually to the brilliantly pigmented alpines at the edge of the permanent snows. There are red-spotted burnet moths everywhere and an occasional alpine accentor or a flock of snow finches. At intervals a piercing outburst of bird-like whistles announces a colony of marmots: Pliny's *mures alpini* (mountain mouse), from which the Romans derived their *murment* and we our marmot. Plump, round-headed, bewhiskered and hairy-cheeked relatives of ground-squirrels, they vary from 22 to 30 inches in length, including the short 6-inch tail, and from seven to twenty pounds in weight, according to race and sex. Rolling in fat, they are made to appear even plumper by their thick coarse coats of short under-wool and longer dark-brown guard-hair, and by their very short stocky legs.

Marmots are not only the most characteristic colonial mammals, where the soil is suitable for burrowing, on sunny grassy slopes with a southern aspect around and above the tree-line almost to the permanent snow in the Alps (predominantly in the west) and Carpathians, but also at great heights in the mountains of central and north-east Asia. In Pakistan there are, for instance, large colonies of the golden marmot, which is a rich orange-red in colour with an admixture of black hairs on crown and back and a ring of black hairs framing the eye and contrasting with pale-gold lower cheeks; these inhabit alpine scrub or meadows among the rocks between 10,500 and 16,000 feet. In the Tibetan Himalaya, bobac marmots — which are rather larger though shorter-tailed than those in the Alps — have indeed been seen with half-grown young at 18,000 feet in what might be described as alpine desert conditions. But in addition to the fourteen races of marmots in the Old World there are also others, such as the hoary and the yellow-bellied in the North American Rockies. There, though sometimes inhabiting the steep sides of canyons or rocky enclaves in the subalpine forest, they usually live above the timber-line on alpine slopes carpeted with the white flowers of mountain avens and the bright yellow of rock-roses, and cluttered with large rocks and jumbles of boulders at the base of the screes. Large isolated rocky outcrops may harbour several groups of hoary marmots, though extensive intervening areas remain uncolonised. The colour-pattern of these marmots — brownish-grey with the tips of the hairs slightly silvered, a black patch across the nose and black feet — may have some camouflagic value, for it is often difficult to see them, particularly when they are motionless against a background of rock with crustose lichens.

All races of marmots live in small colonies, with each family of perhaps one male, eight females and two yearlings occupying a separate burrow among the boulders or scree that has accumulated soil and become stabilised. Alternative burrows for summer and winter use — the latter at a lower altitude — are excavated by the animal scuffling out loose soil with the strong curved claws of its hind feet and shoving this out with its rump. The summer burrow, in which two to five young are born at the end of April or early in May, consists of a branching passage from three to twelve feet long. According to some observers there are invariably look-out posts in strategic positions near the dens and overlooking regular grazing areas, and each group of marmots has a sentinel on top of a high boulder, from which it broadcasts warning of danger with that long, clear, shrill whistle (uttered with mouth closed), which echoes around the walls and crags of a rocky amphitheatre or narrow canyon and which caused the French-Canadian voyageurs to name the marmot *Siffleur*. One tends to have reservations about the posting of animal sentries, but a flat-topped rock is a prominent feature in the vicinity of a marmot's burrow and is used both as a look-out and for sun-bathing, in which marmots indulge for much of their time when not feeding; and they are extremely vigilant, frequently sitting up on their hind feet to peer around if a clear view of a suspicious object is not obtained at first. Their long flat feet enable them to stand erect with ease and also allow the females to suckle their young in a sitting position like bears. Both sight and hearing are acute, and their alarm whistles, which increase in intensity as an intruder approaches, result in an entire feeding colony scuttling back to its burrows, to disappear with what Ronald Kaulback has described as a whisk of their rat-like tails: 'so absurdly small for such lumbering creatures. Then, safe in their holes, they poke out their heads and emit peal after peal of derisive whistles, terminated in a throaty chuckle.' However, a Kalmuk of Kazakh can excite a marmot's curiosity sufficiently, by waving a fox's brush, to fascinate it until he can approach closely enough to shoot it.

It has been suggested that the marmots' bulk precludes their rapid escape into their burrows or into small crevices, and that they are therefore especially vulnerable to the attacks of such predators as golden eagles and foxes; but they are too watchful and too responsive to the whistles of their fellows to be often caught by either predator and too large to be tackled by most stoats or weasels, though the Asian large weasel is reported to prey heavily on them in the Altai mountains. The naturalist, Brian L. Sage, observed that though hoary marmots would become particularly alarmed at the appearance of a golden eagle, whistling from all sides — as if the eagle was an habitual predator — he never saw an eagle attempt to seize one, nor ever found marmot remains at eyries, though the corpses of ground-squirrels were invariably present. Morerover the marmots' slow rate of reproduction — since they do not breed until their third year, and may thereafter have only one litter every two years — coupled with the probable long life-span indicated by the twenty years of one in captivity, also suggests that they do not suffer heavy mortality from predation.

As the first warmth of the morning sun falls on each burrow the occupants emerge and usually spend the next hour basking and grooming before beginning to feed; but in cloudy or stormy weather they remain in their burrows. On warm sunny days they sprawl out on the rocks in postures of abandon, some on narrow flattish ridges on which they lie with all four legs hanging over the edge. But even on these occasions they are watchful, and Sage recalls an incident when half a dozen or so were sunning themselves on a rock outcrop on a hot afternoon. Suddenly two alarm whistles rang out, every marmot instantaneously rushed for its den, and a moment later a rough-legged hawk closely pursued by a gyrfalcon flashed overhead.

The marmots often feed at some distance from their burrows, gnawing at roots with their brownish-red incisors, though grazing mainly on grasses, sedges and herbaceous plants; according to one nineteenth century alpinist, they are particularly partial to a saxifrage. They stuff the vegetation into their mouths very rapidly, pausing only for an occasional look round, and after feeding for a couple of hours break off for another session of grooming or desultory digging. Or they may play, and Sage often saw one that was grazing suddenly stop, run across to another, and take part in a brief bout of wrestling. This, if taking place on a steep slope, might result in the two combattants rolling downhill for some distance in a close embrace. In Mongolia this behaviour has been described by more than one observer as two marmots standing erect, grasping each other with their front paws and waltzing around. Other forms of play include gentle face-to-face nibbling, stand-up sparring matches and swift chases by several individuals. During the last two or three hours of daylight there is a final feeding session.

Although their compact well-furred forms with extremities reduced to a minimum — short legs, blunt head with small round ears — are admirably adapted to withstand cold and conserve heat, the marmots move down to the timber-line in the Alps as early as the end of September or the middle of October in order to excavate their labyrinthine winter burrows, which are usually under a large rock, and extend for 25 or 30 feet to a round chamber at a depth of from 4 to 10 feet underground, and include short lateral passages to serve as latrines; but before finally retiring for their long hibernation, some 3 to 6 feet of the burrow entrance is blocked up with a plug of stones and earth or grass as a seal against the cold and flooding. The entire family, or in some instances a group of ten or fifteen individuals, hibernate in the nest of dry grasses in a temperature of 45 to 50°F, subsisting until the following April on their reserves of fat. If their metabolism resembles that of ground-squirrels, then during their deep sleep their body temperature will fall to the low 40s or 50s°F. In their Himalayan and Pamir habitats, however, they cannot emerge from hibernation until most of the snow has melted in May and the flush of new vegetation is available. In the Rockies the majority go into hibernation early in September or in the middle of October, before the first snowfall but when the leaves and stems of alpine plants have begun to shrivel and the grass has been browned by frost, for since they feed predominantly on grass and green herbs they probably could not subsist on dry withered vegetation. In the low arid valleys of Alaska both hoary and yellow-bellied marmots endure what must be the longest hibernation of any mammal except some grizzly bears, extending from the middle of June — reportedly after a fortnight's preliminary starvation — until the following March or early April! Moreover, on emerging they may have to dig their way out through several feet of snow and subsequently produce their litters of young by early May.

Chapter Six

CHAMOIS AND IBEX

The shrill penetrating whistles of the marmots serve as alarm-calls not only to other marmots but also to other mountain animals, such as chamois and ibex, which may be feeding in their vicinity between the upper limits of the timber zone and the permanent alpine snow. With powerful thickset bodies clad in short greyish-brown hair in the summer and long shaggy black hair in winter, and with slender eight-inch horns rising vertically from the skull to curve back like hooks at their points, chamois resemble antelope but are in fact considered to be neither antelope nor goat but members of an oddly assorted tribe consisting of the mountain goat of the Rockies and the goral and serow of Asian montane forests and jungles.

As an adaptation to the rugged terrain it inhabits, the two main toes of a chamois' hoofs, which are concave on the underside and as hard as steel, can be widely splayed. Additional traction is provided by two subsidiary toes or dew-claws on each hind foot which, though not touching the ground when the animal is on the level, and not coming into use in most hoofed animals, grip steep, grassy slopes. With lower legs acting as springs, contracting and bearing the weight of its body, a chamois can leap more than 20 feet over bare rock surfaces and jump 13 feet up the face of a crag. Their agility, the visual alertness of their large protuberant brown eyes, and their responsiveness to the sibilant nasal whistles of their companions, together with their craggy habitat, preclude the chamois from any significant predation by such carnivores as wolves. Today there are in any case few of the latter in most of the chamois' European haunts: less than a dozen, for example, and only two or three pairs of golden eagles in the chamois' last stronghold in the Appenines — the Abruzzo National Park — where between 300 or 400 graze over the Park's 140,000 acres, which rise to over 7,000 feet. In Europe shooting, and harrying by shepherds' dogs, prevent the chamois from extending their range and establishing colonies outside the various Parks. A fox or a bear may occasionally take a sleeping kid at night, but if the chamois are attacked during the daytime the adults form a circle around the young ones, striking at the attacker. It is improbable that brown bears — of which there are still between sixty and eighty in the

Abruzzo — were ever significant predators, and in the days when these bears were common in Europe they were often to be seen grazing peacefully in the alpine meadows with chamois and the domestic herds of cattle, sheep and goats. However, it is alleged that one in twenty of those bears that still forage during the summer months on the alpine pastures high above the forests in Bulgaria become habitual sheep killers, just as those in the Himalaya may prey on ponies, sheep and goats when these are driven up to the mountain grazings in the summer.

The present day life-history of those chamois in the Abruzzo has been outlined by Sandro Lovari in *Oryx*. It is in the late spring, according to his observations, that the chamois leave their winter quarters in the beechwoods on the valley slopes. Groups of between ten and forty yearlings are led up to the alphine pastures by from one to five barren females more than eight years old, while pregnant females move to separate kidding places. Rocky and inaccessible to most animals, these are pitted with hollows and small caves, sparsely covered by mountain pines and juniper, and rendered predator-proof by almost vertical walls of cliff. In such retreats the chamois give birth to one kid, or two, in May or early June. The latter can follow their mothers almost immediately after birth, leaping from rock to rock and skidding on their haunches down the snowfields; and late in May or in June they join the groups of yearlings in the alpine meadows, where on grassy slopes or on shady north or east-facing cliffs they browse the grasses and herbs, especially clover, though during the heat of the day they lie on patches of snow or enjoy the breezes on knife-edged ridges. At this season the various bands are very shy, fleeing at the first sign of any intruder, though they become less shy as the kids grow older and become more independent. Late in the summer or early in the autumn the herds reach their maximum size when the previously solitary males begin to rejoin the females, prior to the rutting season from October to mid-December. The males demarcate rutting territories by rubbing their horns against rocks, trees or shrubs and depositing scent from the glands behind their horns; and also warn rival males by erecting the so-called 'beard' of long thick hair, glossy black except for yellowish-white tips, along the ridge of the back. Finally in December the various herds migrate to their respective winter-quarters on eastern and southern slopes within the upper forest zone, though visiting the higher ground on sunny days when the snow melts sufficiently to expose some patches of grass, picking their way one by one across snowfields that are avalanche-prone. However, young males and some adults apparently remain in the forest, where there is no danger from avalanches, for most of the year, feeding on lichens and mosses and on buds, bark and pine needles. In some parts of Switzerland the chamois appears to be in process of becoming a forest animal, but in this respect one has always to bear in mind that the habitats of so many wild animals are constantly being adjusted by man's persecution and infiltration of their natural environment. Chamois have been hunted in the Alps for hundreds of years and have been forced to retreat to the highest and most inaccessible crags and slopes. Today, under protection, they should be expected to concentrate in those alpine zones that offer the best forage.

As long ago as 10,000 BC the common wild goat was a member of the European fauna too, since its range extended from Crete and the Cyclades to the rocky arid hills of Sind and Baluchistan and an environment of jagged rock, loose stones and thornbush with little water — a furnace of heat in the summer and bitterly cold in the winter. The foremost ancestor of all domestic breeds, the wild goat is also known as the Grecian ibex or pasang or bezoar. From the latter name is derived bezoar stone: an agglomeration of fibre and hair found not only in the stomachs of goats but also in those of chamois and the Andean vicuna, and formerly employed in all three cases by local inhabitants as an antidote to poison and as a remedy for various diseases. Today probably no pure-bred stocks of wild goats remain in Europe, though everywhere in Asia Minor flocks of up to a hundred crop the grass, browse on berries and top the shoots of small oaks and cedars among the rocks, shrubs and scattered conifers of the *maquis,* 2,000 or 3,000 feet up the steep mountain-sides, though usually at no great distance from high forest. Amazingly agile, with the ability to check and balance on a knife-edge of rock after a great leap, the bezoars are as shy and wary as all goats. A flock of twenty or thirty, led by a long-bearded billy, moves from one feeding place to another with extreme caution, and only after the billy has surveyed the ground ahead for possible danger from such predators as leopards, bears, lynxes or wolves; and when the flock rests, it does so on a commanding ridge, where a sentry can stand guard. Sentry duty is said to be undertaken by the youngest billies first and the oldest last! The life-history of these genuinely wild goats tends to be legendary rather than factual. As protection against the attacks of golden eagles the one, two or three kids are born, in May, in dense forest, and are strong enough to follow their mothers within 48 hours of birth to the lower ridges, while the adult billies summer higher up in the mountains and often above the snow-line which, in regions such as Iran, may be as high as 13,000 feet. The billies, which stand three feet at the shoulder and weigh up to 170 pounds, are equipped with splendid scimitar-shaped, near-black horns up to fifty inches long that sweep back in a graceful curve, and during the rut in the autumn and early winter they are reported to fight so violently that the blows from their heavy keeled horns sound like those of an axe on a tree, and two may roll on the ground with their arcuate horns entangled.

Attractive though the chamois are, they must surrender pride of place to another true wild goat, the magnificent ibex, with whom they share many of their European mountain sanctuaries. Ibex still inhabit the summits of the wildest mountains and most precipitous crags, upon which even the chamois do not venture, as far west in Europe as the Spanish cordilleras, the Pyranees and the Alps. Massive, muscular, heavier-bodied and thicker-set than other goats, the males are superbly equipped with stupendous, dramatically swept-back and thickly knurled horns like trumpets. Three feet or more in length, these curve back to form a full half-arc in Caucasian ibex and a three-quarter arc tapering to thinner points in those in the Himalaya, whereas those of Alpine ibex are much straighter. The ridges or growth lines encircling their horns may indicate a normal maximum life-span of 20 years or exceptionally two or three years longer than this; but these ridges are not reliable indicators, since it is possible for two or three to be added in one year and in aged beasts they may be so worn down as to be almost invisible. By contrast the females' horns are thinner and straighter and no more than twelve inches long, and since their small horns are not apparent in silhouette, their dark brown or reddish pelage is camouflagic.

An ibex's stocky legs terminate in short hoofs which, like those of the chamois, are as hard as steel, rough on the underside and capable of expanding widely. Moreover, the soft and supple pads of the hollowed heels cling to steep surfaces like rubber suction-pads, and an additional grip is obtained by the dew-claws. Thus equipped, an ibex can scale the steepest and slipperiest rock slabs and almost sheer cliff faces with marvellous agility and surefootedness, traversing at full speed across iced crags and precipices that appear impassable and mounting rock walls on which no visible foothold exists; whereas a chamois, in descending a 'chimney' in a vertical rock face, may be said to 'flutter' down, as it jumps from side to side, an ibex does so in bold bounds, alighting on minute projections spaced far apart. The American hunter-naturalist, James L. Clark, has described a herd of fifty female and young ibex fleeing over steep rocks above a precipitous ridge, leaping 12 or 15 feet at a bound — never seeming to choose a spot where next they would alight, as they sped upwards towards the face of an almost perpendicular precipice. He was amazed to see that females and kids alike made their way at this furious pace directly across the front of a pointed cliff that thrust out 'like the prow of a Brobdingnagian battleship' and did not appear to offer the slightest foothold. As rocks rolled and thundered down the cliff, he fully expected to see some of the ibex lose their footing, but on they raced to the very point of the rocks, and, though unable to see what lay ahead of them around the sharp point, made a marvellous turn and alighted safely. They then galloped on without a moment's hesitation, and finally disappeared from sight, while the rocks that they had dislodged were still thundering down the 200 feet of cliff below.

In Europe the ibex's habitat extends from the dwarf pines, willow, birch and rhododendron of the upper tree zone around 5,000 feet to grassy strips among the rocks on the highest alpine pastures and to those dry sunny slopes shunned by the chamois. There they can feed on grass, herbs, sedges and lichens, and also the shoots of the wild strawberry plants, though salt rocks and licks are essential too; and according to Abel Chapman, the ibex of the higher Spanish sierras never descended as low as the tree zone, but frequented the lower mountain ranges, covered with scrub and pines up to their 5,000-foot summits, lying up in the fastnesses of broom, gorse and *abolaga*. During the heat of the day, or from early morning until late in the evening, most herds of ibex rest up in some safe sanctuary high up on a summer snowfield, where a rocky outcrop or crag provides a good lookout — though whether guarded by sentinels is, again, problematical. However, the American explorer-naturalist, Roy Chapman Andrews, recalls how one morning in the Altai mountains he watched forty ibex graze up an almost perpendicular mountainside until the last foot of shade had disappeared, and then dispose themselves comfortably among the rocks:

They were plainly visible while they were standing, but one by one they faded from sight and seemed literally to sink into the ground. Only two bucks were left. They climbed lazily to the highest peak and took station side by side facing in opposite directions. One surveyed the vast complex of mountains to the south; the other gazed over the plain, which stretched away like a calm sea. For two hours they stood motionless, living statues silhouetted against the sky. Then, at the same moment, they left the sentinel post and lay down. We watched a similar performance with a herd of sheep (argali). In that instance one ram remained on guard. He climbed to the topmost pinnacle of rock on the highest hill nearby and stood as if carved in stone.

James Clark has described the difficulties experienced by the adult male ibex in attempting to relieve their neck muscles of the weight of their heavy horns by resting them on the rocks, reclining in unusual positions in order to do so, or even dozing on their feet with their heads tilted down so that the horns are supported by a rock. A male's ranking within the group of his fellow males is rigidly defined and mantained by the length of his horns, which he demonstrates by turning his head to present a side-on view to a challenger. However, it must be said that a challenger with shorter horns does not always accept the superiority of a longer-horned male, in which case the two fight furiously, rearing up on their hind legs to charge and clash horns.

The seasonal habits of ibex vary somewhat from one mountain range to another. In some parts of the Alps they descend from the heights only when driven down by heavy winter snowfalls, but in the Gran Paradiso National Park in Italy the majority, after summering at almost 10,000 feet, go down into the forest in the winter, though rarely below 6,500 feet. In the forest there is not only feed but, as in the case of chamois, safety from avalanches. Although a newborn kid may occasionally be seized by a golden eagle, the main mortality among the wary ibex is caused by prolonged rain, heavy snowfalls, falling rocks and avalanches. In the course of one winter (1958-9) in the Gran Paradiso no fewer than 136 perished in blizzards or avalanches, and it is possible that the ibex themselves sometimes precipitate avalanches by crossing ravines filled with loose snow, as Rocky Mountain goats, inhabiting similar terrain, have been known to do. Except during the rut in the late autumn and early winter the sexes live separately, with the adult males, sometimes solitary, sometimes in herds, often at higher altitudes than the females, kids and young males. Heavy snowfalls may therefore prevent the former from joining the herds of females during the rut, with the result that fewer kids than usual will be born towards the end of the following spring or early in the summer. A band of males, grazing among the choughs, can be approached fairly closely, but the females are shyer and when they have kids — up to three each — station themselves on unapproachable rock faces, which are seldom below 9,000 feet. On such exposed heights the kids jump around like shuttlecocks until, on a danger scent being carried by a veering wind, one of the females utters a bird-like chirrup and the group takes flight at an incredible speed up the steep mountain slope.

Though almost exterminated in the Alps during the nineteenth century there are now more than 3,700 ibex in the Swiss Engadine Park, to which they were reintroduced in 1914. Similarly, although the ibex in the Gran Paradiso were reduced to just over 400 by partisans during the last war, the majority of those that survived were the less easily approached females, with the happy result that under protection they have been able to breed up to a total strength of 4,000, so that it has proved possible to export a surplus to other European national parks. In prehistoric eras ibex were widespread throughout Eurasia and North Africa until at some period — during the Ice Age perhaps — they were split up into isolated populations in their present montane habitats. Although some authorities consider there to be eight different races of ibex, these are all so closely related that they interbreed in captivity and there are only marginal differences in their behaviour and food preferences. Species-splitting has indeed resulted in a multiplicity of both goat and sheep races, the validity of which is dependent upon individual choice.

The most easily identifiable distinguishing feature, evolved in isolation, between the various races of ibex is the shape of the horns, though the colour of the pelage also differs according to habitat. In order to obtain the finest heads of ibex, with which to adorn (and moulder on) the walls of their trophy rooms, Victorian sportsmen travelled to the Caucasus — where there are still reported to be 15,000 or 20,000 ibex — or to the great mountain ranges of central Asia, from north-east Afghanistan, through the Pamirs and the Tien Shan to the Altai, and to the western Himalaya and Tibet. The males of these Asiatic ibex are further distinguished by the addition of pale silver saddles and rump patches to their chocolate-brown pelage, and both sexes grow thick woolly beards in winter. At the present time, according to the American naturalist, George B. Schaller, ibex are the most widely distributed and numerous mountain ungulates in the Pamirs, 'because they are mainly confined to the alpine zone between 11,000 and 16,000 feet, and therefore elude casual shooting, though persistently persecuted by meat hunters in their fragmented habitat of tiny oases of green hidden in wastes of rock and snow'. Further east they are restricted to the rather arid mountains of the inner Himalaya, where even at heights of over 22,000 feet they are able to subsist on tussocks of grass among the crags and on the meadows just below the snow, though they may come down as low as 8,000 feet in the spring to graze the new grass. Because the snowfall is heavy on these inner ranges, herds of as many as 200 ibex may also descend to the forest zone during the winter, when the adult males rejoin the bands of females and young for the rut, which in this region extends from late December or mid-January until the early spring. In the forest they can browse the leaves, or nibble at the leafless twigs of wild currant and alpine willow on sunny southern slopes above the forest. Younger males may, however, stay high, gnawing the lichens and grass from snow-free rocks warmed by the sun, and sheltering in holes and crevices. With their very thick winter pelage of coarse guard-hair and dense undercoat of fine wool-like hair trapping layers of insulating air, they are well protected against the lowest temperatures and can lie up among the rocks, half buried in snow, during a twenty-four hour blizzard; but one must question whether they can, as alleged, break through and traverse snow-drifts after a blizzard, and descend to more wind-swept slopes where they can expose clumps of grass by scraping in the shallower snow, for their short legs would result in their floundering belly-deep in soft snow.

To complete their collections of ibex heads the sportsmen could have obtained specimens of other races nearer home — on the parched crags and ravines flanking the Avara Valley in Israel, in Sinai, the Red Sea hills and the Yemen, in the Sudan and in the fantastic mountains of Ethiopia.

Chapter Seven

THE RAVAGED MOUNTAINS OF ETHIOPIA

On the high, cold, wet and isolated volcanic range of the Simien mountains, rising almost a mile out of the plains of northern Ethiopia, a few Abyssinian or walia ibex have survived incessant persecution during the past 50 years. Eleven hundred years ago the walia had carried on their backs holy books brought by the saint, Kedus Yared, on his return from Jerusalem, and it was then prophesied, according to Clive Nicol and other sources, that foreigners would come to Ethiopia to protect the walia, that a white man would ride on one into the church of St. Michael in Amba Ras, and that the walia, after being almost exterminated, would thrive once again. It is difficult to discover what exactly is happening in Ethiopia today, but with a measure of protection inaugurated by white men, the walia were actually increasing in numbers to a complement of nearly 400 at the most recent count despite the fact that they have also had to contend with the almost total erosion of all accessible land and forest, up to a height of nearby 12,000 feet in places; for Ethiopia has been more ravaged by primitive agriculturalists than virtually any other country in the world.

The extensive original range of the walia consisted of numerous segmented pockets, separated by deep valleys and cultivated fields; and in isolation at high altitudes they have developed a longer coat of dark chestnut-brown hair than the Nubian ibex in their hot habitat on either side of the Red Sea, and have also developed in physique, with a male walia weighing up to 270 pounds and carrying thick curving horns up to 44 inches long, Deprived of their strongholds, the walia have retreated from one locality to another, until today the Simien is their only habitat in Ethiopia — as it is of the red-legged choughs, which roost on the cliff faces but forage on the plateau above, for, as Nicol has pointed out, the Simien is a meeting place of representatives of the flora and fauna not only of Ethiopia, but of Europe, East Africa and South Africa. The wild flowers of the St John's-wort mingle with everlasting flowers and jasmine; red-winged starlings, mountain chats, augur buzzards and thick-billed ravens and lammergeiers are augmented by migrating harriers and kestrels; ibex by spotted cats, baboons, grivet or velvet monkeys, colobus monkeys and

42

the Simien fox.

The massifs of the Simien, lifted to 15,000 feet by volcanic upheaval, are broken by stupendous gorges and immense rock walls with escarpments falling 2,000 or 3,000 feet to gentler slopes of grassy banks, forested with gigantic tree heathers. Leslie Brown has described how the main north-west rampart of the Simien rises in three tiers behind this jumble of monstrous, unscalable blocks of rock and spectacular crags and pinnacles, deep gorges and chasms carved out by torrents and waterfalls. The final tier is one sheer monumental crag — broken into innumerable towers and buttresses and 3,000 to 5,000 feet in height — which soars up and up to the very top of the summit plateau, from which there is only one precarious way down the precipitous rock faces, though the walia have been seen to bound down more than 1,000 feet of these in less than two minutes.

The walia, and also a few of the small rock-loving klipspringer antelope, range over the 40-mile length of this great north-west rampart at heights of from 8000 to at least 11,000 feet. To Nicol the fascination of the walia lay not in the animals themselves, but in the fact that they live and move with such easy grace on the cliffs, which seemed fit for eagles and lammergeiers but not for hooved animals, running as if on air up the rock faces, defying and almost ignoring them. However, according to Brown, the walia appear to avoid the highest crags and almost vertical cliff faces, preferring the lower ledges or the 2,000-foot-high buttresses, because striating the rock faces and encircling the buttresses are broad green ledges, some of which, though steeply angled, are spacious enough to carry several acres of grass and herbs and are blue with scabious under the giant heath trees that, twisted by the strong winds, lean out towards the abysses, thousands of feet deep. The walia graze on these ledges in the early morning and again in the evening, after sheltering in caves or beneath overhangs or down in the forest during the heat of the day. They select their forage with care. A dozen may climb out along the more horizontal trunks of the heaths, festooned with beard lichens, or stand on their hind legs to reach the lower branches. Nicol noted that though the new tips of the heath trees were vividly green, the older foliage was duller, almost metallic; grey, yellow, pale green and soft brown lichens had etched intricate patterns, as delicate as those on Japanese pottery, on the blackish-brown hard red wood of the trunks.

The male walia, which associate in groups of up to eight for all the year except during the rutting season from March to May, feed at a higher level than the more wary females with kids. The females indeed seldom venture up to the plateau top until the rut, and with the birth of the kids six months later, retreat to the most inaccessible crags and gulches.

The only other ungulate endemic to Ethiopia, the mountain nyala, does not inhabit the Simien but the Bale mountains in the south of of the country and one or two other regions south and east of the Rift Valley, though it formerly ranged over most forests and moors above 9,000 feet in the south-east Highlands. Nyala, relatives of the kudus and bushbuck, are huge brown or grey-brown antelopes, weighing 400 to 500 pounds, though the females are much smaller, and carry magnificient lyrate horns. The 2000 or so on Bale are at home in a wide range of habitats between 9,000 and 14,000 feet — in the dense forests of cedars, in the higher forests of huge hagenia trees, 50 or 60 feet tall, with trunks 8 feet in diameter and massive branches flaring horizontally near ground level and then soaring skywards to umbrella-shaped crowns; and higher still in the open forests of St John's-wort which grow to a height of 50 feet and include patches of giant heath; but it is in the latter cold wet zone that they are most numerous, and are therefore permanently resident at a higher altitude than any other large animal in Africa. There, according to Brown, small herds of up to a dozen — adult males are solitary — feed on the fresh tufts of grass on recently burned heath and grassland and also on the four or five foot tall heather, which has been regularly burned for centuries. They also forage for such plants as vetch and lady's-mantle, the latter of which forms a trailing carpet at high altitudes, and whose silvery 'down' perhaps protects the plant from frost and shields it from the sun. At higher levels they nibble at the withered leaves of the giant lobelia, but their prime grazing is on the lush grass and clover growing around old well-manured cattle kraals.

The giant heath also provides the shy nyala with essential cover, and during the daytime they usually bed down in its scattered stands, with each member of a group facing in a different direction. It is perhaps not surprising that in such inaccessible country the wary nyala was, despite its considerable bulk, the last large animal to be encountered in Africa, for its discovery in 1908 came eight years after that of the okapi and four years after the giant forest hog's. It is possible that the groves of heath also harbour a few of the mysterious spotted lions, which a native tracker in the Aberdare mountains has described as lightly built like cheetahs, with whiskers instead of true manes, and spotted all over with rosettes. A dressed skin from the Aberdares measures only 8 feet 7½ inches in comparison with the 9 feet 6 inches of a good-sized lion, and as sound a naturalist as Leslie Brown does not dismiss the spotted lion as necessarily a creature of myth.

On both the Bale mountains and the Simien the summit plateaus at an altitude of between 11,000 and 14,000 feet are composed of rolling moors, often waterlogged, over which the winds whip during the day, while at night the temperature drops below freezing point. The monotony of the moorlands is broken by low shrubs, occasional stands of red-hot pokers with flame-coloured or orange-red spikes twelve inches long and three inches thick, and the wierd giant lobelia, resembling enormous artichokes when immature, but later developing huge inflorescence spikes. Clusters of alpine tarns, some filled only during the rainy season, lie in the hollows among the numerous small rock outcrops and prominent volcanic plugs. Waterfowl, including many pairs of the endemic blue-winged geese, crowd the lakes and streams, huge wattled cranes probe the soft soil, spot-breasted plover and sandpipers feed on the banks.

The loose earth between the rock outcrops supports a thin turf, spangled with small flowers and scented with aromatic herbs. The turf and the tussocks of longer grass are honeycombed everywhere with the holes of grass-rats, which Brown describes as standing at the entrances to these like minature marmots and chirping their shrill bird-like warnings, before diving into their holes at the last possible moment as the intruder's feet break through the crust into a burrow. Some burrows on the Bale plateau are associated with one or several piles of plant debris two feet or more in diameter, which may possibly be bedding discarded by giant mole-rats, though are more probably superfluous food. Although first described as long ago as 1842, the giant mole-rats' life-history was virtually unknown until W.D. Yalden made a brief study of them in December 1971. At that time of year he observed that there was no sign of activity in a colony of mole-rats until about 9.30 a.m., when, some three hours after dawn, the night frost had usually melted; but then a head would appear at the mouth of a burrow, pushing up loose soil, and the rat would proceed to gather in food by tearing away with its large incisors the grass immediately around the hole, seldom actually leaving the hole to do this, and backing into it at the slightest sound. After feeding in this manner for five minutes at most and taking in a dozen mouthfuls of grass, the rat would disappear underground for an hour or longer. Three or four of these feeding spells would exhaust the supply of vegetation around the hole, and the rat would then open up another one; one very large and distinctively coloured individual opened up five different holes the first day and four the next. In several instances holes around which the supply of grass had been depleted served as vents for the disposal of loose soil. As the heap of earth was pushed above the snow, so a hill-chat would arrive. Two or three of these birds were in constant attendance on the colony throughout the day and the appearance of one beside a burrow was often the first indication that a rat was at work. After a hole had been cleared it was plugged with soil and the majority were sealed by the early evening. Since a few of these blocked holes were reopened the following day, Yalden suggests that they were sealed in order to maintain an equable temperature inside the burrow during the cold nights, when it is well below freezing and the rats are probably inactive; and that reopening is not only for the disposal of unwanted soil.

Both mole-rats and grass-rats are preyed on by migrant kestrels and steppe eagles from Europe, by the large black Verreaux's eagles and red-tailed augur buzzards hovering gracefully above the colonies or perched on 20-foot spikes of giant lobelia, and by lanner falcons whizzing over the moors so low that they almost brush the grass as they attempt to capture the rats before they can dive into their burrows. The rats are probably also the exclusive prey of the so-called Simien fox — better known perhaps as the Abyssinian wolf — which survives precariously in only four areas of Ethiopia. There are possibly fewer than a score of foxes on the Simien, though between 350 and 475 on the Bale plateaus, most of which are inaccessible to and unsuitable for pasturing sheep and cattle. Certainly these foxes are to be found in greatest numbers in the zone of open moorland above 9,000 feet in which rats are most abundant. Their long and lightly structured jaws are adapted to snapping up any small rodents and birds, and there is no evidence that they prey on the brown hares, which are also extremely numerous on the Bale moors, where as many as thirty, usually solitary or in pairs, may be seen during the course of a day's tramp. The foxes are mainly diurnal, though that term includes moonlight in the animal world, and evince little fear of man except in such regions as the Simien where they are subjected to interference. Mole-rats, as we have seen, rarely come right out of their burrows to obtain food, and according to P.A. Morris, the fox's method of hunting rats in general is to walk slowly over ground on which they are particularly plentiful, pausing frequently to investigate a hole or a grass tussock and cocking an ear at the rats' high-pitched alarm squeaks. Ultimately it crouches stealthily towards one with short tense steps, then freezes with belly pressed flat to the ground for as long as ten minutes, before making a final dash over the last few yards to grab its prey. In longer grass, in which the rats are probably located by ear, a fox may 'jack-knife' and pounce with its fore-paws; occasionally one attempts to dig out a rat, either by a few desultory scratches at the entrance to a hole or by completely destroying a set of burrows and scraping up a mound of earth three feet high.

A Simien fox, though slightly larger and longer-legged than a European fox or jackal — to the latter of which it is probably most closely related — is not wolf-like, resembling, rather, a handsome red coyote the size of an Alsatian dog. With its bright rufous or yellowish-red coat, long black bushy brush and white legs and underparts, it is conspicuous as it moves at a swift trot over the grey and green moorland, barking from time to time or giving vent (in broad daylight!) to a loud screaming yelp or shriek, recalling the unearthly scream of a European vixen or of a jackal. These foxes do not apparently lair in earths, and their coats and brushes are luxuriantly thick to counter the nights, that are cold all the year round on the high moors, and the days when the sun's heat may be intense.

A feature of the Simien massif, as of other mountains and rocky ravines and gorges north and west of the Rift Valley, including the 15,160-foot summit of Ethiopia's highest peak, are the large, heavily built gelada baboons. The fourth of the mammals endemic to Ethiopia, and possibly forming a link between the African baboons and the Asian macaques, the geladas resemble monkeys facially, for their relatively short, rounded muzzles contrast with the dog-like snouts of other baboons, such as the still larger, ash-grey hamadryas that replace them in the Bale mountains. The male geladas, weighing more than 60 pounds, are a shaggy dark brown, varying to gold or near-black. With impressive leonine manes or capes of pale fawn fur falling about their shoulders as mantles, and long, tufted tails, they indeed slightly resemble lions as they lumber over the grasslands. The vivid red hourglass-shaped patches of bare skin on chest and neck — responsible for their popular name, 'bleeding-heart' baboons — are of a more intense shade in adult males and sexually receptive females, and the latter are also distinguished by bare, coloured hindquarters.

Huge troops of as many as 400 or 500 geladas rest at night in caves or under overhanging ledges on the cliff sides of the gorges that carve up the Ethiopian highlands. In the early morning some may begin foraging on the grassy ledges that straddle the colossal rock faces, but the majority climb up 1,000 feet to the alpine grasslands of the plateaus. There, according to Michael Nathan, they immediately head for the outcrops that are catching the first morning rays of the sun and begin to groom each other's fur, with a number of females attending to one adult male lying on his back; for the troops include harems of from two to six females, in addition to bachelor groups of males. Nathan has described how during the hours of daylight they never seem to stop grooming or stuffing themselves with food, and there is a ceaseless turmoil of noise and activity as the hunched forms, dotting the rough green pastures, shuffle along on their bottoms, a foot or so at a time, plucking bundles of grasses and plants and digging up roots so meticulously that after a troop has fed over a piece of ground it appears to have been grubbed up with a hoe.

It has been suggested that the geladas retreat to the impregnable fastnesses of the cliff faces at night in order to be safe from the attacks of predators rather than for shelter; but what predators? Leopards, though well known as montane predators in other parts of Africa — Mount Kenya for example — are extremely rare in the Ethiopian highlands, and while a young gelada might possibly be sized by a Verreaux's eagle or a lammergeier, that is certainly not a frequent occurrence. On the other hand the geladas, like so many wild animals, are apparently terrified of domestic dogs. In Nathan's experience, 'the mere sight of a dog sends the whole herd scurrying for the cliff line where the females and juveniles literally throw themselves to the safety of the steep slopes'; yet the Cape hunting dogs' range does not at the present time extend as far north as Ethiopia.

The geladas' reactions to man are variable. Nicol's presence, for instance, produced a similar reaction to that of dogs, for when close to a herd, any movement on his part evoked warning cries — 'the females and adolescents are awful shriekers' — and if the movement appeared threatening, the entire herd would bolt for the cliffs:

> The sound of the hundreds of feet was like thunder as they leaped and tumbled down impossible faces of rock and crashed . . . through the cliff-ledge tree heathers. Their quickest way of getting down a cliff was to fall, occasionally arresting the fall by grabbing for a rock or a tuft of grass here and there.

On the other hand adult males allowed Leslie Brown to approach to within thirty yards, though drawing back their lips to expose white gums and teeth in a grimace, which served both as a startled response to an alarming situation and as recognition signal. His own reaction was that any of the big males could have overpowered a man, while had the troop been aggressively inclined they could have torn him and his companions to pieces. This comment recalls Charles Darwin's report that a troop of geladas successfully repulsed the Duke of Coburg-Gotha's riflemen in the mountain pass of Mensa by rolling down boulders until the pass was blocked.

The phenomenon of gigantism in plants, exemplified by the heaths, St John's-wort and lobelia, reaches its height of extravagance on the East-African mountains of Kilimanjaro, Ruwenzori (Mountains of the Moon) and the Virunga volcanoes. There, in the alpine zone between 11,000 and 14,000 feet, one might be in the Scottish Highlands were it not for the monstrous growth of plants as big as trees. In this fantasy world Patrick Synge has described St John's-wort with flowers nearly as large as tulips hanging delicately like orange lanterns from the ends of the branches, and dense stands of giant lobelias on 6-foot stems with clusters of narrow leaves pointing skyward like candles, and flowering spikes, resembling open fir-cones, 7 or 8-feet long, covered with tiny purplish or powder-blue flowers. The latter attract and are no doubt pollinated by brilliant irridescent, turquoise blue and green sunbirds — the African counterpart of hummingbirds — which climb agilely round the great spikes and insert their long beaks into the flowers. When the sun strikes the dewdrops on the flowers and grey bracts the whole spike glitters with a silvery radiance and the sunbirds become emeralds and sapphires. When gashed, the lobelia stalks exude a sticky and extremely bitter fluid that burns the eyes, though this does not deter the mountain gorillas from attempting to eat them.

There, too, gnarled stems of giant tree-groundsels, 20 or 30 feet high and perhaps 200 years old, are twisted and contorted into all manner of weird shapes that ramify like stag's-horn coral. At the apices of the branches are clusters of large, ovate polished leaves, 3 feet long and a fierce shade of metallic green; the immense 4-foot-long flower spike carries florets resembling those of an English groundsel, except that there may be a hundred or more 1½-inch blossoms on one spike, and emerges from a cabbage-like mop of foliage, which includes the old leaves, dangling as a dead, slowly decaying mass around the trunk below the mop.

There is, I believe, no satisfactory explanation for this rampant growth which, is paralleled by the bromeliads of the Andes; for they also thrive in a cold alpine zone of the tropics, where water oozes everywhere and mist and fog maintain a humidity only rarely dissipated by the sun. Perhaps this montane gigantism is induced by a combination of such factors as fairly constant low temperature, very high humidity, high ultra-violet light intensity and an equatorial location.

Where Zaire, Rwanda and Uganda adjoin, two separate mountain massifs arise from the Albertine Rift: Ruwenzori, and to the south, the chain of the eight Virunga volcanoes, which rise to a height of nearly 15,000 feet and form a dam across the rift north of Lake Kivu. Five of these volcanoes harbour an ever-decreasing stock of some 225 or 250 mountain gorillas; there are no gorillas on Ruwenzori, though chimpanzees range to the tree limit between 10,000 and 11,000 feet.

The Virunga gorillas' adaptation to their montane environment will be of significance when we come to consider that of the Yetis in the Himalaya; and I have written of the gorillas' life-history in an earlier book, *Life in Forest and Jungle*. With an inexhaustible supply of vegetable food available to them the year round, the gorillas wander about the forest seasonally, and up into the bamboo belt between 7,500 and 10,000 feet with its thickets of wood-nettles. Although these stand six or eight feet and are virulent enough to sting through two layers of a man's clothing, the gorillas wade through them, incorporate them in their sleeping structures and eat the stems and leaves, bristling with stinging hairs, with apparent impunity. The young asparagus-like shoots of the bamboo are an important item in the gorillas' diet and, shredding and peeling them like bananas, they discard the tough outer sheath and eat the tender white bitter-sweet pith. The bamboo is supplemented by borage roots, vine leaves and particularly the juicy though, again, bitter interior of wild celery, six or eight feet tall, together with thirty or more other mainly bitter plants, which, though scarce in the bamboo belt, are common in the still higher zone of the bushy yellow-rosed St John's-wort, growing to a height of 10 or 25 feet. From time to time the gorillas climb up into the sub-alpine zone in order to sample the ripe though sour blackberries, which grow in extensive clumps 10 or 12 feet high.

Chapter Eight
THE MARKHOR OF THE HINDU KUSH

Up to this point we have been dealing mainly with the inhabitants of montane environments below 15,000 feet; but in Central Asia we explore regions that include the highest mountains in the world, commencing in the west with the Hindu Kush, which form the backbone of Afghanistan. More than 2000 years ago Alexander's soldiers named them Parapamisus, the mountains over which no eagle could fly. Later, the Arabian theologian and traveller Ibn Batuta — Sheik Abu Abdulla Mohammed of Tangier — who crossed the range in 1332 or 1334, stated that Hindu Kush could be translated as 'Hindoo-slayer' because 'so many of the slaves, male and female, brought thither from India died on the passage of this mountain owing to the severe cold and quantity of snow'; but its origins are in fact Persian.

Although the Hindu Kush rise to more than 20,000 feet, with snow — exceptionally slight in recent years — lying on them for eight or nine months of the year, and with freezing temperatures almost every night above 12,000 feet and subzero temperatures at Kabul in the winter, the summers are hot and dry below 15,000 feet. It is indeed a wild and desolate country of great peaks and rocky mountain spurs, which turn gold, pink and mauve as the shadows lengthen after the day's intense sunlight; of high barren plateaus; deep, narrow and fertile valleys with stretches of beautiful green turf here and there at higher altitudes; of precipitous gorges with magnificent forests of deodar, pine and larch; of grey-green torrents and wide, open flats of sun-baked desert.

In the north-east the Hindu Kush merge into a complex of high mountains that include the Russian Pamirs, with the grotesquely named Pik Communism rising to more than 24,500 feet. To the south-east of the Pamirs are the Karakoram or Black Gravel in Turki, in allusion perhaps to certain glaciers blackened with debris in sunless chasms, though they are in truth the whitest of all mountain ranges, with the greatest concentration of high peaks on Earth and four out of the five largest glaciers in temperate regions. Hindu Kush, Pamirs and Karakoram all meet in the north of Pakistan and Kashmir to form a colossal mountain mass, of which, because they are reached by the rains of the summer monsoon, the southern hills carry forests of oak, fir and pine up to a height of about 13,000 feet. The big game hunter, G. Burrard, has described how some fifty years ago, when autumn settled on the hills around the Vale of Kashmir, within a few days of the first heavy fall of snow soon after the middle of September the forests would ring to the war-cry of the barasingh (the Kashmir stag or hangul), which come down from the alpine pastures to rut. It was a wonderful and awe-inspiring cry, more like a drawn-out shriek than the genuine roar of its relative, the red deer.

To the north, beyond the frontier towns of Chitral and Gilgit, where precipitation, mainly in the form of snow, drops to less than 20 inches a year, George Schaller, when watching markhor, found the mountains bleak and cold and composed of glaciers and rock sparsely dotted with aromatic *artemisia* and other low-growing shrubs, though meadows and groves of birch and willow bordered the banks of streams or grew in places dampened by melt-water from the permanent snows. Yet the region was densely populated, with the result that most of the forests had been felled and the vegetation further denuded by the exploitation of junipers and other shrubs for fuel. Even in arid areas irrigated crops were being grown up to an altitude of 11,000 feet, and sheep, goats and yaks foraged on the sparse coarse grasses to over 15,000 feet, near the upper limit of vegetation.

The presence of the immense flocks of sheep and goats severely restricts the wildlife, though marmots are conspicuous. The majority of the few mammalian species are herbivores such as ibex — which are mainly diurnal because of the cold nights — and another wild goat, the markhor, which replaces the common wild goat eastwards of Baluchistan. Now that cheetahs and tigers have been exterminated, predators include only a few leopards, weasels, foxes and wolves, which hunt in ones and twos in the mountains during the summer, but rove in bands during the winter, often approaching the hill towns. Nevertheless, the Hindu Kush still hold the world's largest population of markhor, though the construction of new major roads has inevitably resulted in the decimation of their herds in the lower parts of their winter range. Elsewhere there are small isolated groups in the east of Afghanistan, in the Pamirs, and in the Pir Panjal range in Kashmir. A male markhor, standing 40 inches at the shoulder, is perhaps the most impressive of the wild goats, with heavy beard flowing down over throat and chest, shaggy mane falling from shoulder to knee, and massive, dark, spiralling horns up to 65 inches long on the outside curve, flat in section and twisted like a sword fashioned into a corkscrew. Those of the Afghanistan race indeed form a true corkscrew in contrast to those in Astor, further east, whose horns diverge widely into an open spiral.

1. Lammergeier (Bearded Vulture)

2. Andean or Great Condor

3. Chough

4. Pika

5. Blue Mountain Hare

6. Bighorn Ram

7. James's Flamingos

8. Female Mouflon

Since, like such mountain sheep as mouflons and urials, the markhor grows very little underwool during the winter beneath the long outer coat of thick, wiry iron-grey hair (which turns reddish-brown in summer and whitish with age) and loses this underwool after the summer moult, it could be argued that it is not a true goat like the ibex, despite its rank hircine stink; moreover when alarmed, it grunts nasally like sheep by expelling air through its nostrils. However, Schaller observed that when markhor were resting — which one may do for an hour or more at a time, after pawing the ground a dozen times to scrape a 'bed' — it does so in a typical goat manner with one or both forelegs stretched out in front of its body; and, when threatening other males it, like ibex and tahr, rears bolt upright on its hind legs with chin tucked in and head twisted to one side while facing its opponent, and may strike with its forelegs from this position, though not usually clashing horns.

Markhor also differ from mountain sheep in their choice of habitat, which usually comprises the rock sides of precipitous gorges with juniper scrub, above the sparse oak forest but below 13,000 feet. They never, however, climb up to the aery fastnesses of ibex and seldom venture on to the snow, though the absence of underwool does not prevent them from ranging over the barren Pakistani Sulaiman Hills with their contrasting cold winters and fiercely hot summers. Elsewhere they usually move up above the tree-line only during the summer months, when the males go up alone or in bands of half a dozen to heights inaccessible to females with kids born late in May or early in June. In the winter, when they collect in sexually mixed herds for the rut, they go down below 7,000 feet to sheltered valleys, densely forested with pine, birch and evergreen oak. There they graze in grassy glades or display typical goat agility in climbing to a height of 25 feet in the brushy holly oaks, jumping from bough to bough or balancing along swaying branches in order to obtain the acorns and leathery leaves that are a staple food, especially when the snow is deep. Schaller has described how a markhor will rear upright on its hind legs to reach a low bough or hook a foreleg over a branch and hold it down while nibbling the leaves. Half a dozen may pass an hour browsing the same tree, before ultimately jumping down from a height of 6 or 9 feet; and he observed one yearling male that climbed 12 feet up into an oak in order to rest with its legs dangling down on either side of a branch.

Chapter Nine
THE HAYMAKERS

Collared pikas (also known as mouse-hares or pygmy hares) are common in some areas of the Hindu Kush and become progressively more numerous eastwards, until in the highlands of the frontier country between Nepal and Tibet they are the most conspicuous animals, as they bask in the sun on the edges of moraines, and are the only common mammal on the less stony parts of the 14,000-foot terrain between Sikkim and Tibet. Ronald Kaulback, when at about 12,000 feet on the upper Salween in the south-east of Tibet, came across a gigantic pika warren that stretched in a half-mile wide swath for five miles along the floor of the valley:

> The ground was riddled with burrows, and hundreds of the little fellows went scurrying away as we approached, scuttling over the boulders like clockwork toys, dashing back to their holes and popping up again in a second, like marmots, to watch us go by. . . A small fox was running about, apparently quite aimlessly, among the holes. . . and five or six hawks were eternally wheeling overhead.

Pikas are no doubt the main food source of mountain foxes and also of the small short-tailed weasels, though the latter venture above the snow-line in the Himalaya only during the summer months, when they raid over a wide area in search of the nests and eggs of snow partridges.

Another Tibetan explorer, Henry Hayden, found the plains among the great lakes north of Llasa similarly perforated everywhere a few inches below the surface with networks of burrows resembling grandiose mole-runs:

> 'Except where the ground was completely waterlogged, there was hardly a square foot of flat country without them; as one rode along, the plain was alive with rats, which at our approach made for their burrows, where they sat and watched us, disappearing underground if we came too near.

The pikas are the highest resident mammals in the Himalaya. Howard-Bury recorded them at 20,000 feet on the Tibetan side of Everest, and Charles Stonor, a member of the *Daily Mail* 'Abominable Snowman' expedition, saw 'thousands' among the rocks up to a height of 18,000 or 19,000 feet on the approach route to Everest from Nepal, although the only vegetation appeared to be a sparse growth of lichens; and some were still present at that altitude during the winter, sunning themselves on moraines. Presumably these high-altitude pikas are emigrants from over-populated colonies at lower levels.

There are a dozen species of these engagingly fearless little animals in Asia, from Iran to Manchuria and from the Himalaya to the arctic coast of Siberia; and in these various regions they have been able to adapt to such contrasting environments as damp forests at an altitude of only 5,000 feet, hot arid steppes or cold mountainsides. Similarly, the two species scattered over the scree slopes of the North-American West from Mount McKinley, where they may occupy the same habitat as the hoary marmots, to northern New Mexico, range from 13,500 feet down almost to sea-level. Although belonging to the same order as rabbits and hares, and therefore known as coneys or rock rabbits in the Rockies, they more resemble miniature guinea-pigs or hyraxes, since they are only six to eight inches long and weigh only 4 to 9 ounces. Guinea-pigs in rabbits' fur they have been termed, being tail-less and with their feet concealed by their long hair. Their rounded vole-like faces are heavily bewhiskered and their ears protected inside and out by thick hair. Since their hind legs are as short as their front legs they hop over the rocks like balls of grey fluff in brief quick dashes with a stiff hobbling gait. Nevertheless, they scamper with extreme agility over the most precipitous places, vying with lizards in their contempt for vertical rock walls, for their hairy soles give perfect traction and also insulate their feet from snow and frozen rock.

On mountainsides, plateaus and valleys alike their habitat is open rocky ground, on which they may be almost invisible against a background of lichen-encrusted boulders. On these they rest for hours at midday, sitting hunched up with back higher than head, preferably in a partly protected place such as the crest of a backward-slanting rock, which affords a wide angle of view below and yet allows them to tumble back into the shelter of the boulders if endangered. But they cannot tolerate excessive heat, retreating to the cool interior of the rocks if the temperature climbs into the nineties, and are most active in the early morning and evening, and also on moonlit nights.

Remarkably, considering the altitudes at which they live, pikas, unlike marmots, do not hibernate and are out every day throughout the winter in such cold environments as that of Tibet — their nostrils can be closed in severe weather — collecting fragments of vegetation. However, in some regions they evidently move down to lower levels in the autumn, for Kaulback observed that as the snow melted in the spring and fresh greenery appeared at 13,000 feet in the Chutong valley between Burma and Tibet, pikas came trekking up from lower down the valley and after a week or ten days moved on again, as the snow receded from further stretches of grassland, to a pass 1000 feet higher; and in one locality at 12,000 feet in Sikkim they disappear in winter. But wherever they winter they are able to survive the long cold by practising refection like hares and rabbits. During the daytime their droppings are green and dry, but their night droppings are covered by a layer of mucus that keeps them moist. When exposed to the air, the bacteria in these night droppings form essential vitamins that, when swallowed, mix with fresh food during redigestion. It has been asserted that without refection the pikas would starve after about three weeks during the winter. Nevertheless, not only do they tunnel under the snow from one patch of roots or greenery to another, but probably rely mainly on the 'hay' that they harvest on warm dry days during the late summer:

> From the numerous cracks and crannies, which honeycombed the conglomerate, scampered innumerable pikas [wrote Douglas Carruthers, watching them at 9,500 feet, just below the snow-line in the Karakoram]. Being diurnal in habits, the whole colony was at work, for this was their harvest-time. . . The were, literally, making hay while the sun shone, running out onto the hillside, collecting loads of grass, and racing home with bundles as big as themselves.

Green plants such as iris and cinquefoil, together with the leaves of shrubs and at lesser elevations, green shoots from the lower branches of trees, form 80 per cent of a pika's hay, though quantities of seeds and grasses are also collected. Victor Cahalane has described how the individual haymaker, after pausing at the edge of the moraine housing its burrow, suddenly rushes out to a plant. Clipping it off with its sharp incisors, the pika carries it to another plant and then to others until, in less than a minute, it has amassed a large bundle. Holding this crosswise in its mouth, with 4-foot-long stems folded four times, trailing beside or behind it, it races back to the moraine, hops across the rocks and places this fresh green food on the steadily increasing pile laid out on a flat boulder to dry in the sun. The haymaker undertakes trip after trip, rarely venturing more than a few yards from edge of the rocks though occasionally several hundred feet. When it has finally completed its haycock this, when dried, may contain as much as a bushel of material and be nearly two feet high; but though very compacted its contents normally cure evenly, since only the quantity that will dry properly is cut each day. Once the hay is dry it is then stored in a place that will be easily accessible during the winter to a family or possibly a community of pikas, since as many as six adults and one juvenile have been trapped at a single store. This will be sited in a deep, dry, well-drained yet airy crevice or hollow in the rocks or, more frequently, in a sun-trap free from running water below and protected above from snow and rain by a tilted overhanging shelf of rock. It is fascinating to note that the pikas' haymaking and curing technique preserves not only the natural colour of the plant material unfaded, but also the fragrance of well-cured hay free from mould, despite the fact that in some cases the stack may include the twigs and needles of conifers.

While they are haymaking the pikas chatter with plaintive nasal bleats, which have been likened to the high-pitched creaking of a rusty hinge or the clinking of two flakes of granite. However, the Tibetans call pikas *shippi* or whisperers, perhaps because of the ventriloquial nature of their calls, which are associated with a violent jerking forward of the whole body and a twitching upward of the ears, as if considerable exertion is required to expel air from the lungs.

According to the Everest naturalist R. W. G. Hingston, the pikas' haymaking and burrowing habits have led on the high-altitude steppes of Tibet to an amicable relationship with such birds as ground choughs, horned larks, desert chats and at least three kinds of mountain finches, for the choughs, chats and finches nest in the pikas' burrows, frequently at a considerable depth, and all are attracted by the hayseeds lying around and in the burrows.

Chapter Ten
THE GREAT SHEEP OF
THE PAMIRS

The Pamirs can be considered as a westerly extension of the Himalaya and as the knot from which radiate those other great mountain masses — the Hindu Kush, Karakoram, Kun Lun and Tien Shan. Their arid but sunny western slopes, with their sparse woodlands of longeval junipers, wild apple and pear trees, walnuts, pistachios, almonds and maples belie the fact that the Pamirs have long been known as *Krysha Mira* or, in Persian, *Bam-i-dunya*, the Roof of the World, which has changed little in the seven centuries since Marco Polo wrote in 1273:

> The plain is called Pamier, and you ride across it for twelve days together, finding nothing but a desert, without habitations or any green thing, so that travellers are obliged to carry with them whatever they have need of.

Nevertheless, the 35,000 square miles of sky-high plateaus, intersected by line after line of parallel ridges rising to 15,000 or 20,000 feet, are not one vast tableland, but a series of troughs or valleys, of no great width, shelving downwards to a river-bed or lake and uniformly framed on either hand by mountains that have been eroded into immense, rather smooth hills perpetually covered with snow to a depth of sixty-five inches above 15,000 feet — as Lord George Curzon discovered more than eighty years ago. The mountains terminate in steep shingle slopes, and George St George has described in *Soviet Deserts and Mountains* how at the snow-line the ground is strewn with broken moraines of former glaciers and pitted with round holes or cirques filled with ice or water, but otherwise bare except for gnarled shrubs hugging the cold ground.

Thus, the Pamirs in fact comprise eight lofty shallow valleys 10,000 or 15,000 feet high, each of which incorporates a more or less level expanse of spongy soil, usually covered with coarse yellow grass, stretching away on either side of its river or lake. These plains, green and flower-strewn during the summer, are interspersed with areas of sand, clay and stones, which in many places are overlaid with a powdery encrustation of magnesium salts

58

that glitters in the sun like hoar-frost. The plains and valleys are so high that St George found that he was rarely aware of the great altitude of the latter, but always conscious of the illimitable spaciousness of the brown wastes of sandstone rocks, 'decorated here and there with low cushion-plants of sombre colour varying from dark green to violet', though otherwise almost devoid of vegetation except where ravines provided shelter for a few Siberian primroses and golden-headed mountain onions, which are extraordinarily common in sandy places in some parts of the Pamirs and Tien Shan and whose leaves are covered with a fine frost-proof 'fur'.

Nevertheless, there is an abundance of pasturage on the Pamirs, providing the finest grazing in central Asia, particularly in the milder Alai Valley with its enormous snowfall. This, Marco Polo also noted, stating that: 'And when he is in this high place he finds a plain between two mountains, with a lake from which flows a very fine river. Here is the best pasturage in the world; for a lean beast grows fat here in ten days.' But in winter icy blizzards sweep the grazings and for more than half the year they are buried under snow, with the passes blocked and lakes frozen. On the high central and eastern desert regions, however, little snow falls — less, according to St George, than in any other area of Soviet Asia, with only an inch of precipitation at Lake Kara-kul, one of the highest lakes in the world. Although its 'black' waters are set in sand-dunes the lake is surrounded by snow-patched mountains and the cold is intense, with temperatures falling below freezing every night except for a couple of weeks at midsummer.

As a consequence of their location on the extreme north-west of the Central Asian mountain system the Pamirs and the Celestial Mountains of the Tien Shan form a barrier between the palearctic and oriental faunal zones and, at the same time, a meeting place for fauna from such diverse regions as the Siberian taiga, the deserts of Central Asia and India, the mountains of the Himalaya and the high plateaus of Tibet and Mongolia, with the result that about 120 species of mammals have been found in these two ranges. Inevitably, alpine marmots are everywhere, established in colonies comprising hundreds of burrows; but the Pamirs are above all the home of the great mountain sheep, as indeed is the whole Central Asian plateau from the Pamirs to Tibet and the Altai.

Although as few as six and as many as thirty-six races of mountain sheep have been recognized it will be simplest to assign them to five groups: the mouflons and urials ranging from the Mediterranean and Iran to western Pakistan, and not usually living above 10,000 feet; the argalis or ammons inhabiting the highest mountain masses in Central Asia; the Siberian bighorns or snow sheep frequenting all the ranges from the Yenisey east to Kamchatka; the thin-horned Dall's and Stone's sheep of Alaska, the Yukon and northern British Columbia; and the bighorns of the Rockies south to Old Mexico.

There can be no doubt as to the ovine ancestry of all these sheep, though the reddish-brown adult rams of the mouflon, carrying horns with heart-shaped curls 30 inches long, are distinguished from all other wild sheep in their winter pelage by white patches on either flank. They and the Cyprus urials are also unique, at the present time, in being the only sheep living in partially forested country. The flocks of twenty or thirty mouflon led by an old ewe are, for example, restricted in Corsica and Sardinia to scrub-covered mountain tops around 6,000 feet. There, in grassy glades interspersed among thick heather growing to a height of 6 feet, they feed on coarse grasses, heather, broom, leaves and the shoots of young trees, supplemented by acorns and beechnuts in the autumn. Similarly, the Cyprian urial is confined to the dense, dwarf-evergreen Forest of Paphos, lying at an altitude of 6,000-7,000 feet on the steep mountains rising from the centre of the island. Eleven valleys, radiating approximately from the centre, serve as wintering grounds. In the case of both mouflon and urial the more or less inaccessible cover has probably saved them from extinction, affording them sanctuary from persecution at lower levels and in more open parts of the islands. The various races of Asiatic urials in Iran, the Punjab, Baluchistan and Afghanistan, for example, which inhabit either gently rolling, grassy mountain slopes above or below the tree-line or rocky scrub-covered hills and barren stony ranges, have been subjected to a persecution that has reduced the immense nineteenth-century Ladakh population of shapu urials, distinguished by their great black or grizzled ruffs, to their present complement of less than a thousand.

According to some authorities the mouflon was originally a forest animal on the mainland of the eastern Mediterranean and not indigenous to Corsica and Sardinia, while the present restriction of wild sheep in general to mountainous regions is the result either of expulsion from lowland areas by persecution or of the absorption of those inhabiting lowland regions into domesticated flocks. In this respect the mouflon, the smallest of the wild sheep, is probably the ancestor of the domestic sheep — it somewhat resembles the Soay sheep — and has thrived in the environment of European forests as if they were its natural habitat. Thus, whereas there are to-day only about 300 mouflon in Corsica, those that have been introduced to a number of forests in central Europe have multiplied a thousand-fold. Beyond the confines of Europe sheep country at the present time consists predominantly of open grassy slopes that are not too steep, on the sunny side of mountains, but with rocky outcrops in the vicinity to which the sheep can retreat if surprised by a predator. Wild goats, on the other hand, prefer rougher, more precipitous slopes, backed by crags, and feed on a coarser type of vegetation, leaving the shorter, sweeter grasses to the sheep. However, it must be admitted that a wild sheep can bound down a steep slope strewn with rocks with the speed and grace of an antelope running over the plains, and in the Altai argali can be seen in rocky ibex country, though ibex are never seen on the rolling grassy sheep hills. The American naturalist, Valerius Geist, has summed up wild sheep as generalised mountaineers that roam over all typical alpine terrain and are capable of running at high speed for short distances, but which jump rather than climb like goats when fleeing through crags and cliffs.

In his account of his travels along the Silk Road over the Pamirs, Marco Polo stated that:

There are great numbers of all kinds of wild beasts; among others, wild sheep of great size, whose horns are good six palms in length. From these horns the shepherds make great bowls to eat from, and they use horns to enclose folds for their cattle at night.

He did not apparently see the sheep himself, though the Fransiscan friar, Father William, had done so twenty years earlier, and five and a half centuries were to elapse before the great *poli* sheep of the Pamirs were rediscovered by Europeans in 1834. Three years later the first pair of *poli* horns were brought back to England by John Wood, who, while exploring the source of the Oxus, had picked up the head of a ram killed by hunters in the Wakhan region between the Hindu Kush and the Great Pamir:

We saw numbers of horns strewed about in every direction [he wrote], the spoils of the Kirghiz hunters. Some of these were of astonishingly large size. . . The ends of the horns projecting above the snow, often indicated the direction of the roads; and wherever they were heaped in large quantities and disposed in a semi-circle, there our escort recognized the site of a Kirghiz summer encampment.

The Kirghiz stacked cairns of *poli* heads everywhere, just as their ancestors under Gengiz Khan built mounds and pyramids of their dead enemies' skulls. Marco Polo's grey sheep, protected in winter by long white plaids covering neck, chest and shoulders, are among the largest of all wild sheep, standing twelve hands (4 feet) at the shoulder and weighing up to 300 or 350 pounds, though not much more than 200 pounds in the spring after a winter's semi-starvation, since their bones are surprisingly light and brittle. The rams carry massive, deeply wrinkled, open spirals of horns, the colour of old ivory, which coil round to form a more-or-less complete circle, with the points flaring out to the side in a graceful curve to give a horn length of 60 inches on a large head and 75 inches on an exceptional one, and a circumference at the base of 15 to 20 inches. Old cast horns are commodious enough to house foxes, say the Kirghiz. Although the rams' necks are slender and not particularly muscular, deep strong withers enable them to bear the weight of these great horns and also to take up the shock when pitching down from a rock on to their forefeet. When during the rut from December to early January two rams fight, backing thirty or forty paces from each other and charging again and again — like domestic black-faced rams on a Highland stance — they clash head-on in stupendous collisions with cracks that can be heard a mile away; but though these contests may continue for several hours until one or both combattants are exhausted, no serious injuries are suffered. This is a phenomenon to which we shall return when considering the American bighorns, whose behaviour has been much more extensively studied.

At the conclusion of the rut the rams wander away in twos and threes, eventually to summer near the permanent snow-line. James Clark actually climbed to 20,800 feet, when the temperature was 14⁰ F below zero, in order to shoot *poli* near Chapchingal on the Chinese border. This led him to comment that the pursuit of wild sheep takes a man to the top of the world, where the towering mountain peaks sweep on to the horizon and vast valleys plunge thousands of feet below; and that the man who hunts low will never bag the biggest of big rams, which tuck themselves away in the highest and most inaccessible hidden amphitheatres surrounded by rocky walls, though with an opening at the lower end through which a small stream drains the area.

In the spring the winter flocks of a hundred or more *polis* break up into groups of a dozen or so ewes and younger beasts and are led by one of the older ewes, whose short horns curve like sabres, to the summer pastures of the Kirghiz nomads — those fearfully bleak, undulating valley-plateaus, which the fourteenth-century Chinese described as 'midway between heaven and earth; the snow-drifts never cease winter or summer; the whole tract is but a dreary waste without a trace of humankind.' Up there, on the roof of the world, the *polis* graze the dry grasses, alpine plants and nine-inch-high *boortza* scrub, feeding, like ibex, from dawn until the sun is high, when they sleep in the shade until two hours before dark, selecting where practicable a saddle or a depression on a ridge where the wind reaches them from every side. 'There was no tree, no bush, no lowly shrub to break the sweeping expanse of scree and brown earth', wrote H. W. Tilman of typical *poli* country at 14,000 feet in the north of Hunza. 'Grass there was, but the blades were so sparsely scattered that even at this time of high summer ones eyes received only the vaguest impression of anything green.'

On these open hills the *polis* can wind their most dangerous predator, the wolf, at a range of a quarter of a mile, and can sight one at a much greater distance with eyes equivalent to 8x magnification binoculars. If wolves stampede them the younger sheep, which can easily outdistance them, may run for ten miles before halting. Around Kara-kul, according to Sven Hedin (who was exploring central Asia in the 1890s) the wolves, though killing some ibex and hares, preyed mainly on the *polis;* but one questions his account of the hunting methods they employed:

In hunting the wild sheep the wolves display remarkable craft and intelligence. Having enclosed the sheep in a wide ring, they begin to howl, so as to make their presence known to them, and gradually close in upon their prey. When they get near enough, they cut off two or three of the sheep and force them to take refuge in a narrow, out-jutting crag. . . If the crag is too steep for them to scale it, they patiently wait at the bottom until the wild sheep's slender legs become numbed. . . and they roll down the precipice into the jaws of their ravenous persecutors.

The *polis* are more vulnerable to the attacks of wolves in the winter when heavy snowfalls force them to migrate to lower valleys or to more southerly ranges, where they can feed on scattered tufts of grass among the rocks and screes on high, wind-swept slopes with a southern aspect. In these conditions, when they are much hampered by the deep snow, they are liable to be driven by packs of wolves into corries or snow-drifts, where those weakened by the poor winter fodder, particularly the older rams with their very heavy heads, become easy prey. In writing of his experiences in the Karakoram, Carruthers observed that whereas derelict horns of ibex were usually to be found in the valley bottoms and in streams, where they had been deposited by time, wind and weather, those of sheep, by contrast, were nearly always in the places where their owners had died, since the very nature of the terrain in which they lived prohibited any or much movement after death: 'Those Golgothas, which one occasionally comes across, where horns lie in hundreds, are nearly always in places situated close under escarpments, where deep snow-drifts would be likely to accumulate, and therefore to become traps for unwary or hard-driven beasts.' According to nineteenth-century big-game hunters they were also decimated by wild dogs and it is possible that eagles may takes some lambs and snow leopards kill some of the younger beasts in the spring. Wolves, snow-drifts, avalanches and hunters must preclude all but a few *polis* from attaining to their potential life-span of fourteen years.

Marco Polo would find parts of the north-eastern Pamirs little changed today; but although the Great Pamir and the western Himalaya were until recently the main stronghold of the *polis,* the construction of the Karakoram highway from Pakistan to China during the late 1960s has resulted in their flocks being decimated and they are now only sporadic visitors to the fresh spring grass in Pakistan from Sinkiang, where they are protected.

Far to the east of the Pamirs, rolling plateaus, at altitudes of up to 16,000 feet, composed of flat steppes, tilted levels and round-topped hills, stretch for 2,000 miles from southern Tibet to Outer Mongolia. This monotonous terrain, broken here and there by immense swamps and stupendous mountain masses, is the habitat of the even larger, antelope-like *nyan* — the Tibetan great sheep, weighing up to 400 pounds, standing twelve hands at the shoulder and, despite their long legs, as bulky as small ponies. The white-ruffed brown rams carry outward-curving horns, which, while shorter than those of the *polis* and never exceeding a single curl, have a wider span than a man's outstretched arms.

> The chief point which impressed me [wrote Burrard] was their wonderful length of leg, compared with animals such as burrel, thar, ibex or shapu. They seem built for galloping over open country, and ... the best place in which to find them are vast open spaces interspersed with hills in which there are valleys to provide shelter from both sun and wind.

Such terrain is found on the uplands of Tibet where, as another big-game hunter, A. A. Kinloch, wrote nearly a hundred years ago:

> For hundred of miles not a tree is to be met with; where in every direction, as far as the eye can reach, there is nothing but a vast expanse of barren soil, rock and sand; where there is no shelter from the glare of a cloudless noon, nor from the freezing winds that sweep the naked hills with relentless force towards the close of day; here; in the midst of solitude and desolation, where animal life has apparently to struggle for existence under every disadvantage, is the home of this great wild sheep.

We do not know very much about the habits of the *nyan.* According to Mongolian nomads in the Altai, some flocks cross ten or fifteen miles of desert from one mountain mass to another in the winter, but the majority migrate to the lower valleys and in the spring feed along the river banks in ravines or follow the receding snow upwards. After the lambs have been born in May or early June the rams summer near the limit of vegetation at 19,500 feet in flocks of sixty or more. There they graze in the early morning and evening and rest during the heat of the day on bare hillsides, pawing out scrapes in dry stony places and supporting their great horns on the ground.

Chapter Eleven

BLUE SHEEP AND SNOW LEOPARDS

The habitat of the blue sheep — the bhurel or bharal of the big-game hunters — extending from the Karakoram in the west along the northern ranges of the Himalaya to Mongolia, Szechwan and Shensi and including almost the whole of the Tibetan plateau, is one of the most desolate regions on Earth, lying between 11,000 to 21,500 feet and characterised by extreme winter cold and summer aridity. A montane steppe of rolling downs and low, blue and brown hills that stretch away as far as the eye can see in the clear light, with here and there an encampment of herdsmen, it is associated with broad, stony valleys and shale ridges at the bases of the higher peaks. Primulas, gentians and large yellow poppies, with petals encased in ice, bow before the searing winds that sweep down from the eternal snows of the peaks. Nevertheless, despite the arid terrain, nine-tenths of the blue-sheep country is grass, providing summer grazing for their flocks of from thirty to a hundred, especially on slopes facing south, from which the snow melts more than a month earlier than those facing north. Even in winter, grass, though withered and dead, remains their staple food, augmented by the tips and leaves of juniper and other shrubs at the upper limits of the tree-line. To find a blue sheep actually within woodland would no doubt be exceptional, but one must accept with reservations a report that in the valley of the Yangtse a dwarf race has evolved at a distance of only 500 yards from the main body of the parent stock because it has been isolated by a belt of forest.

Being as agile as goats, and indeed resembling Rocky Mountain goats in being short legged, broad backed, quick and neat footed, blue sheep can climb rougher and steeper slopes than any of the true sheep and are able to graze on the ledges of precipitous rock faces and cliffs. They nearly always feed in the vicinity of rocks, on which, according to L.A. Waddell, sentries can stand, and to which they can retreat if threatened by predators.

As we made our way along a moraine ledge under these cliffs [wrote Eric Shipton when at 18,000 feet on Nanda Devi in the central Himalaya] we were alarmed by the ominous whirr of falling stones accompanied by some shrill whistles, and, looking up, we saw a number of bharal high up among the crags above us. Never have I seen a more extraordinary display of rock climbing. The cliffs on which these animals were sramb-ling about looked from where we were to be utterly unclimbable; and yet here were... young and old running about them as if they were horizontal instead of being almost vertical... Although I had often watched chamois in the Alps I never before believed that these animals could move about on the rock faces of such appalling steepness... It was difficult to understand what brings these animals to such altitudes. Three thousand feet below was perfect grazing, and neither man nor beast to molest them... one would expect them to be fat and lazy down below; instead of which they seemed to spend most of their time climbing about precipices of astonishing steepness, risking their necks on crevasse-covered glaciers...

Unlike *polis* and *nyans,* some of the summer flocks of blue sheep may include a few adult rams, though the majority of these associate in all-male groups of from half-a-dozen to as many as forty at higher levels near the permanent snow-line from June until the rut in November-December, when they round up small harems of ewes. The rams, standing three feet at the shoulder and weighing 140-165 pounds, are majestic animals with demonic gold or orange eyes, heavy cylindrical horns that arc outwards almost horizontally for 30 inches or more from broad bases to backward flaring tips, and a strikingly coloured winter pelage of brownish-grey tinged with slaty-blue on the upper parts, which are separated from the white underparts by a horizontal black stripe. This pattern renders them barely visible against rocky outcrops, though it is offset by the conspi-cuously blue-black stripes down the fronts of their white legs. During the summer, when the under-wool is shed in ragged patches, the blue-grey changes to reddish-grey.

Few naturalists have been priviledged to watch blue sheep, but Peter Matthiessen did so on the mountains of Dolpo on the Nepalese-Tibetan frontier west of Mustang, and he has described in *The Snow Leopard* how one morning early in the winter he crouched for a long time high on a mountainside in order to be with the sheep when they were resting for their habitual hour's cudding. A black redstart was bobbing and flaring its rufous tail on a nearby rock and a flock of fifty or more choughs were lilting and dancing and squealing on the wind, before plummeting out of sight, filling the silence with a rush of air. All the sheep except two were lying down, and four big rams, a little uphill of the rest, faced him unalarmed, as they chewed their cud, with the sun glowing on the coarse hairs of their blue coats and 'carved faces sweeping back to the huge cracked horns.' Eventually the sheep began to graze again, twisting their necks in search of tufts of grass under the bush honeysuckle, though a few browsed the shrub's small yellow-green leaves; but when the lead female emerged from a hollow not ten yards uphill of Matthiessen, she suddenly caught his scent and turned quickly to stare round-eyed at his motionless form below, the black marks on her legs quivering with tension. When a ram approached her, he also became alarmed and whirled round with a jump as his tail shot straight up in the air. Stamping his right forefoot, the ram gave a weird, harsh, high-pitched whinny — resembling the chatter of a squirrel or sharp shrill whistle of an ibex rather than the bleat or 'sneeze' of a sheep — and stepped boldly forwards to investigate. The remainder of the flock followed, 'until the mountain blue is full of horned heads and sheep faces.'

But, as in the case of the markhor, we have to ask whether the blue sheep are in fact sheep or goats or an intermediate form of goat-sheep. Although they, and in particular the ewes with their short spindly horns, resemble sheep in their general appearance and do not have the typical beard, knee calluses and strong body-odour of goats, they on the other hand lack the small face glands just below the eye of true sheep and display more numerous affinities with goats. These include the shape, structure and colour of the rams' blue-black horns, which do not have any surface corrugations; the large dew-claws and the striped markings on their legs; the hairless tail (except for the tip) which is raised goat-like when the rams are excited; and their voice and behaviour when rutting at midwinter, for, as Matthiessen has pointed out, they rear up and run on their hind legs before crashing down into the impact, as true goats such as ibex do but unlike true sheep that usually charge on all fours. However, it must be said that Rocky Mountain bighorn rams, instead of completing their rutting charge on all fours, sometimes cover the last few yards reared up on their hind legs. Why, asks Matthiessen, should Nature have devoted so many thousands of years to the natural selection of characters that favour head-on collisions over brains?

The blue sheep are the main prey of the snow leopard; they are also hunted by wolves in Tibet — where bears are reported to kill some — and by wild dogs. On one occasion, when Shipton was on a grassy alp on the flank of a glacier at an altitude of some 14,000 feet in the Karakoram, he found that he was stalking the same flock of sheep as six wild dogs; and early in November Matthiessen watched a pair of wolves racing straight downhill to cut off the rearmost of six sheep bounding across the snow towards some cliffs. Although the ewe appeared to be moving much too swiftly to be caught, the wolves were gaining on it over the hard snow, and as they tore through the matted juniper and down over steepening rocks, it seemed that the bharal must be intercepted and bowled over. However, at the last moment it reached a narrow ledge, where it could not be followed, and after a brief gaze around, the wolves returned up the mountainside. There, on being joined by two other members of the pack, all four paused to romp and roll in dung on the yak pasture, before trotting away and disappearing behind a snowy ridge, on which, after a short run in alarm, a band of fourteen sheep formed line on a high point and watched the wolves depart; but it was not long before all, including the six that had been chased into the precipice were browsing again.

The beautiful snow leopard is rather smaller than the common leopard, standing four feet at the shoulder and weighing up to 160 pounds, and is distinguished by a higher forehead, shorter muzzle, enormous paws and a furry tail, three feet long and thick to the tip. Its eyes are pale and frosty, its dense, velvety fur of misty grey-brown or smoke-grey hair is marked with a cryptic pattern of black spots and rosettes, which are clouded by the depth of the fur pile. Snow leopards are now rare or uncommon throughout their range from the Hindu Kush and Pamirs to the northern Himalaya and the high plateaus of Tibet, the Tien Shan, the Altai and the Sayan Mountains near Lake Baikal on the Siberian frontier with Mongolia. According to Schaller, probably fewer than 250 remain in Pakistan, while during their 250-mile late-autumn expedition from Kathmandu to Dolpo, he and Matthiessen saw only one snow leopard out of a possible 150-300 inhabiting Nepal, where, though legally protected, they are still killed by means of poison-tipped spears implanted in the trails of their extensive hunting circuits. They may, however, be less rare in that wilderness of rocks, snowfields, glaciers and alpine meadows between 10,000 and 15,000 feet on the northern slopes of the Himalaya. In the summer they range from the treeline at 12,000 feet over the alpine steppe to the snow-line at 18,000 feet or more in the Himalaya, and to 20,000 feet in the Altai, preying not only on the blue sheep but also on argalis, urials, markhor, ibex, young yaks and musk deer, which are to be found as unusually high as 19,000 feet on the hills of south-east Tibet, and on such small mammals as marmots, pikas and hares. When they move down to winter in the oak scrub or spruce forest in the upper valley bottoms between 3,000 and 6,000 feet, domestic sheep and goats are attacked if not guarded, and snowcock, pheasants, chukor partridges, monals and tragopans are also stalked and captured with huge leaps if there is no cover from which to ambush them. But there appear to be very few first-hand observations of snow leopards. Tom Longstaff, who saw their tracks higher than 19,000 feet above the Inner

Sanctuary of Nanda Devi, states that they are difficult to approach because during the day they search for game by lying out on some high rocky spur commanding a wide view over the country below; and he cites an instance in Kumaon of two lying side by side on top of a cliff watching a flock of urials feeding on the slopes below. On the other hand, when Shipton was crossing the Chichilik Pass, deep in snow, between Hunza and Sinkiang on an autumn evening in 1940, two snow leopards suddenly walked out from behind a buttress of rock not 50 yards ahead of him; 'They paused for a moment and looked at me, then ambled on across the snow, apparently quite unconcerned. It was the first time I had seen these beautiful creatures. In that wild and lovely setting it was a most moving experience.'

Since Richard Meinertzhagen also saw two crossing a stream in the Karakoram, the assertion by some writers that they usually hunt alone and are nocturnal, lying up in a rocky lair by day, is evidently not invariable; and it is indeed contradicted by other sources which state that they roam over vast territories — as they must do in view of the scarcity of prey — especially when hunting the blue sheep, and den up at night.

If we know little about the actual hunting habits and life-history of the snow leopard, we know still less about those of that rarely seen predator, the clouded leopard, which inhabits dense evergreen forests from Nepal eastwards to south China and Malaya. This leopard has a tail almost as long as its body — a useful balancing aid when climbing after small mammals and birds; but why, though considerably smaller than a snow leopard and weighing only about 45 pounds, is it equipped with enormous upper canines that are relatively the nearest in size among the large cats to those of the sabre-toothed tiger, and would appear to be unnecessarily formidable for the killing of deer and domestic stock?

Chapter Twelve

TAHR AND TIGERS IN THE HIMALAYA

The Himalaya and their spurs present a southern barrier to many of the animals of temperate regions and form the northern boundary for much of the tropical fauna. They also mark the most westerly limits for such oriental species as lesser red pandas, snub-nosed langurs, takin and two species of goat-antelopes related to the chamois — the goral from as far east as Manchuria and the serow, which also inhabits Indo-China, Sumatra, Taiwan and Japan; and the most easterly limits for such Eurasian species as urials, and for markhors and the dusky-brown tahr.

The tahr is another of those strange goat-antelopes, or perhaps a link between them and the true goats; for although a typical-looking goat with stocky body and powerful fore-quarters (and also the strong-body odour of a goat) the tahr has closely set, laterally compressed horns 12-15 inches long, curving sharply back in both sexes, instead of the long scimitar-shaped or spiralling horns characteristic of true goats. It also lacks the hircine beard, which is replaced by long tufts of hair at the jaws, and in the Himalayan race by a magnificent shaggy ruff and mane of coarse hair up to twelve inches long that flows from neck, shoulders and chest down to the knees, and from back and rump down to flank and thighs. Moreover Schaller, who studied tahr in the Himalaya and also on the Nilgiri Hills, observed that when two were fighting, they usually lowered their heads and lunged at each other from a distance of two or three feet, like sheep, to clash horns with a crash. On the other hand, two would sometimes stand side by side, though facing in opposite directions, while circling rapidly and jabbing at each other's flank and abdomen like Rocky-Mountain goats; or, like ibex and markhor, rear up on their hind legs, with chins tucked in, and, plunging downwards, crack horns together.

In addition to being widely scattered throughout the Himalaya as far east as Sikkim, other races of tahr, distinguished by silvery saddles, inhabit such distant outposts as the rolling grass tableland, 6,000 feet high, of the Nilgiri Hills and the high grassy plateau, surrounded by precipices on three sides of the Eravikolan range 60 miles to the south, whose population of 500 makes it the largest single tahr colony in the world. Still more distant is the 400-mile stretch of coastal mountains in northern Oman, where an estimated 2,000 tahr live. It would therefore appear that tahr are 'goats' which, with their incomparable climbing ability, have established themsleves in an environmental niche of often arid, always vertiginous mountains in which no other large herbivore could survive, for they have been described as 'desperate climbers' about the ledges and rock faces of the steepest precipices, especially grassy cliffs broken by small stands of oak, box, rhododendron and dwarf bamboo. Their hoofs, with very soft pads set in a hard horny rim, are well designed for gripping rocks, and additional traction is provided by the large dew-claws. Schaller, when watching tahr for three weeks in a Nepalese valley whose sides rose in sheer cliffs more than 3,000 feet high, observed that one, balancing along a ledge only an inch or two wide, could leap with precision on to a small tussock of grass growing on a sheer cliff six feet below; or when confronted by a smooth, sloping rock face, might sway backwards and forwards before suddenly propelling itself upward with a series of leaps, in which it gripped the rock briefly with the calluses on its knees rather than with its hoofs. When sliding in a squatting position down a steep incline other calluses on the hocks were employed to supplement the hoofs as brakes. In the Himalaya tahr are therefore among the most inaccessible of animals, lying up by day in thick scrub in the highest oak and juniper forests, emerging only in the early morning and again in the evening in herds of a dozen and occasionally more than a hundred, to graze in recesses among the crags on their staple food — dry grass and sedge, which they apparently prefer to green vegetation, though they also browse on shrubs, oak leaves and bamboo, and in Oman on fruits and seeds. When they do come out of cover they are restless and on the *qui vive*, whistling shrilly by expelling air through their nostrils when alarmed, and racing away along the cliff edges.

Inhabiting such rugged terrain, tahr cannot often be hunted by predators other than an infrequent snow leopard or wolf, though it is true that wolves, like the leopards, hunt very high in the Himalaya. Howard-Bury watched one wolf stalking a snowcock at 19,000 feet and saw another at 21,000 feet. A few pairs of the very large Tibetan wolves, capable of tackling a yak, regularly infiltrate Nepal over the permanent snow by way of such high passes as the Nangpa La, which, though its summit lies at over 19,000 feet, was at least before the Chinese annexation of Tibet, the Sherpas' trading route from Thyangboche Monastery in Nepal to Ronguk Monastery at the base of Everest in Tibet, and probably the highest such route in the world. These wolves also traverse the glaciers and rear their cubs in caves on the high frontier. According to Charles Stonor, they prowl openly around the Sherpa villages, 'conspicuously creamy white against the grey rocks and tremendously agile as they leap from boulder to boulder with long springing strides.' He describes an incident at a village early in spring when in the late afternoon sun all was tranquil, with

> smoke curling from the grey roofs, walls and fences being repaired, fire-wood being gathered and the yaks and sheep being driven in for the evening. But... only a hundred yards above us on the mountainside, two great Tibetan wolves, almost white in their luxuriant winter coats, bounded out from the rocks and made off, weaving nimbly upwards.

Two days later these same wolves raced down at midday to the very fringe of the village and in the space of a few minutes killed seven sheep and made off with two lambs. The wolves' attacks and ability to bolt their kills are much too rapid to be prevented by shepherds or Sherpas, and a big-game hunter and excellent naturalist, C.H. Stockley, has described one wolf spurting suddenly in the most amazing manner into the middle of a flock of sheep and pulling down one after another with such wonderful speed and dexterity that there were five lying on the ground within a distance of thirty yards: 'He came right up to the side of each sheep... and seizing the galloping sheep behind the right ear, jerked its head downwards and inwards so that it pitched on its nose.'

In the winter, when the tahr descend as low as 5,000 feet, and in the spring when they herd in valley bottoms for the first early bite before the snow has melted from higher ground, some are killed by tigers — or were in the days when tigers were numbered in thousands instead of tens and ranged from the jungles in the Terai at the base of the Himalaya up to 6,000 feet in the foothills. Early in the nineteenth century, indeed, a few tigers were reported to be living as high as 10,000 feet, preying mainly on wild boar and black bears. Although most of these tigers went down to the forest with the onset of the autumn snows, a few were reputed to have wintered for years at a time only just below the snow-line in the western Himalaya. About 1876, for instance, a tigress in the Mandali district of Kashmir is said to have restricted her activities throughout her ten years as a man-eater to a narrow beat some 25 miles long, which included a group of villages stretching from the Jumna valley to a spur immediately above the hill station of Chakrata: never leaving this beat along the ridge from 8,000 to 10,000 feet high to visit the numerous villages skirting the valleys of several mountain streams. She may have arrived at Mandali while following the Kashmir herdsmen, who were at that time extending their summer hill-grazings; and this 'stranding' of tigers in unsuitable terrain may have been responsible for a number of man-eaters in mountainous country.

Such tigers were usually the young, the old or the injured, which had been driven up to the barren hills, where game was scarce, by stronger tigers from breeding forests at lower levels. During the summer the Mandali tigress preyed on cattle and also sheep and goats, though she disappeared for months at a time when she found game. During the winter snows from December to the end of March she was accustomed to go down to the Jumna valley, but since she did not follow the cattle into the forest, found it difficult to kill sufficient natural game at this season if she had cubs to feed. After four years of this seasonal alternation of plenty and semi-starvation she began man-eating at a time when she had three cubs, and by 1883 was beginning to ignore the herds of cattle in favour of their herdsmen. When she was finally killed in 1889, when not less than seventeen years old, she was in miserable condition, with all but one of her canines worn down to stumps.

Other tigers reached still higher altitudes when passing from Nepal into Sikkim and back again, while following herds of wild elephants; and a few went even higher in north-west Sikkim, where summer grazings at 13,000 feet bordered snow-bound hills and glaciers. When the snow began to recede from the grazings at the end of April herds of yaks, sheep and semi-wild breeding horses were driven up from the forests to these fresh pastures. In pursuit of stragglers from the herds, and perhaps an unwary bharal, came the predators, tigers among them: their great pug-marks imprinted one and a-half inches deep in the snow of the steep paths, winding some 5,000 feet up through the forest. So regular was this spring ascent of the tigers that the Bhutia herdsmen venerated them as *devtas* or gods.

Even 13,000 feet may not, however, have been the altitudinal limit of tigers, for in 1934 a tiger, having killed a mule on the Sikkim road between Gangtok and the Nathu La pass, almost certainly went over the pass at a height of more than 14,000 feet and down into the Chumbi valley, where later a large domestic bull yak was found dead, though not eaten, with fang marks in its throat. Inevitably the killer was believed to be a *mirta* (yeti), though this was not by any means the first yak to be killed by a tiger.

Chapter Thirteen

BIRDS IN THE HIMALAYA

Jungle tigers can be linked with mountain tahr because in the Himalaya an almost complete range of climatic zones is concentrated within the four or five miles of vertical ascent from tropical jungle to frozen peaks and glaciers. At 5,000 to 6,000 feet the character of the vegetation in the forest zone changes, with oak, magnolia, laurel and birch (festooned with lichens and mosses) replacing the sal and silk-cotton trees and the giant bamboo of the foothills. At 7,000 to 12,000 feet, varying according to the height and depth of intermediate ranges and valleys and the influence of the monsoon rains, one climbs into the temperate zone of blue pine, silver fir, yew and juniper with an undergrowth of scrubby rhododendron and dwarf bamboo, though all damper localities are dominated by evergreen oak. At its upper limits the oak merges into the silver fir, growing to a height of 150 feet in deep gorges, with their impenetrable jungles of 20-foot bamboo. In this temperate zone the bulk of the tropical Indian fauna is replaced by such Indo-Chinese species as serow and goral, and in Nepal plants and animals from Afghanistan and Kashmir meet those from Burma and China. However, since Nepal was closed to Europeans for about a hundred years after 1850, 5,000 square miles or more still await investigation by naturalists, and in the intervening period vast tracts have been totally deforested, just as deforestation and peasant farming are devastating much of the remaining forest in the western Himalaya up to a height of 7,000 feet.

In late winter and early spring rhododendron forests stain whole mountain sides in the Himalaya crimson red or pink, yellow or white, with 60-foot-tall tree-rhododendrons standing out as flaming torches — as Stonor saw them — against the bright green and silver of the birchwoods, fringed with the paper-white of cherry trees and the butter-yellow of barberry bushes; and between 13,000 and 19,500 feet in all the wooded valleys and on all the mountain slopes along the frontier with Tibet, are the rose-coloured, almost mauve, flowers of the Rhododendron of the Snows.

Between the tree-line and the snow there is, too, an extraordinary abundance of alpines. Nigel Nicolson has described how early in the spring, primulas, with buds and leaves wrapped in scaly protective sheaths, push up through the winter snow before it has melted and subsequently burgeon into purple-pink, blue, white or yellow flowers at the bases of cliffs or in sunny places in the lee of great boulders. By July the alpine meadows between 12,000 and 15,000 feet are starred by millions of potentillas and by anemones, aconites, edelweiss, saxifrages, irises, asters and blue, lilac and white gentians.

The Himalayan forests harbour a wealth of such gorgeous pheasants as the crimson-plumaged, pink-legged tragopans or horned pheasants, which are equally at home in steep, wooded and shrubbed mountain slopes and ridges or cold, often wet forest and rhododendron jungle between 3,000 and 12,000 feet from Kashmir eastwards to Szechwan in particular. Being more arboreal than other pheasants, they make use of the old nests of crows high up in the trees and may also forage among the branches for acorns and berries, though they feed mainly on fern leaves. The exotic plumage of the cock is exaggerated when displaying to the brown hen, for while jerking neck and wings and uttering bleating cries it puffs up two small fleshy, bright-blue horns, which at other times are concealed in the feathers on either side of the crown, and also inflates a neck pouch of bright-blue skin edged with salmon-pink blotches, resembling an embroidered piece of silk.

With ringing squeals huge blue and chestnut, peacock-headed monals or impeyan pheasants rocket down like capercaillie over the thickets of oak, rhododendron, box and dwarf bamboo from the grassy slopes above. Despite their bulk the brilliant iridescent and metallic blues, greens, purples and copper-reds of the cocks' plumage rival those of birds of paradise, sunbirds or hummingbirds, and contrast with their velvet-black underparts, white rumps and chestnut tails, and with the brown plumage of the white-throated hens. To the Nepalese, the monal is the national bird of nine colours; to the Himalayan hill tribes, and also to the Chinese, it is the oak-charcoal chicken or the fowl of burning charcoal, because the colours of its neck and mantle resemble the intense glow of a charcoal fire. From Nepal to China the habitat of the numerous races of monals extends from the highest open forests of conifers, oak and bamboo at round 8,000 feet in the winter to the alpine pastures, moorland and scrub at 16,000 feet in the summer. In these zones they dig with their strong, curved beaks for grubs, roots and tubers and particularly for *fritillaria* bulbs, but do not scratch for these with their feet like other pheasants. According to Stonor, a favourite spring haunt in Nepal of the whistling monals, slinking in and out of the juniper scrub, were the moss-carpeted groves of great knotted and twisted birches growing alongside a stream in the Dudh Kosi valley, flanked by the jagged brown and white ranges of hills. The stream's almost endless cataracts of foaming waters powered a chain of water-mills, by means of which the hill villagers of Porche, above the Thyangboche monastery, ground their barley flour at an altitude of more than 15,000 feet.

There, too, were blood pheasants, so named from the large, deep crimson splotches on the cock's grey-green breast plumage streaked with black and white. To this riot of colour are added a daub of vivid crimson round the tail and from one to three crimson spurs on each leg. No larger than partridges, and behaving more like them, the blood pheasants with their curiously transparent plumage are almost ethereal in comparison with others of their kind and merge into their typical background of granite rocks encrusted with pale greenish lichen and dull, crimson fungi. Small coveys of from five to twenty, including the dull-plumaged brown hens, call incessantly with prolonged wheezing whistles, not unlike those of marmots, or rally to cover with high-pitched clarion squeals, as they file through the conifer forests and rhododendron jungles and particularly the bamboo stands, or through the thicker juniper scrub above, foraging for insects and digging with their strong beaks in the deep snow for mosses, lichens, ferns and pine and juniper shoots and buds. They move up and down with the snow-line, from 7,000 feet in the winter to 15,000 feet in the summer. Though roosting as high as 20 feet in the pines or rhododendrons they seldom take wing when alarmed but run quickly to hide among the rocks, except in the vicinity of Tibetan monasteries, where all wildlife is protected and where they scratch about tamely on patches of ground among the houses. At the Thyangboche monastery, 14,000 feet up on an isolated spur above the junction of the Dudh Kosi and the Imja Khola, which drains the southern flanks of Everest twelve miles distant, Stonor saw them in the first light of dawn strutting to and fro along the tops of the walls surrounding the monastery courtyards, peering down at the sleeping lamas in their sanctuary of encircling gigantic peaks of rock and ice.

To the south of Thyangboche and its green meadows starred with gentians, the forested slopes of rhododendron, fir, tree-juniper and birches, silvered with mosses, fall steeply to the gorge of the Dudh Kosi and are alive with beautiful butterflies and birds, including the Eurasian cuckoo, whose nostalgic call may be heard as high as 12,500 feet — a thousand feet higher than the Himalayan cuckoo's; and on moonlit nights, according to Stonor, the wild tormented cry of the large hawk-cuckoo 'echoes and re-echoes through the highest forests... up and up to a crescendo, until one can hardly wait for the next shriek.'

Of other birds in the Himalayan woodlands there are laughing thrushes, warblers, flycatchers, bulbuls, bush-chats, nuthatches, doves, woodpeckers and scimitar babblers bouncing about on the ground among the bamboo and piercing the rhododendron flowers with their long beaks. Tiny metallic-green, fire-breasted flowerpeckers dart from tree-top to tree-top in search of parasitic growths; minivets — the males scarlet and black, the females bright yellow and grey — hunt for insects in the crowns of the oaks; yellow-backed sunbirds, with green heads and scarlet breasts, suck the nectar from the scarlet flowers of the colquhounia bushes with the almost tubular tongues of their curved beaks, and also snap up insects attracted to the flowers.

Higher in the woods, in the subalpine zone of birch and nesting in the rhododendron bushes, are fire-tailed sunbirds, whose tropical plumage is a kaleidoscope of deep blues, metallic blues, bright yellows and fiery reds, culminating in an ultra-long, pointed bright-red tail. Stonor has described a swarm of these brilliant little birds hovering like moths before the crimson bells of a dendron to suck the nectar or clinging to the twigs while craning their scimitar beaks round into the flowers:

> Darting and hovering, they flicked jerkily across from bush to bush... flashing like gems in the shafts of sunlight streaming through the black pines. The dazzling tropical plumed birds among the equally splendid flowers, intermingled with the sober spruce trees; a few drifts of snow still on the ground below, and, in the background, a deep gorge overhung with giant, slowly thawing icicles, breaking off occasionally with a metallic crack that reverberated through the valley as they shivered to fragments in the cliff-ledges below.

In this zone too are willow warblers, brown bullfinches with black wings and tails, treecreepers and tail-less, scaly-breasted wren-babblers. In the Himalaya, as in other parts of its wide range, which extends right across Eurasia and into North America, the true wren (*Troglodytes troglodytes*) pops up in all manner of unexpected places — among the rocks and boulders in the fir, birch and rhododendron forest near the tree-line, and higher still in the dwarf juniper zone, nesting as high as 15,500 feet. Showell Styles indeed watched one popping in and out of the 16,500-foot summit ridge of a peak near Annapurna, chirruping frantically to an invisible brood, and Stonor saw one flitting over the scree at the edge of a retreating glacier at 17,000 feet. Even in winter these Himalayan wrens do not descend lower than 7,000 feet.

> The bird I particularly associate with piled moss-covered boulders and desolate scree ... is the tiny Nepal wren [wrote Tilman]. It creeps like a mouse over, and often beneath, boulders and disappears from view for

seconds at a time to reappear in a quite unexpected place some yards distant. Its shrill chirrup was a pleasant reminder that there was life among these wide Himalayan wastes.

Only at an altitude of about 12,500 feet, where in the more open country the villagers have their *kharkas,* does one pass out of the zone of tropical birds into that of the temperate species, which extends into the alpine scrub and dwarf rhododendron above 14,000 feet; but even at that altitude, and more than 3,000 feet higher in Tibet, birds of tropically brilliant plumage, the exquisite grandalas — glistening purple or turquoise-blue with black wings and tails — swirl about the grey rocky slopes above the forest and below the dazzling white peaks. Their closely knit flocks of from five to fifty are ever on the move, swooping down as one bird, flowing over the ground like starlings as they feed, then up again to whirl away in a musically chattering band. Though reputed never at any season to descend below the high boulder-strewn alpine slopes or as low as the tree-line, restless swarms of several hundred do in fact visit woodlands temporarily in winter and are often composed entirely of males. Such a flock, blue against the soft, shallow snow, in which while probing they bury their heads, must be one of the memorable sights of a naturalist's world.

This alpine zone is also frequented by pipits, accentors, grey and pied wagtails and the sooty-brown Himalayan dippers, recognizable by the absence of white gorgets. Perching on midstream rocks, they fly under the clear grey-green water which, though prevented from freezing solid only by the force of the current, harbours water-bugs and snails, active even in midwinter. In placid reaches of these swift hill streams, where the torrent broadens and flows over stones, that curious high-altitude wader, the red-legged ibis-bill, runs over the boulders and breast-deep into the water to thrust its long, slender red beak (almost as sickle-shaped as a curlew's) under the stones to pry for food, or curves it round a stone and inserts it from the side. Feeding in streams as high as 14,500 feet, it nests in old glaciated valleys above 10,000 feet.

And bobbing and hopping over the boulders amid the rushing waters or between drifts of snow on most Himalayan streams from 6,000 to 16,000 feet, and even higher, are white-capped redstarts. They vary their short erratic fly-catching flights from rock to rock with brief visits to the wet mossy cliffs or steep marshy hillsides flanking the stream: in contrast to the slate-blue male and blue-grey female plumbeous redstarts, which only rarely leave their torrent for the bank or the branch of a tree. Behaving like grey wagtails rather than redstarts, they flit from rock to rock, dipping their conspicuous tails (chestnut in the case of the male, brown and white in the female) and intermittently darting up in pursuit of passing insects. From time to time the male utters its short, sweet, jingling song from a rock in midstream or while flying in a slow parabola with rapidly vibrating wings from one rock to the next. No stretch of Himalayan stream between 3,000 and 13,000 feet is without its pair of plumbeous redstarts.

Characteristic of the higher Himalaya and rarely below 5,000 feet are the flocks of grey and white snow-pigeons, picking tamely about the potato fields between the Sherpa houses at 15,000 feet and on the terraced cultivation of the upland valleys at the edge of the melting snow. Regularly every morning, even when a snowstorm is raging, they fly down to their feeding grounds from their colonial roosts in the cliffs flanking the valleys above the snow-line, where they are safe from their main predator, the golden eagle, and back up again at dusk.

To these hill-village oases of shallow streams, fields and small groves of juniper, set in amphitheatres of mountain ranges rising to near 20,000 feet, they also plane down the valleys in the early morning, with curlew-like whistling calls, flocks of 20 or 30 or more bulky grey and white snowcock — those giant partridges the size of guineafowl or small turkeys and weighing five or six pounds. Having drunk at a lake, they then return up the steep slopes, almost to 20,000 feet, to pass the day digging for roots and tubers. Snowcock are widely distributed above 9,000 feet over the mountains of central Asia. Shipton encountered them in such contrasting habitats as pine forest in the summer and on mountain tops covered by a deep mantle of snow in the early spring, when no clear ground was to be seen for miles. Their echoing call, a long ascending note, when heard at dawn high up on a mountainside, was the most thrilling sound known to him, reflecting the wild grandeur of the country they inhabited. They may go higher than 20,000 feet, for they have been seen flying down from the rocks and ice of the gorges above the Rongbuk glacier, lying at 17,000 or 18,000 feet, and Shipton met with them many miles up other great glaciers and among barren mountains where water was very scarce. According to a Tibetan saying, when March snowstorms have driven the snowcock down to lower levels:

You know the depths of the snow on the pass
By the cry of the snowcock below.

Shipton found them difficult to stalk because one member of a flock would usually sit perched on a rock commanding a view over all the mountain-side, ready to give the alarm to the remainder while they were feeding, cackling incessantly. They are noisy birds, particularly in the late-winter months when, being paired as early as February, they chase around in circles. If alarmed, they usually run uphill — rather than take flight — with a waddling, goose-like gait, jerking up their tails as if moorhens, and revealing their white undertail coverts. However, Shipton observed that if startled into flight, or when removing to another feeding ground, they would, with a shrill gobbling cry, launch themselves from a nearby rock in a steep downward glide, whose impetus would carry them across the valley without any apparent movement of their wings, and which, if they had not previously been stooped at by a golden eagle, might extend for several miles.

Snow partridges, which somewhat resemble red-legged partridges, probably range even higher than snowcock, for Stonor recalls finding a nest and eggs at a height of nearly 19,000 feet, and they are also present on the Chang-Tang; but they are as at home on open grassy hillsides in low hot valleys as on stony screes with a sparse growth of barberry bushes or on the permanent snowfields. They crouch very tightly on the snow if suspicious, prior to shooting up almost vertically with a loud whirring and clapping of wings and hurtling downhill at breakneck speed. Stonor watched a covey of twenty 'climbing' the sheer face of a cliff with extraordinary dexterity by gripping with beak and claws and flapping their wings violently, while probing every slightest crack in the rock in order to extract seeds from the shrivelled remains of the previous summer's plants. In Nepal, after packing together in the autumn, they apparently survive the winter without retreating to lower altitudes, despite the fact that 70 per cent of the high country is then under snow; but in this respect it has to be remembered that the winters in Nepal up to 18,000 or 19,000 feet are little more severe than in England. However Carruthers, writing of the Zarafshan valley in Turkestan, stated that when the snow partridges were forced down to lower altitudes in search of food in winter, the natives trapped them by sinking large earthenware jars up to the neck in the ground and baiting them with grain. The hungry partridges, lured by the bait, dropped down into the jars, but were unable to clamber out again. Three thousand five hundred miles to the west, poachers in the Scottish Highlands were at that time employing an almost identical technique to catch ptarmigan.

Carruthers also refers to an experience in the Karakoram, when snow partridges were calling with ringing musical chuckles and wild shrill whistles all around him, and what he presumed to be a cock alighted on the patch of snow beside which he was lying:

He then proceeded to cross it a run, with head bent low and his tail cocked up, every now and then stopping and uttering the loud whistle so typical of these highlands. He was coming to feed on the same dozy patch where the other birds (finches and larks) were, but the sudden appearance of a hawk, probably a hobby, of which the only evidence to me was a shadow passing over the sunlit snow, broke up the breakfast party. The cock went, like a bullet, straight across to the opposite side of the valley, a mile away... Then silence, except for marmots whistling and the thunder of a snow-slide. Down in the valley below the day had not yet begun.

Even during the winter months there is a considerable variety of bird life over high Nepal, including such scavengers as lammergeiers, for ever swinging and floating, solitary or in pairs, over the glaciers and up and down the valleys; griffon vultures following man and his livestock wherever they go, and domestic yak range wherever there is a scraping of vegetation — as do the wild bharal; and ravens strutting over the snow of the highest passes, with far below them the endless vista of cone-shaped hills, valleys and rolling tablelands that is Tibet.

Chapter Fourteen

YETIS: APES OR HOMINIDS?

The Nepalese and Tibetan Himalaya may harbour one or more species of primates — great apes or subhumans — unknown to science, but widely reported by the native peoples.

Old Indian maps designate the mountainous northern frontier of Nepal along the Nuptse-Lhotse range as the Mahalangur Himal: the Mountains of the Great Snow Langur.

According to members of the ancient Sikkim forest people, the Lepchas (of Tibetan or Mongolian ancestry), their forebears spoke of an ape-like mountain beast they referred to as *Thloh-Mung* or *Chu-Mung*, the Glacier Spirit, still worshipped in the Lepcha pantheon. Lepchas working in Darjeeling told Charles Stonor that this 'Mountain Savage' was reputed to live alone or with a very few of its kind, and only in the higher mountains, where it foraged both on the ground and in the trees. Although it closely resembled a man it was covered with long dark hair; it was larger than a monkey and more intelligent. However, when the human population increased, felled the forests and occupied the wild country, the *Thloh-Mung* disappeared, though many people said that they were still to be found in the mountains of western Nepal, where the Sherpa peoples called them Yetis.

In 1958 Emmanuel Vlcek, a Czechoslovak anthropologist, while researching in the library of a former lamaistic university, discovered a Tibetan 'Anatomical Dictionary for recognizing various diseases' at least 200 years old. In this work a systematic discussion of the fauna of Tibet and adjacent regions included, among a group of arboreal monkeys, an illustration of a biped primate standing erect on a rock with knees slightly bent and one arm stretched upwards. Described in the accompanying text as a man-animal, the head is full bearded and the entire body, except for hands and feet, is covered with long hair. In another edition of this medical natural history printed a century later, the textual reference to the illustration has been translated by Vlcek as: 'The wild man lives in the mountains, his origin is close to that of the bear, his body resembles that of man and he has enormous strength. His meat may be eaten to treat mental diseases and

83

his gall cures jaundice.' It is significant that among all the other illustrations of animals in this dictionary not a single mythological or fantastic creature is included: all are of known living species.

The Sherpas are a Mongolian people, possibly originating in eastern Tibet, since *Shar* is east and *Pa* people. At the present time their eighteen clans live in the hill villages of Nepal's frontier with Tibet. To all of them yetis are as real as wolves, snow leopards or wild goats, or as tigers are to Indian aboriginals, though the European finds it difficult to distinguish between fact and fiction in their accounts of yetis, and equally difficult to locate a Sherpa who has actually seen a yeti with his own eyes. One of the more factual descriptions of a creature watched through a large crack in the wall of a stone hut was given to Stonor by a villager of Pangboche a couple of miles north of Thyangboche. It was squat, thickset, of the size and proportions of a small man and covered with reddish and black hair, which was not very long. Its head was high and pointed, with a crest of hair; the face bare, except for some brown hair on the sides of the cheeks and the nose 'squashed-in'. It had no tail and moved about with long strides, stooping slightly, with its arms hanging down by its sides.

Stonor was given a further description by a Tibetan merchant, from a district not many days north of the Nepal border, of a yeti he had watched at a range of 200 or 300 yards on some flat ground sparsely covered with rhododendron bushes. This one was also the size and build of a small man with long hair on the head, the middle of the body and thighs, and walked nearly as upright as a man. On seeing the merchant and his companions it uttered a loud high-pitched cry.

In what can be termed the anecdotal, embroidered category of yeti lore is that told by the deputy Abbot of Thyangboche Monastery to Wilfred Noyce, who took part in the successful 1953 ascent of Everest and who, one evening, heard whistles ascribed by his Sherpas to yetis. According to the Abbot, the yetis, which were about five feet six inches tall with shaggy reddish hair, would come quite low down for food and had been seen playing in the snow near the monastery, though at the sound of the monastic horn they would make off. They would sometimes eat a yak, which they skinned carefully, leaving its horns stuck in the ground. On one occasion the inhabitants of a village in Tibet had been much plagued by yetis, which used to come and do the same things at night, only in a disorderly fashion, as the villagers had been doing during the daytime. Thus they would play about in a field of potatoes which had been planted during the day. Finally the exasperated villagers prepared a great bowl of *chang* (fermented liquor) and pretended to drink it. The yetis, coming that night, did in fact drink it, with the inevitable result, and were easily disposed of; but since that time the killing of yetis had been prohibited in Tibet.

There are many versions throughout the Himalaya of this use of liquor to get rid of yetis, and one should perhaps add that in China 'monsters' were being caught with the bait of wine as far back as 200 BC. One Himalayan account from the Jalap valley in Sikkim relates how after a large ape-like creature had been drinking regularly at night from a cistern, the villagers doped the cistern with *chang*, and on one of the beasts collapsing in a drunken stupor, lashed it to a pole; but it subsequently sobered up and escaped. Peter Matthiessen was told by one Sherpa that yetis had formerly been common in the Khumbu region to the north of Thyangboche; but in his grandfather's time, after the yetis had been raiding the crops, poisoned barley was put out and this bait killed them off: 'There were dead yetis everywhere.'

Let us now turn to the European evidence for the existence of yetis, though first noting that they, or possibly similar creatures known as *almas* — from the Mongol *ala* (to kill) and *mal* (cattle) — are not restricted to the Himalaya, but have also been reported, mainly by Soviet observers, from the Caucasus, the Pamirs and the Tien Shan eastwards to the high rocky plateau of the Altai-Gobi in Outer Mongolia, and from the Karakoram to the Tsinling Shan in western China and the upper Salween on the Burma-Tibet marches.

It was in the 1870s that the Russian explorer, N.M. Przewalski, had returned with accounts of almas — 'human-like animals or animal-like humans' — in Mongolia, where they had in fact been reported intermittently for more than six centuries; and from where there have come a mass of witnesses, many of them recent and reputable, all of whose descriptions agree on an anthropoid rather larger than a man and with a stooping, bent-kneed gait. It is described as covered with dark reddish hair, sparse enough to reveal the skin, but longer on the head, and having prominent eye-ridges, a low forehead and powerful jaws.

According to Odette Tschernine, who has made a special study of the Soviet evidence of yetis and almas, early reports of these were 'lost' in scientific archives prior to a full investigation in the 1950s. They included one by a Russian geologist of his experience in 1934 when he was at an altitude of between 8,000 and 9,000 feet on a plateau in the Parmirs. Tschernine's translation states that the geologist, B.M. Zdovik, came upon a small area of ground on which the grass had been completely flattened and parts of it dug up as if with a spade. On the path were drops of blood and scraps of what looked like marmot fur, and then, right at his feet, an unknown creature, about 5 feet long, lying fully stretched out on its stomach on a heap of freshly dug earth. The whole of its body was covered with shaggy reddish-brown hair, redder than any Zdovik had seen on a bear and more like yak's wool than a bear's pelt; its head and front limbs were hidden by a withered *grechika* bush, but the legs and bare black front feet were too long and too well shaped to be those of a bear.

After the 1950s, sponsored research and the examination of alleged sightings of almas in the Pamirs were again banned, for reasons peculiar to the Russian mentality, though in 1954 a Chinese photographer had reported seeing two almas at 20,000 feet in the Pamirs and in August 1957 a Soviet scientist had seen a bipedal anthropoid, covered with reddish-grey hair and with very long arms, in these mountains. However, Tschernine states that research has since been renewed in the Caucasus, Azerbaijan and other regions of the USSR and also in Mongolia, and that there have been more than 300 reports of almas from remote farming areas and tea plantations in the Caucasus and the Chatkal mountains east of Tashkent in the Tien Shan. These have included the discovery in the 1960s of food hoards cached by almas in densely wooded terrain surrounding isolated orchard and dairy holdings in the Caucasus, where fruit bitten into by a briefly glimpsed young female indicated a much larger than human jaw and larger, stronger teeth; and as recently as the summer of 1979 a camp of Ukranians in the Pamiro-Ala mountains in Tadjikistan is reported to have been visited several times at night by a hominid leaving prints nearly 14 inches long.

The first European to hint that yetis might actually exist in the Himalaya proper was that excellent early naturalist, B.H. Hodgson, who was British resident at the Court of Nepal from 1820-43 and who in 1832 reported that his native hunters, while collecting specimens for him in northern Nepal, were frightened by what they called *Rakshas* (demons), which walked erect, were tailless and were covered with long dark hair.

Subsequently L.A. Waddell, a major in the Indian Army Medical Corps and also a Doctor of Law and an FLS, stated that when in the late autumn of 1887 he was at an altitude of about 17,000 feet on the Lachoong Pass between Sikkim and Tibet: 'Some large footprints in the snow led across our track, and away up to the higher peaks. These were alleged to be the trail of the will hairy men who are believed to live among the eternal snows.' However, Waddell dismissed these 'so-called wild men as evidently the great yellow snow-bear, which is highly carnivorous and often kills yaks.'

Since those early reports by Hodgson and Waddell more than fifty mountaineers and naturalists have come upon the tracks of yetis and in a few instances appear to have seen actual specimens; and almost every Himalayan expedition has referred to unidentifiable footprints in the snow.

Let us consider the more important of these. In 1906 Henry Elwes who, in addition to being a well-known Himalayan explorer was a botanist and geologist, is said to have seen and sketched a yeti in Tibet and to have deposited with a Royal Society very full descriptions of the appearance of yetis and of their footprints, and also of their habits and the localities in which they were to be found. These notes were apparently seen by members of a number of Royal Societies, but have since been curiously mislaid. But in 1915 he communicated to the Zoological Society a letter he had received from J.R.O. Gent, a forest officer near Darjeeling, in which the latter described what the local coolies working in the forest called *sogpas*: 'These lived above the tree-line and were humanoid creatures about 4 feet in height and covered with long yellowish-brown hair, with a stride of from 1½ to 2 feet on flat ground, but in steep places appeared to "walk on their knees".' However, the tracks they left in the snow were not those of the large Nepalese langur monkeys and the *sogpas* were probably a dwarf race of human rather than yetis.

1921 — Hugh Knight, an English explorer about whom nothing appears to be known, described in *The Times* an encounter with what may also have been a humanoid rather than a yeti near Gangtok in Sikkim eight years earlier:

> I stopped to breathe my horse in an open clearing... and watched the sun, which was just setting. While I was musing, I heard a slight sound, and looking round, I saw some 15 or 20 paces away, a figure... Speaking to the best of my recollection, he was a little under 6 feet high, almost stark naked in the bitter cold — it was the month of November. He was a kind of yellow all over... a shock of matted hair on his head, little hair on his face, highly splayed feet, and large, formidable hands. His muscular development in the arms, thighs, legs and chest was terrific. He had in his hand what seemed to be some form of primitive bow.

1921 — Howard-Bury, when on his reconnaissance of Everest, reported possible tracks of a yeti between 20,000 and 21,000 feet on the Kharta glacier.

1925 — A.N. Tombazi, who has been variously described as a British photographer and Fellow of the Royal Geographical Society or a Greek or Italian in charge of a forestry project in Sikkim, when camped at 15,000 feet not far from the Zemu Gap between Sikkim and eastern Nepal, was summoned from his tent by his Sherpa porters to see a yeti:

> The blinding sunlight and intense glare from the snow prevented me at

first from seeing anything, but I soon spotted the 'object', two or three hundred yards away down the valley. There was no doubt that its outline was like that of a human being: it walked upright, bending down occasionally to pull up a withered dwarf rhododendron bush. Against the snow it looked dark and apparently wore no clothing. Within a minute or so it had moved into some thick scrub and was lost to view. Such a fleeting glimpse unfortunately did not allow me to set up the telephoto-camera, or even to fix the object carefully with the binoculars; but a couple of hours later, during the descent, I purposely made a detour so as to pass the place where the 'man' or 'beast' had been seen. I examined the footprints, which were clearly visible on the surface of the snow. They were similar in shape to those of a man but only six or seven inches long by four inches wide at the broadest part of the foot. The marks of five toes and the instep were clear, but the imprint of the heel was very slight. I counted fifteen such footprints at regular intervals ranging from 1½ to 2 feet, undoubtedly those of a biped... From enquiries I gathered that no human being had been in this area since the beginning of the year... I am at a loss to express any definite opinion. I can only reiterate with certainty that the silhouette... was identical with the outline of a human figure.

1935 — Ronald Kaulback, when at 16,000 feet on the upper Salween in the south-east of Tibet, discerned five sets of tracks descending a very steep hillside to the valley bottom. Slightly obscured by drifting snow, they resembled those of a bare-footed man and were not those of a bear or snow leopard.

1937 — August 18: H.W. Tilman (exploring the Karakoram with Eric Shipton) was in the vicinity of Snow Lake, that huge expanse of glistening ice that gives birth to the great Biafro glacier at an altitude of around 13,500 feet. While contouring round the foot of a ridge between two glaciers they came upon tracks nearly 12 inches deep in the snow of an 'Abominable Snowman'. These were 8 inches in diameter, almost circular, without sign of toe or heel, and 18 inches apart. As they were three or four days old, melting had probably altered their outline. To Tilman the most remarkable thing about them was that the prints were in a straight line one behind he other, with no right or left 'stagger', because although a quadruped, walking slowly, would place its hindfoot in the track of its forefoot there was always some mark of overlapping; nor would a quadruped's footprints be precisely in front of each other. These 'yeti' tracks led from a glacier pool, at which the animal had evidently drunk and disappeared on rock after a mile; but the next day the same spoor was picked up on the north side of the lake. Since they were not the tracks of any species of Himalayan bear, and since there was no game of any kind, nor grass, within 15 miles of the lake, and the nearest village was 40 miles away, Tilman could offer no explanation for their presence, particularly when a few days later he was at lower levels and found bear tracks to be common and recognizable as such by himself and also by his Sherpas.

1937 — John Hunt (Lord Hunt of Everest), when at 19,000 feet on the north side of the Zemu Gap, came upon two lines of apparently human tracks, although it was known that no man except members of his own party were anywhere in the vicinity at the time.

1942 — August: a polish officer, Slavomir Rawicz, and his companions, when on the Sikkim-Bhutan border, observed two bipedal animals more than 8 feet tall with powerful chests and grey-tinted, reddish hair. Although Rawicz's account of this incident in his book, *The Long Walk*, was discredited by reviewers because it contained so many unacceptable facts regarding the anatomy of these animals and also of the route he followed through the Himalaya after his escape from Russian captivity, he subsequently affirmed that it was true.

1951 — Shipton and Michael Ward photographed tracks of yetis on one of the Menlunga La glaciers, which are set in a vast amphitheatre near the border between Nepal and Tibet, in the course of a reconnaissance of Everest. These tracks were also seen by W.H. Murray and Tom Bourdillon a few days later. According to Murray, the party had withdrawn from Everest into Sola Khumbu in Nepal early in November in order to explore the unsurveyed ranges lying 30 or 40 miles to the west. The party then split up and Shipton and Ward penetrated into the heart of the Gaurisankar range — a wild tangle of high and icy peaks — by crossing a pass of 20,000 feet, the Menlung La. At 18,000 or 19,000 feet on the lower part of the glacier they came across the tracks of two or more bipeds, moving side by side at one point and then criss-crossing. They followed the tracks down the glacier and, as they descended, the depth of the snow gradually diminished, until barely an inch covered the ice. Higher up the individual footprints had been rather shapeless in soft, heavy snow, but on the thin, frozen snow at lower levels many prints were so sharply defined that they could hardly have been clearer had they been made in wax; nor had there been any distortion by melting, as they could see by comparing one print against another and by their clearcut outline. The prints were very fresh and had not been made more than 24 hours earlier, because little balls of snow that had been dislodged had not melted into the surface, despite a warm sun all day. At one point one of the creatures had jumped across a three-foot-wide crevasse, leaving the mark of its take-off and on the other side a clear imprint of where it had dug in its toes on landing. According to Shipton, the actual footprints — 9 or 10 inches apart and pointing down the glacier — displayed a rounded big toe, projecting a little to one side, with the next toe well separated from it, and three small toes grouped closely together and probably joined near their bases. His photograph shows the medial toe to be the longest, as in the case of the human foot, which the print much resembles, though 12½ inches long and broader, being 7½ inches across, whereas the average human foot is about 10 inches long and not more than 4 inches broad.

For a quarter of a mile the tracks kept more or less to the middle of the glacier, following the easiest route through the crevasse system: striking sharply left or right to avoid broad crevasses and detouring round small ice cliffs and pinnacles; but (according to Murray) after two miles the glacier became excessively riven and the tracks diverged on to a lateral moraine and were no longer discernible. Shipton had previously attempted to follow sets of these curious footprints on many occasions, both in the Himalaya and the Karakoram, but had invariably lost them on the moraine or rocks at the side of the glacier.

1952 — Both the First and Second Swiss expeditions to Everest saw a number of inexplicable tracks, including a fresh set not unlike a bear's, on the Khumbu glacier on the lower slopes of Everest.

1954 — Ralph Izzard, a member of the *Daily Mail* expedition, followed the tracks of a biped, which proceeded purposefully and, like Tilman's, in a straight line with no trace of 'stagger' for 80 yards over the Khumbu glacier to a lateral moraine. The prints were 10-11 inches long and 5-6 inches wide, and at one point the creature had halted with its feet in a position of 'ten to two'. Had the animal been a quadruped, placing its hind feet exactly in the tracks of its forefeet and thus simulating those of a biped, such a position could not have been attained.

1955 — May: Abbé P. Brodet, geologist to the French expedition to Makalu, 12 miles south-east of Everest, followed the tracks of a 'yeti' for more than a kilometre through fresh snow on the upper edge of the rhododendron jungle in the Barun Valley, until visibility was reduced by fog; a second set of tracks led to a lake, 'where the animal had evidently stopped to drink'. The first comprised nearly 3,000 footprints almost 8 inches long, imprinted 4 to 6 inches deep in the snow and somewhat resembling the human foot; and at some points these indicated that the animal had jumped over obstacles. Brodet took photographs, which showed the more or less circular marks of four (not five) toes, much larger than human toes, and a roughly elliptical sole, rounded underneath. The first inside toe was larger than the others, which lay on the front edge of the sole and very close to it, and there were no claw-marks, invariably present in bear tracks. In the clearest imprints little ridges of snow dividing the toe-marks indicated that the toes were slightly separated when the creature walked.

1955 — June: an RAF expedition encountered fresh tracks of many prints at a height of 12,375 feet in the Kulti Valley. The 12 inch by 6 inch prints included five toes a quarter of an inch wide and were 11 inches deep in the snow, though those of the mountaineering party were only 1 inch deep.

1960 — A. Cram, a Scottish magistrate, was reported to have seen a yeti in October and photographed tracks at 18,000 feet in the west Lahoul region.

1970 — March 25: at about five in the evening, when it was beginning to get dark, Don Whillans (deputy leader of the British expedition to Annapurna in Nepal) had just dumped his load at base camp on the south face of the mountain when he heard a noise on the ridge behind and whipped round in time to see a dark object dropping behind another ridge, and as it vanished, two lines of black crows flew up. Although described by Chris Bonington, the leader of the expedition, in *Annapurna South Face* as tough, self-sufficient and utterly realistic, Whillans was 'quite nervous — dead worried' about the presence of a yeti. In his own words subsequently: 'There had been a peculiar atmosphere about the place ever since we had arrived at the Base Camp'.

On reconnaissance the following day up a valley — known to the local inhabitants as the Valley of the Great Ape — between a bank of moraine and the smooth, easy slope of very soft snow on the mountainside, down which there had been an avalanche several weeks earlier, Whillans had been walking for only a few minutes when he was stopped dead by the appearance of a set of deep tracks, similar to those made by his own party, which came down from the crest of the ridge at 15,000 feet to about 13,000 feet at that point where he had seen the dark object the previous evening. Although he photographed the tracks for their entire length, it was impossible to obtain a clear picture of any one print because the snow had tumbled into each 12-inch-deep hole; but he estimated them to be about the same size as his own small, size 6 foot.

That night, according to Bonington's account of Whillan's experience, the moon was so bright that it was possible to read small print: so, after pondering about the tracks, Whillans eventually stuck his head out of the tent, although it was 'fantastically' cold. The moon was shining directly on to the hillside with the tracks and after a while he noticed that one of the dark spots of possible rocks or trees, whose positions he had previously memorised, had begun to move towards a clump of trees. With a mono-cular he was able to distinguish the limbs of a reasonably powerful animal bounding along on all-fours very quickly and perhaps hunting for food as it wandered from one clump of trees to the next. Finally, when it came out into the moonlight and moved diagonally downhill in the direction of some cliffs, Whillans decided that it was an ape or ape-like creature, before it disappeared into the shadow of some rocks. He later described it as a dark, hairy biped, resembling a cross between a gorilla and a bear.

1979 — According to a report in the *Daily Mail*, the members of an RAF Himalayan expedition, Dr. John Allen and Squadron-Leader John Edwards, were at 17,250 feet in the Hinku Valley 20 miles south-east of Everest and were beneath an overhanging rock that formed a small cave about 200 yards from the main track, when, in John Edwards's words:

'I rounded a corner and was absolutely amazed to see prints. From their formation, it seemed as if the creature had jumped from the rock, bounded through the snow and across a stony outcrop where they disappeared. They were about 8 in. by 4 in. and were obviously freshly made, and cut three or four inches into the snow, indicating the creature was standing upright and weighing around 11½ stone.'

Nearby were droppings that were not those of any animal known to inhabit the area.

Edwards continues: 'As we were photographing the prints a few minutes later, we heard a high-pitched scream. It came from close above us. It was loud and piercing... more like a woman's voice than an animal cry.' After the sightings their Sherpas refused to stay high on the mountain after nightfall, as had also been the case in Don Whillans' experience.

From the various accounts of Europeans, Sherpas and Tibetans, together with photographs of tracks, there would appear to be two or three types of yeti — certainly two: one large, one small — though it is possible that these may represent different age-groups, sexes or geographical races of the same species. From these reports we can build up an identikit of an anthropoid ape. To those Tibetans living in Sherpa country the yeti is known as *Teh* — which, however, is also the Tibetan for bear — from which the Sherpas derived *Yeh* (rocky place) and *Teh* (this type of animal). Therefore *Yeh-Teh* is that type of *Teh* living in rocky places. Under this general name the Sherpas recognize two kinds of yeti, of which the larger is the *Dzu-Teh* and the smaller and much more commonly seen, heard or imagined is the *Mir-Teh* or *Mi-Teh* (man-like beast or possibly man-bear). The latter occasionally comes into contact with man, especially when the winter snow is deep, and it reveals its presence near a Sherpa hill village by its distinctive loud mewing or drawn-out howl, which has been compared to the cry of a sea-gull, though not, significantly, to that of the ubiquitous chough; a series of short, slightly warbled chirps have been likened to the chatter of monkeys. However, Mir-Tehs are normally shy and retiring unless provoked or cornered when, like gorillas and chimpanzees, they stage an impressive threat display but seldom carry this through to actual attack.

By all accounts a Mir-Teh is squat, stocky, tail-less and ape-like, 5-5½ feet tall and very heavy, to judge by tracks several inches deep in the snow. It is covered with stiff, bristly, coarse hair varying in colour from fawn to chestnut-brown, reddish-brown, greyish-brown or even blackish, though paler on the chest and tending to be longest on head and shoulders and around the waist; its flat face being mainly hairless. The 'squashed-in' nose is monkey-like and the ears lie close to the large head, which is pointed or conical with a pronounced saggital crest. It has a bull-neck, slightly prognathous jaw with very powerful muscles and a very wide mouth, but no lips, and its teeth though large are not fangs. It arms are long, reaching to the knees, and its feet very broad, with the heel nearly as broad as the forepart of the sole. Although the very thick great toe is separated from the other toes, it is not opposable to them as in the case of most monkeys. It normally walks erect like a man, though leaning forward slightly, taking strides of from 9 to 18 inches with a shuffling or unsteady rolling gait, but if frightened and hurrying or negotiating deep snow or rocky ground, may drop to all fours and bound along — as Whillans noted.

In the case of the larger, reputedly aggressive and dangerous Dzu-Teh, Dzu can indicate either a large hulking beast or one associated with live-stock as a predator that sometimes kills yaks or cattle. This yeti is rarely or never seen in Sherpa country, and the numerous reports of it all come from very high altitudes in the extreme north of Sikkim and Nepal, but mainly from eastern Tibet and Mongolia, though there are also hunters' tales of big, hairy wild men in the Chatkal range of the Tien Shan, The Dzu-Teh is reputed to stand 7 or 7½ feet (more than 8 feet according to Rawicz) with long arms and huge hands, and a powerful body covered with thick, shaggy reddish-brown or dark brown hair, which is sparse on the ape-like face. Its oval-shaped head, with beetling brow, runs up to a point, and the imprints of its feet resemble those of a human giant except for two subdigital pads under the first toe; a footprint photographed in the clay shore of a mountain lake in the Chatkal was 15 inches long and 5.2 inches broad, with the second toe much larger than the big toe.

By saddling the yeti with the ridiculous sobriquet of 'Abominable

Snowman' — a mistranslation of the Tibetan *midre* (man-bear), to which *kang mi* (glacier man) is added — westerners have fostered the no less ridiculous myth that the Mir-Teh's habitat in the Himalaya is the zone of permanent snow ranges, peaks and glaciers, in which it is obvious that no primate could exist for any prolonged period; and this absurd assumption has resulted in searches for yetis — which are in any case certainly few in number — being mounted in the wrong type of terrain. When their tracks have been located on the snow at great altitudes — as high as 23,000 feet — they are not those of residents but of migrants, possibly with no settled abode, traversing glaciers or making use of high passes to cross from one valley to another. The fact that there are so few practicable routes through this high country for beast or man accounts for the quite frequent confluence of yeti tracks with Sherpa or European mountaineers or explorers. Shipton's photographs, for instance, were taken in a region of alpine moorland, free of snow in the summer. The Yeh-Teh of the Sherpas is the beast of rocky places, preying on such small mammals as pikas and marmots, which are very numerous in the higher mountains, and also searching for what the Sherpas describe as a 'saline moss' growing on the rocks of the moraines, but which may be in fact a lichen containing Vitamin E. There is ample food for an omnivorous animal at these high altitudes. In the course of its activities the yeti leaves its tracks across the snowfields, as do wolf, fox, snow leopard, deer or tahr; but none of these animals is commonly seen. As Stonor has pointed out, the fact that the *Daily Mail* expedition failed to locate a yeti did not disprove its existence. Snow leopards, for example, were reputed common in the area of investigation, but none were seen; only some members of the expedition saw wolves, despite the fact that wolves were preying on domestic stock throughout the expedition's time in the Khumbu region of Nepal; and only two or three foxes were seen, although the commonest of the larger alpine mammals.

Yetis — 'sightings' or tracks of which range from 12,000 to 23,000 feet — have as their *lebensraum* an inconceivably vast terrain, virtually unknown and unexplored by man, from the snow-line down to the almost uninhabited and trackless montane cloud forest between 9,000 and 14,500 feet. This zone does not invite exploration, since it is riven with thousands of deep canyons where the vegetation is not only so dense as to be termed impenetrable but harbours myriads of leeches and stinging and biting insects; and every steep mountainside is savagely gouged out by streams and rivers, like the terrain south and south-east of Everest and Makalu. It is significant that the Dzu-Tehs are reported to live in impenetrable thickets in the highest forests, though they too may perhaps go up on to the snow in order to obtain lichens from the rocky moraines. Nevertheless, according to *Oryx* (May, 1973), the very few expeditions that have explored the high forests in search of yetis, have found their tracks, faeces, sleeping sites and hair. The few aboriginal inhabitants say that the yetis in this zone lair up during the day-time, but their peculiar whistling calls are heard at night. However, the anthropologist, John Napier, has pointed out in his entertaining and informed book on the yeti, *Bigfoot*, that while the mountain gorillas in East Africa may climb as high as 13,500 feet in passing from one forested zone to another, vegetable food is available to them all the year round; but comparable forests in the Himalaya to those inhabited by the gorillas are not to be found much above 5,000 or 6,000 feet; for while the floor of those gorges transecting the Himalaya from north to south may be heavily forested with tropical montane vegetation, this degrades above 6,000 feet into bamboo, and thence upwards into rhododendron, moorland and finally permanent snow between 13,000 and 20,000 feet.

In addition to the Himalayan cloud-forest there are the thousands of square miles of the alpine zone above the tree-line but below the permanent snow. These include the greater part of the higher Himalaya and far exceed the area of ice and snow. Though strewn with rocks this is not — as Stonor has pointed out — a barren zone, but alpine country with plants and grasses and in places a 'profusion of sage-green dwarf juniper covering whole slopes raggedly', and numbers of birds and mammals. The Sherpas pasture their yaks as high as 17,000 feet on the less precipitous slopes of this zone, but they never venture into the rocky valleys, which are impassable to their herds.

In considering the problems presented by the existence of such a large, unknown animal as a yeti it is not without significance that of the twenty-one species and subspecies of mammals collected in the Khumbu region by the *Daily Mail* expedition four were new to science. Sceptics have argued that yetis, if they exist, are either bears or large monkeys; and it is true that wall paintings in monasteries and temples depict two types, one of which resembles a bear and the other a large monkey. But the few descriptions of the living animal and the numerous descriptions of their tracks, together with the photographs of the latter, cannot be assigned to bears or monkeys. Sir Edmund Hillary and Desmond Doig, who took part in an expedition to Makalu, partly for research into human reactions to prolonged living at high altitudes and partly to search for yeti, were finally convinced that all so-called yeti tracks were in fact the result of hot sun fusing the pug-marks of such small mammals as foxes and enlarging them out of all proportion to their original size. Wherever they found tracks that the Sherpas asserted were those of a yeti, these were 'quite obviously' those of small quadrupeds, which the effects of sun-melting and Sherpa imagination had transformed into those of yetis. Doig cites, as one example of Sherpa fantasy, a track that they followed when at a height of 18,400 feet on the Ripumu glacier. On the shaded side of a snow ridge the 'footprints' could not be mistaken for anything other than small pug-marks, but on the top of the ridge they had expanded under the influence of the sun into huge 15-inches 'feet', in which the slightly misplaced pug-marks formed the toes and heel. It was on gradual slopes and at the top of passes where the tracks were on a more or less single plane of snow, and where their angle of exposure to the sun was the same, that they retained their huge yeti shape with a regularity sufficient to convince any observer that they had indeed been made by a very large biped. But, in rebutting this theory, John Napier has demonstrated, after making numerous practical experiments, that the signs of sun melting tracks are so obvious that no one with any experience could confuse a melted footprint with a fresh one, because in the former the outline becomes woolly and the details in the floor of the print become blurred.

Of known animals, with which it has been suggested yetis and their tracks have been confused, the brownish-grey Himalayan langur monkey — a large male of which may be 30 inches long and carry a 34-inch tail — is familiar to most Sherpas and to Himalayan travellers, with its distinctive purplish-black skin around eyes, cheeks and muzzle, framed by a ruff of radiating creamy white hairs that conceal the bare black ears. Lithe and lean with very long legs, it walks daintily on all fours, with its great tail terminating in a tuft, also creamy white, held aloft; and runs very swiftly with tail curved in a road arc over its back. Even at a distance of several hundred yards it is unmistakable and no descriptions of yetis can be attributed to this monkey, with the possible exception of a single, never substantiated report by two Norwegian prospectors that in 1948 when near the Zemu Gap, and therefore at an altitude of about 19,000 feet, they followed a double set of man-like tracks in the snow and attempted to lassoe two large brown-haired 'apes with long furry tails', with the result that one man was knocked down and mauled. Although gibbons and all the apes are capable of walking bipedally, none of the reported yeti tracks could have been made by a langur's long, elongated, narrow feet, and the tracks photographed by Shipton most closely resemble those of the mountain gorilla. Moreover, langurs usually associate in small bands — led by the males — and being specialised leaf-eaters, never venture very far away from the trees, though in the summer they may move from their wintering woods at 7,000 feet to the upper edge of the conifer forest at 12,000 or 13,000 feet, higher than which they have hever been seen; except that in November 1903 a companion of C.G. Rawling was positive that he had watched through binoculars a troop of monkeys on the *north* side of the Brahmaputra where, to the north-east of Everest, the terrain consisted solely of grass and rocky hills.

Toni Hagen, who travelled over most of Nepal during the eight years of his geological survey, reported seeing long-haired 'apes' at an altitude of 12,000 feet; and Ivan Sanderson has stated that the mainly unexplored plateau and mountains of the Kun Lun, demarcating the border between Tibet and Sinkiang, are inhabited by a very large species of macaque, mature males of which are reputed to stand 6 feet high. He suggests that there could be a giant species of macaque in the Himalaya, and possibly also in the Karakoram, another source of unknown animals. Although the tracks made by a macaque would not resemble those of a yeti, it is worth noting that while this monkey normally struts on all fours, it sometimes walks on its powerful hind legs when there is snow on the ground because, like other monkeys, and apes, it may dislike getting its hands cold in the snow. Points of physical similarity with the yeti are the apparent absence of a tail, which is so small that it is concealed by the macaque's long, reddish-brown or orange coat, and the head, which is flattened from side to side between the beetling brows and pointed crown. From the region of the macaque's eyes, however, immense domes of long hair sweep back to the neck to join a profuse mane, and the pink skin of the hairless face turns bright red in heat and bluish when cold.

The bears in the Himalaya and adjacent regions are the sloth bear, which is confined predominantly to the lower jungles, the black bear and various races or colour variations of the brown bear: referred to as red, isabelline (perhaps the red bear in its pale, yellow-brown winter pelage) and blue, which is the much rarer large Tibetan bear, standing 6 or 7 feet high. Although most blue bears are in fact golden-brown with bluish undertints and an ivory band across the shoulders, the 5-inch-thick fur of some individuals is a very pale blond or platinum-blond sprinkled with black hairs that impart a bluish tinge to it. However, the blue bears' range does not include the Himalaya, with the possible exception of Bhutan, and they are only reliably known to inhabit eastern Tibet — where it is perhaps significant that *Dzu-Teh* is one name given to this bear — and the almost unexplored mountains of Kham, Amdo, Tsing-hai and Szechwan. Thus, to both Sherpas and Europeans, blue bears are virtually known only from their skins.

Black bears, on the other hand, are commonly distributed in the forests just below the Sherpa country and from the Hindu Kush to Assam, but have rarely if ever been seen above the tree-line in the Himalaya. In the winter the majority go down to the lower valleys around 5,000 feet, where food is always available. Brown bears, by contrast, prefer montane moorland, and are seldom found below 10,000 feet during summer in the Himalaya, where they range from Kashmir south-eastwards to the upper reaches of the Ganges near Kamet and Nanda Devi, but probably only occasionally wander into northern Nepal. Thus the Sherpas have no name for this bear and are mostly acquainted with the black bear. Unlike the latter, and also the yeti, brown bears are obliged to hibernate for three or four months in caves or among snow-covered rocks at around 6,000 or 8,000 feet in the valleys; but after emerging in the spring, she-bears and cubs move up to the high yak pastures to graze the new grass in glades near the edge of the tree-line, or on the sites of old sheep-pens, as the melting snow recedes, and plough up great tracts of hillside in search of roots and tubers. They have been known to climb above the snow-line to 16,500 feet. So too the blue bears — some of which winter in the montane prickly-oak forests of Szechwan when the alpine vegetation is under snow — summer on Tibet's tree-less steppes of sandy hills and coarse grass at heights of over 16,000 feet, grubbing up tubers, digging out voles, marmots and pikas from their burrows and hooking fish out of the streams.

Against the argument that yetis and their tracks can be assigned to bears are the facts that reports of yetis are most frequent in wintertime when brown bears are hibernating; that, while capable of shuffling along in an erect posture for short distances, no bear would raise its feet alternately in a stride, and certainly could not walk upright for several hundred yards, as indicated by the tracks followed by Tilman, Shipton, Brodet and Whillans; and that the absence of claw-marks in yeti prints, together with the alignment of the toes, in which the inside toe is longer than the others, precludes the possibility of their being made by bears. Nor can all of the prints seen over the years by reputable observers be attributed to the effects of melting on the tracks of such animals as snow leopard, wolf, fox, bharal, ibex or giant panda, or any other known animal except gorilla or man.

One of the more ludicrous suggestions as to the identity of yetis is that they are giant pandas, despite the fact that the latter are almost exclusively forest animals, whose altitudinal range between 5,500 and 14,500 feet is closely associated with that of the bamboo jungle and the mixed fir and broad-leaved forests of central and northern Hsi-fan — as the wild western region of Szechwan is known to the Chinese — and the Tsinling mountains fringing the south of Kansu and Shensi. This territory of upwards of a quarter of a million square miles — lying about 1,000 miles east-north-east of the Everest region — contains the world's entire population of giant pandas, and the bulk of them are concentrated in only one-tenth of this area to the east of the 25,000-foot mountain, Minya Konka; but according to

Chinese sources they number only between 400 and 1,000, though one would suppose this to be an under-estimate, particularly since 140 are reported to have died when the bamboo crop failed in 1977.

Because the bamboo normally provides them with an inexhaustible supply of food it is probably true that they seldom move far from those precipitous slopes of bamboo and spruce rising at angles of 45 or 70 degrees from the rivers and their deep gorges, where, say Chinese naturalists somewhat improbably, they drink so heavily that they can only waddle along after drinking or actually become unconscious. However, giant pandas, like the little red pandas, frequently kill small mammals and birds, and they may well venture out of the bamboo jungle more often than reported, for there have been a number of sightings of them in trees near farmhouses and wood-cutters' huts, and they also raid the villagers' beehives for honey, although the hives are fashioned from hollow tree-trunks and protected by strong fences. Some apparently move right out of the forests during the summer, for in June 1940 a Chinese zoologist encountered a panda with two cubs at an altitude of around 15,000 feet on the steppe at the upper source of the Yellow River at that point where it connects two lakes, Tsaring Nor and Oring Nor, between the immense ranges of Bayan Kara Shan and Anne Machan Shan, and in the extreme north-west of known panda territory:

After jumping over rills we came to a boggy tract. Suddenly our guide and bodyguard uttered a loud cry of surprise. About 2-3000 metres south-east of our route there emerged a queer beast. Hurriedly I took up my telescope and got a clear view of the beast with two cubs. "Giant Panda! Giant Panda! Look quick! How beautiful she is!" At that moment we were on this side of one branch of the Yellow River . . . The mother with her cubs was just turning away from us, doubtless on account of the noise we made. In the course of their retreat the mother panda sauntered . . . leisurely and stubbed plants . . . Her fur is sparklingly bright as the sun shines upon it. Further away, near the lake, the Oring Nor, many antelopes and wild asses were to be seen . . . Two blue bears appeared on the opposite bank of the stream, where we were to ford across . . . The two cubs . . . followed and suckled their mother.

This panda was feeding on a variety of the abundant steppe plants, which probably included gentians, irises, crocuses, the matrimony vine and such tufted grasses as bents and rice-grass, and was no doubt also grubbing up bulbs and roots.

We do not know whether those pandas inhabiting bamboo jungles bordering the steppes are regular summer visitors to these, like the blue bears that follow the camps of explorers and are constantly to be seen digging out pikas. One assumes that the pandas' visits are made, not because bamboo culms are unavailable during the summer — which is not the case, for young shoots continue to spring up from June until the end of September — but merely for a change of diet, vegetable and animal. Weather conditions may also be an influential factor. An animal with a slightly oily, very thick undercoat and an extremely dense, woolly outer coat lying long and close and two inches or more thick in places, does not voluntarily tolerate heat; and even within the bamboo zone some pandas go higher in hot weather and lower in cold, although in the main the Hsi-fan summers are cool, damp and wet, and the winters very cold.

While there is no *hard* evidence that the yeti is a member of the Himalayan fauna, since accounts by the Sherpas are in the main too closely associated with their mythology, there is an abundance of what Napier has termed *soft* evidence — eyewitness accounts, tracks and photographs of footprints — that only apes or subhumans could have been responsible for at least some of those tracks found at high altitudes on snowfields and glaciers. What would a brown bear or even an Indian *sadhu*, capable of existing stark naked in the Himalayan snows, be doing bounding about on all fours in the 'fantastically cold' moonlight of a late winter's night at 13,000 feet on the south face of Annapurna? Add to this soft evidence only a small percentage of the numerous sightings by Soviet citizens in the Caucasus and Pamirs and other regions of the USSR, and one finds it difficult to rule out the existence of creatures unknown to science — possibly, though there is no supporting evidence, descendents of, related to, or in the case of the Dzu-Teh, an actual *Gigantopithicus:* the huge anthropoid that inhabited south China and India some half-million years ago, when the Himalaya were still in process of formation, and to the sanctuary of which it was driven by the evolving *Homo Sapiens.*

Chapter Fifteen

LIFE ON THE ULTIMATE SUMMITS

As one climbs to high altitudes in mountainous country, so the skin of soil over the rock becomes progressively thinner, fragmented by frost and dragged downwards by boulder slippages; it also becomes poorer in nutrients, leached out by heavy rains. Trees become stunted and are replaced by shrubs, then by alpine meadows and finally by lichens and mosses up to the permanent snow. The upper limit of tree growth varies with latitude and also with regional micro-climatic conditions. In the Alps it lies between 6,000 and 7,000 feet, in the Himalaya and the Andes around 12,000 feet, but in Tibet, with the highest forests in the world, above 15,000 feet; whereas in the Rockies on the same latitude the tree-line is some 4,000 feet lower, while on Mount McKinley in Alaska it does not reach 3,000 feet. Once the limit of tree growth has been passed, the mountain environment becomes very similar to that of the desert. There are extremes of temperature, both seasonal and between day and night; strong winds, increasing in velocity at high altitudes, shrivel up the young shoots of plants; and there is a lack of shelter and a shortage of water, since the moisture contained in ice or frozen snow is mainly inaccessible to plants for the greater part of the year. As L.W. Swan has pointed out, water in liquid form, with the exception of glacial pools or snowfields with an impervious base, is largely confined at high altitudes to the subsurface, for the very small quantities of water vapour in the air may preclude the formation of dew. All these factors result in a short flowering season for plants.

In the Himalaya plant cover of a kind extends as high as 17,000 feet and, though dominated by dwarf rhododendron and juniper, includes various grasses, sedges, buckwheat, gentians and small primulas, together with sandwort, edelweiss, rock jasmine, sagebrush and joint-pines, while on meadows and screes a brilliant blue poppy attracts insects, but straw-coloured spines, protruding from its leafy rosette, stem and sepals, discourage browsing animals. White saxifrages, blue gentians and dwarf blue delphiniums have indeed been recorded in the Tibetan Himalaya as high as 19,800 feet, and a diminutive cushion-plant, *Stellaris decumbens*, collected at a height of 20,130 feet on Makalu by Swan — who was a member of the 1954 American expedition to that mountain — must have been near the tolerable upper limit for flowering plants. Where monsoon showers penetrate the Himalaya, as in the Dhaulagiri — Annapurna region, the mountain slopes between 16,000 and 18,000 feet are gay in June with many small flowering plants. But, as Swan has noted, plant life becomes very sparse at around 19,000 or 20,000 feet and tends to be restricted to two types of niche, congregating either around the bases of rocks or in those places where there is some subsurface drainage of water from a higher snowfield. On dry slopes small communities of plants are concentrated where protruding rocks, dark against their white surround of snow, have absorbed heat from the sun and have melted some of the snow into water that accumulates under them. Plants such as sandwort, edelweiss, gentian and the 'furry', 6 or 12-inches-high *Saussurea*, resembling saw-wort and growing in great clubs of softest white wool, are to be found only in the rock-base type of niche at these higher elevations. Oddly enough, most Himalayan plants are not protected like the *Saussurea*. Swan also noted that lichens, usually considered to be a characteristic feature of desiccated high-altitude rocky slope environments, were scarce, small and often dead above 18,000 feet in the Himalaya, because they depended for their survival on surface water in damper places below the drainage points of snowfields.

Snow is not only the main source of water at high altitudes, but the amount of winter snowfall is a critical factor in determining the plant and animal life because it provides a protective blanket against extremes of temperature and prevents the ground from freezing. In those places where the snow has been blown off by strong winds, plants and insects are exposed to those desiccating winds, with their abrasive snow and ice crystals, and also to very low temperatures. On the other hand, if the snow drifts to too great a depth, it may not melt away during the summer, or do so too late for plants to fructify. Most of the arthropods on high mountains concentrate along the snow-line or near glaciers, lakes or torrents of melt-water flowing from ice or snow, and expose themselves to the sun only in moist places, usually near the edge of the snow. In these they can absorb heat from direct sunshine without being dehydrated in the dry air or harmed by ultra-violet radiation. It is a fair assumption that, without snow, there could be no communities of any kind of life much above the tree-line, whereas with snow, the alpine zone in fact supports a unique and complex life system.

Sizeable insects — such ants, bees, wasps, flies, moths, beetles, aphids, leafhoppers, stoneflies, mayflies and grasshoppers — are common in regions of sparse vegetation up to 16,000 feet in the Himalaya. Bees and butterflies migrate through mountain passes and move up and down the mountain-sides as different plants come into flower. A migratory passage of large white butterflies and long-tailed blues, together with hover-flies and ladybirds, negotiate a 12,000-foot pass in Nepal late in March and fly still higher over the snow slopes; apollos, swallowtails (related to the apollos) and painted ladies migrate over mountain passes at 17,000 feet; clouded yellows and Indian tortoiseshells have been recorded at 19,000 feet on the Zemu glacier in the middle of May and considerable swarms of clouded yellows, apollos and silver-washed fritillaries have been observed at an altitude of nearly 20,000 feet. Hingston noted that a tortoiseshell was sometimes seen at 17,000 or 18,000 feet on the Rongbuk glacier, the surface of which was deeply fissured and largely covered with rock debris, though some grass grew among the fragments of rock and there were patches of lichen on the stones. A number of moths, probably *Anarta,* also frequented the glacier's moraine, and there were larvae of both stoneflies and mayflies in the deep blue pools lying on the surface of the ice, despite the fact that the temperature of these are so low that after sweeping them with a net, the gauze remained frozen in a rigid bag.

The highest breeding butterfly in the world — and also a dominant in arctic regions — must be the diaphanous-winged apollo, *Parnassius acco,* which lays its eggs near ice at heights of over 19,000 feet, though whites are known to do so at over 18,000 feet, as may a few *Vanessa,* which are mainly restricted to wooded areas. All these high-altitude Himalayan butterflies, like those on the alpine meadows in Europe, are diurnal fliers, though their counterparts at lower levels may be crepuscular or possibly even nocturnal; but the behaviour of many kinds of high-altitude insects is influenced by sudden and extreme temperature changes from hour to hour that are typical of their environment. Swan observed that though when the sun was shining they were remarkably active, in cloudy weather they behaved erratically, and in such conditions it was a common sight to see butterflies and flies running over the ground or actually lying torpid beside a rock, and some butterflies would actually lie on their sides in most un-butterfly-like postures. Similarly, on Tibet's 14,000-foot central plateau, *pseudabris* beetles, brilliantly coloured with alternate bands of black and red, normally cling in clusters to vetches while feeding on the young shoots and flowers; but when one of Tibet's frequent gales springs up, they drop to the ground and lie on their sides with heads bent at right-angles to their bodies, apparently lifeless. Yet when the wind decreases they quickly revive, running over the ground and climbing back up the vetches again.

Another characteristic of butterflies in the nival zone above the snow-line is that instead of laying their eggs on the plants that will provide food for their caterpillars, as is customary, they deposit them on the ground. Moreover, the caterpillars shelter under stones on the ground and, if the previous winter's snowfall has been less than normal, are likely to remain quiescent throughout the summer, neither feeding nor pupating. They can indeed survive in a state of dormancy under the snow for a year or longer, compensating for this static period by abbreviating the subsequent stages of their life-cycle.

Perhaps the most remarkable visiting insects to the highest mountains are *Adonia* ladybirds, which not only migrate in swarms in the late autumn through the high passes of such European mountains as the Pyrenees, but deliberately migrate from plains, valleys and forests to certain peaks in the Rockies and the Himalaya. Enormous swarms of adult ladybirds, comprising a number of different species, mount up from the lowlands, even though there may be no up-draught currents to assist them, or even when the prevailing wind is against them, and migrate towards some particular peak, to the exclusion of all others — not in order to feed or breed on it, but to hibernate during the winter in enormous concentrations of 5000 or 9000 in a single square yard beneath a boulder or in rock crevices, which may be overlaid by 30 or 60 feet of snow during the course of the winter. In this respect there is a species of scorpion, found at 13,000 feet in the Himalaya, that can endure the winter under a stone covered by 50 feet of snow; and hibernating insects in the nival zone can survive prolonged burial under ice or snow 45 or 60 feet thick for a year and in some cases two or even three years. Though some insects are capable of withstanding exposure to temperatures in the region of minus 15°F, it is probable that none hibernate in ground that is not blanketed by snow. Nevertheless, immense numbers of hibernating ladybirds succumb to the cold or are eaten by insects or birds or, incongruously, by Himalayan brown bears and in the Rockies by grizzlies. The latter turn over the rocks in search of the ladybirds and also the larvae of the army cut-worm moths (*Agrotis*), besides regularly visiting glaciers to gorge on the grasshoppers that are blown up on to the snow near glaciers every autumn. When the snow melts the following summer, the surviving grasshoppers return to the valleys to breed.

M.S. Mani made the remarkable discovery that the mass swarms of ladybirds in the Himalaya assemble in the same hibernating places year after year, with the result that the latter contain considerable accumulations of dead and frozen beetles from previous years. One such assemblage of seven-spotted ladybirds on a sheltered snowfield at a height of about 14,000 feet on the south slope of the Dhauladar range in the north-west Himalaya was estimated in the middle of May 1953 to contain some 200,000 beetles to the square yard; and since the whole aggregation covered 9 or 10 square yards, and to totalled about two millions, it gave a reddish-brown tint to the snow-field, conspicuous at a considerable distance. The majority of these beetles were alive but inactive, though when disturbed they moved slightly, and a few spread their elytra before settling again.

The altitudinal level of the snow-line varies not only regionally but from one peak to another within a single range of mountains. In the Pyrenees and the Alps there are permanent snowfields down to 8500 feet, and in the Caucasus to around 10,000 feet, whereas in the Himalaya the snowline varies between 14,500 and 19,000 feet. Accounting for this variability in the Himalaya, Swan has pointed out that their southern faces are exposed between June and September to continuous snow, which may accumulate on outlying rocks between 15,000 and 16,000 feet; but further into the range snowfall decreases sharply until, beyond the highest crest in Tibet, the annual precipitation may be less than 15 inches. Thus, in the inner-most Himalaya, where cloud is less frequent and intense sunlight correspondingly greater, there are places where no snow-line can be defined, and where, while tongues of snow reach down to 18,000 feet, immense areas of snow-free rock rise to great altitudes.Indeed, if the slope is continuous and the mass of a particular mountain large enough, snow-free rock may extend as high as 23,000 feet. Photographs taken on the summit of Everest, for instance, reveal a snow-free expanse of gently sloping rock and scree only a few feet from the highest point at over 29,000 feet.

The permanent habitable zone of a mountain might be expected to terminate near the lowest level of perpetual snow, and it is only in recent years, as zoological and mountaineering expeditions have climbed successively higher up the world's highest mountains, that it has become apparent that insects have been so successful in adapting to montane conditions that billions have actually colonised and are resident far above the snow-line. Consider the factors influencing life in this nival zone, which covers about 1½ million square miles of the world's 14 million square miles of mountains. Obviously, the higher the mountain the more rarified the atmosphere, which at 26,500 feet is only three-quarters as dense as at sea-level. This rarefaction is associated with low humidity and a reduction in water-vapour, and therefore intense aridity, since increased ultra-violet light during the hours of daylight not only produces a high rate of evaporation, tending to dehydrate animals, but is followed by extreme radiation at night resulting in wide fluctuations in ground temperatures every twenty-four hours. On Himalayan peaks air temperatures may range from minus 40°F during the night to 219°F in the direct rays of the sun. At 21,200 feet on Everest in mid-May Wilfrid Noyce found it too hot to sit outside the tent in shirt-sleeves, and three years later Jung Marmet and Ernst Schmidt were obliged to remove their down-filled clothing at 28,000 feet, though the members of other Everest parties in other years suffered intense cold at this season. Although such warm conditions can only prevail on calm, sunny days they are not infrequent on mountain summits. Despite the fact that the mean temperature falls by about one degree with every 300 feet increase in height, it may be warmer on a sunny day at a higher altitude, where there tends to be less cloud and less shade from direct sunlight. At 18,000 feet, when the air temperature in the shade was 55°F, Swan recorded 92°F on the rock surface and 60°F at a depth of six inches in the sandy soil; and all these temperatures were higher than equivalent readings at 16,000 feet.

Oxygen starvation begins to take effect above 16,000 feet, at which height many resident vertebrate animals adapt with larger lungs and hearts and more oxygen-absorbing blood cells than their lowland counterparts. However, animals are surprisingly resistant to pressure changes, and this resistance has been emphasized by the recent successful ascents of both Kangchenjunga and Everest by climbers without the aid of oxygen apparatus. It is the wind, increasing in velocity at high altitudes to gusts exceeding 230 mph, that is the main factor determining the presence or absence of birds, for example; and those found at great heights are either powerful fliers such as vultures, eagles, ravens or choughs, or small passerines that take flight infrequently, and when they do so, keep close to the ground, taking advantage of available cover, or like wallcreepers, are adapted to clinging to rocks. Significantly, 60 per cent of all insects above the tree-line are wingless — minute wingless grasshoppers are to be found at 18,000 feet on Himalayan moraines — while even those possessing wings, such as the American cockcroach, may never actually fly, though the male does so in the temperate lowlands and both sexes do so in the tropical lowlands.

Apart from strong winds, the other factor restricting insect life at high altitudes is a combination of low pressure and very high or low temperatures resulting in the loss of body fluids. Most flies are protected from heat loss by being abnormally hairy, since hair absorbs and retains heat, but also retards the evaporation of moisture from the body. The dark colouring of the majority of alpine insects may not only enable them to absorb the sun's heat more rapidly during the early part of the day, but also to complete their foraging before the ground becomes too dry. Yellow or orange butterflies are much deeper in colouring at high altitudes, and in the Himalaya their normal whitish ground-colour is clouded black. Their dark pigmentation also allows these nival insects to absorb heat from the direct rays of the sun without at the same time being subjected to injurious effects both of the sun and of the intense ultra-violet radiation, which, as it happens, is one of the contributory factors in the production of these pigments. Woodlice and beetles have developed highly reflective surfaces as their protective shields against radiation. However, some nival insects are intolerant of light and many are so sensitive to even a slight rise above the normal maximum temperature in their zone that a few minutes' exposure to the warmth of a man's hand is sufficient to kill them. The advantage of being able to absorb heat by being dark colour- ed evidently outweighs any disadvantages. Black-bodied craneflies (phalangids), for example, run about the snow in the sun. Their body temperature may approach 90^0F, whereas the temperature of melting snow is approximately 32^0F in sun or shade. Normally the long stilts formed by their legs preclude their black bodies from melting the snow, but Swan found one individual whose black body had, by some accident, remained in contact with the snow long enough for a hole to be melted, into which it had sunk and been frozen.

At 16,000 or 17,000 feet there is a very marked decline in the numbers of larger insects, but this is compensated for by enormous aggregations, though few species, of small invertebrates that have colonised mountains to a height of at least 22,000 feet. In common with other insects their breathing apparatus consisting of tubes leading from various spots on the external skeleton, are relatively unaffected by the lowered air pressure at high altitudes. Among them are the springtails, also known as glacier fleas or snow fleas. These, which inhabit the ice masses of Greenland and other arctic islands too, and zones as high as 6,000 feet in Antarctica, can actually extract oxygen from the moisture that collects on their skin, and can thus be said not to require air. Also present at high altitudes on mountains, though possibly not much above 19,000 feet, are mites and small centipedes and, as high as the springtails, tiny anthomyiid flies and jumping spiders (salticids). The latter, apparently all immature, were first collected in 1924 at 18,000 feet on the rock and snow buttresses of Everest.

The wingless springtails, the smallest only one-fifth of an inch long, derive their name from a fork-tailed, trigger-like spike folded beneath the abdomen. The fork lies forward and is held with a ratchet-like latch of horny material. When the latch is released, the fork strikes the ground and throws the springtail a few inches into the air. This tiny particle of muscle powering the tail is said to be the strongest material yet discovered. The masses of dark-bodied springtails, soaking up the sun's heat on the snowfields and ever-moving rubble of glaciers, give large areas of these a sooty-black appearance that, like the swarms of ladybirds, is pronounced at some distance. Both springtails and the dark-brown jumping spiders, bouncing about spasmodically over rocks and glaciers, absorb enough heat from direct sunshine during the day to survive freezing during the night, though some springtails are to be seen crawling quite actively over a glacier at night when the temperature is as low as 14°F. However, both springtails and jumping spiders counter drops in temperature by passing into a state resembling hibernation under rocks or stones, which may subsequently be buried under deep snow. In such locations the temperature variation between day and night is lessened. At 17,000 feet, for example, the temperature beneath a rock may vary through only 12°F in twenty-four hours, in contrast to a 44°F range in the air temperature. Oddly enough, ground-hunting wolf spiders, when ascending in small numbers from lower levels to prey on anthomyiid flies at over 18,000 feet, have appeared to be more tolerant of cold than their prey. These spiders normally set out to hunt in the late afternoon when, since the sun has set behind the surrounding mountains, the ground is the warmest environment and attracts flying insects seeking shelter for the night; but on one occasion, when snow was actually falling, Swan observed spiders carrying insects that they had captured, 'having apparently taken advantage of a sun-less period to seize ordinarily more active prey reduced by the cold to a state of numbness and torpidity.'

Since both springtails and jumping spiders normally travel only a few feet or yards they must be permanent residents wherever found, assuming that they are not periodically transported to other localities by the hurricane-force winds that are a feature of their habitat. For that matter, how did they become established in such vast numbers in the nival zone in the first place? The spiders can obviously survive in those barrens above 20,000 feet, where even lichens are virtually non-existent, by preying on the springtails and anthomyzids: stalking the flies in the sun or, when clouds obscure it, hunting the springtails that are sheltering in dark recesses beneath the rocks, detecting them with the aid of their enormously enlarged first pair of eyes. But why are all these high-altitude spiders immature? On what, however, do the springtails and anthomyiids subsist in an environment in which while it might be practicable for them to feed during a period of six or eight weeks in the course of a summer, this period might include only a few suitable sunny hours, and this might be the case in one or two successive years?

The solution to this problem is as fascinating as any posed by high-altitude life, for there is in fact available to them an inexhaustible supply of food in the form of fungi, rotting vegetation and the enormous reservior of pollen, seeds and leaf-fragments, together with refrigerated insects and spiders, which are not only exposed along the edge of the receding winter snow, but litter the surface of snowfields and glaciers and are trapped on the lee or downward side of tilted rocks and boulders. Mountain plants, especially juniper bushes, produce large quantities of pollen — more apparently than the same species of plants at lower altitudes, to judge from the relatively large number of high-altitude pollinating insects; and this pollen is blown up on to the snowfields. But the most abundant food-fall on the highest snowfields and barrens is provided by the all-the-year-round air-lift of arthropods from the plains, valleys and forests. Mounting on thermals or, in the case of the young of some species, sailing aloft on silken filaments, myriads of arthropods are borne into the upper air, where they are immediately frozen. The chill winds may carry their refrigerated bodies hundreds of miles before ultimately dropping them on the mountain snowfields, some of which are 22,000 feet above the plains whence they originated. Much more of this organic material is blown on to the nival zone than off it, and it has been estimated that in some parts of the Himalaya the corpse of a lowland arthropod is falling on every square yard of this zone every 30 seconds. Millions of aphids are deposited on both the Himalaya and the Alps; million of white butterflies, raised by thermals far above the high peaks of the Alps, perish in the cold night temperatures and drop on to the glaciers; immense swarms of grasshoppers have been refrigerated in the Grasshopper Glacier in the Montana Rockies.

The highest resident springtails, and also the few green algae and plants growing on dead matter, can therefore rely for all or much of their nourishment on this constant air-lift of 'manna' from the lowlands; even butterflies suck juices from the 'carrion'. There would not appear to be any impediment to prevent springtails inhabiting the highest mountain peak, providing that rock-bases holding a little moisture were available; icicles hanging from rock faces above 22,000 feet confirm that thawing temperatures are experienced at unexpectedly high altitudes. Indeed, Swan discovered that the springtails have colonised what is perhaps an even more hostile habitat, for at heights of between 17,5000 and 19,000 feet on Makalu he was astonished to find a large form of this enterprising insect among the freshly cut rock rubble covering a glacier, 'where the angular slabs move and tumble, leaving gaping chasms and black voids between the boulders. In this incredible habitat the springtails were sunning themselves on the rocks and then, by strong flexing movements of their bodies, leaping in random bounds to avoid capture. Time and again they fell off the rocks and disappeared into the dark gulfs deep in the glacier.' Presumably they too subsisted on wind-borne debris.

Perhaps weather conditions will permit the members of some future Everest expedition to undertake an hour or two's search for insect life near the summit.

Chapter Sixteen

BUDDHISM AND WILDLIFE

From a Himalayan peak one looks north over a vast expanse of rolling steppes or downs bearing hardly a trace of snow, and naked rocky hills, unnaturally fired in blues, browns or baked ochre-yellows streaked with dull reds and cindery purples. Interspersed with broad flat strips of barren plain, they stretch away as far as the eye can see in the clear light of Tibet: that

> piercing clear light, which cuts every object sharp in its masses [wrote John Hanbury-Tracy, who accompanied Ronald Kaulback on his expedition to the upper Salween] not the unblinking light of the desert with a sky of hot hard tin, but a sparkling light, as of a sun through a fountain, with a hint of blue. The light dances in the spring, drugs you in summer, glares hard in the autumn when the grassland is parched yellow, and strikes brisk and clear-cut in winter when a man may bask in the sun but shiver in the shade a few feet away.

So very small and gently rounded appear the outlines of most of the treeless hills, which carry only a few scrubby thorns and an occasional juniper, that to David Snellgrove — who made a pilgrimage to Himalayan monasteries in 1956 — it was as if he was looking into the heart of a gigantic Cairngorms, for the relative heights of mountains and valleys are much the same, in contrast to the stupendous ranges of snowy peaks, slashed with narrow, deep-cut ravines and wooded valleys, to the south.

However, Tibet can be partitioned into three clearly defined environmental belts, which become increasingly arid northwards. In the south and east the river-gorge country, between 9,000 and 12,500 feet, of well-watered and largely wooded, flat-bottomed valleys, several miles wide, is very fertile, growing abundant crops of corn and fruit; the valleys, fingering steeply up between the hills, are cut off from each other by ranges of forested mountains. In the steeply wooded gorges in the higher juniper zone, and also on hillsides and plateaus where the forest approaches the snow-line, are flocks of white-eared pheasants, sixty or seventy strong and sometimes in company with blood pheasants. In the early morning they shout loudly to each other from hill to hill and, if alarmed, run uphill for several hundred feet before, if still approached, launching themselves into the air to glide downhill, accelerating with intermittent quick beats of their wings. The commonest large birds in this type of country, they vary in plumage from dull grey with black wing-tips to pure white except for black caps, blood-red circlets round the eyes and long, black feathers in their tails.

Buckthorn, dwarf rhododendrons and several kinds of edelweiss grow on the comparatively rich soil in the upper parts of the valleys, and there are also stretches of pasture, free from scrub-jungle, providing four or five months of rich grazing on the short grass for the Tibetan gazelles or goas, which sometimes associate with the flocks of domestic sheep, and in other parts of Tibet range as high as 18,000 feet. Reddish-grey in colour, the goas are distinguished by most conspicuous white blazons on their rumps. When excited or alarmed, and bounding away stiff-legged on all four feet like sheep, the skin along the ribs is drawn forward, thereby extending the blazons into perfect ruffs. Though more widely distributed over Tibet than the antelope, they do not herd in large concentrations like the latter and little is known about them.

North of the fertile belt, and at an average altitude of 14,000 feet, lies the colder, drier and more sparsely vegetated sub-plateau of steppes and wide, shallow valleys. The green of the marshlands around the shores of lakes and along the banks of winding rivers mark depressions between the hills. Many of the lakes are saline and therefore unsuitable for some birds and fish, and hot springs, with temperatures varying between 60° F and 212° F, appear to be inhabited only by a species of snake; but though weed and vegetation may be sparse on the freshwater lakes, pools and springs, which are intensely blue in the deluge of sunlight so often illumining this country north of the cloud-gathering Himalaya, brown-headed gulls and terns fish them in July and August, and great numbers of bar-headed geese and ruddy shelduck swim with their broods. The geese nest in colonies of thousands on flat plateaus of sand and pebbles on islands in both fresh and salt-water lakes, though this does not protect them from wolves and foxes, and also on cliff ledges, where there are no lakes, at altitudes of 13,000 or 14,000 feet. Lakes bordered by cliffs are particularly favoured by both geese and shelduck, and several dozen geese may sit up on the cliffs, just as the duck sit in caverns and fissures occupied by hill pigeons, choughs and ravens. There are solitary snipe with soft, mournful cries, great black-necked cranes and, where rivers enter large lakes, Pallas's fishing-eagles.

Hingston noted that the geese and shelduck, which in India were amongst the most timid of birds, swam about the ponds near Tibetan villages as tamely as in a city park; for since all wildlife was protected by the lamas, animals and birds, especially in the vicinity of monasteries, were fearless — or were before the Chinese occupation. Near monasteries even trees were protected, since the lamas believed that trees once sacrificed their lives to save one another, and were thus Buddhisattras which would be reincarnated in human form. The very soil might not be tilled for fear of taking life. The finches and larks around the pikas' burrows were as tame as the hill pigeons that fed from the hand at an Everest base camp. Howard-Bury mentions hundreds of ravens, magpies, red-legged choughs, hoopoes, tree sparrows, redstarts and wagtails nesting in the walls of a Tibetan fort and protected by the lamas; and Michael Peissel found that in Mustang, that almost unknown Nepalese enclave in Tibet, all the birds would take food from his hand or approach to within inches of him, whether they were the migratory sparrows or the gigantic ravens — the size of 'large eagles' — which perched in the huge branches of two mighty willows that grew outside the great wall around the town of Trenkan at an altitude of about 13,000 feet.

Peter Matthiessen has described how at daybreak early in November, when the White River sought of Samling (on the Tibetan frontier north-west of Dhaulagiri) was sheathed in ice, two ravens would come to perch on tritons on the roof of Shey Gompa (the Crystal Monastery):

> *Gorawk, gorawk,* they croak, and this is the name given to them by the Sherpas. Amidst the prayer-flags and great horns of Tibetan argali, the gorawks greet first light with an odd musical double note — *a-ho* — that emerges as if by miracle from those ragged throats. Before sunrise every day, the great black birds are gone, like the last tatters of departing night ... The sun rising at the head of the White River brings a suffused glow to the tent canvas, and the robin accentor flies across the frozen yard.

Even the ewes of the wildest of wild sheep, the bharal, would venture within ten yards of the members of the 1921 Everest expedition in their base camp at the Rongbuk monastery, and were also fed regularly every morning at the cells of the hermits less than 100 yards from the camp. Numbers of these sheep lived at 18,000 feet on the main shelf of the Rongbuk glacier, grazing on the sparse grass that grew near the melt-pools in the spring, descending 2,000 feet to the vicinity of the monastery in winter. However, it was permissible in Mustang to shoot a predator, such as a snow leopard, if it was in the act of attacking domestic stock; and game was regularly hunted by nomads to the north of Llasa, with the result that the antelope in that region were very wild.

Beyond the valley pastures, where large, vividly green migratory grasshoppers settle in the shimmering sunshine beneath the blue sky, are boundless sandy wastes, ruffled and blown into dunes by the winds, where vegetation is restricted to gorse, growing only 12 inches high in sheets like heather, but so spiny that neither the domestic stock nor the wild kiang will browse it. Brilliant rose-finches sway on its twigs in the eternal wind, partridges whirr over the scrub, sand-plover scurry over the sand between the tuffets — as they do in other high-desert country from Iran to Mongolia — and pairs or parties of six or eight tiny, sand-coloured ground choughs or jays skim over the ground. With their predominantly pink-fawn plumage, marked with black and white, they more resemble jays than choughs and have possibly adapted from jay stock in response to their unusual environment on the high barren or brushy plateaus of Central Asia with their stone-littered hillsides and hummocky country sliced by dry watercourses. These unique ground-peckers, as they are more appropriately termed, are the size of larks with long, strong black beaks, slightly decurved like those of true choughs, with which they can vigorously pick-axe the soil or probe under stones for beetles and hiding insects, lizards and vegetable matter. With long, strong legs also, but short wings, they spend much time on the ground, for they can fly no farther than 100 yards at a stretch; but, sprightly and active, they run very swiftly in long, bouncing hops with body and head held erect, leaping on to a rock or bush from time to time, to bob and curtsey like a chat, flicking open wings and tail. They nest in shrubs or crevices in walls, or in burrows already dug by rodents or which they themselves excavate in steep earth-banks. In the latter case a horizontal tunnel, 5 or 6½ feet long and less than 3 inches in diameter, widens at its end into a nest-chamber stuffed with a large pad of sheep's wool or yak hair weighing as much as 1½ pounds.

The ground-peckers are also to be found near every habitation on the Tibetan plateau, as are tree sparrows, rose-finches and Eurasian cuckoos calling from the telegraph wires. Tame and fearless like the other birds, the ground-peckers perch on roof-tops and piles of stones that mark the boundaries of cultivated patches of land, while uttering their feeble, plaintive whistles. On every plot of cultivation are various species of mountain finches, snow finches and larks — skylarks, calandra, short-toed and shore larks feeding young when the ground is still covered with snow. These ground birds are inconspicuous against the soil, strewn with stones, not only because their colour harmonises with it, but because their shapes are confused with those of the stones, while those birds that are conspicuously marked, such as desert chats with white wing-patches, lose these markings when they alight and close their wings. Orange-beaked choughs wheel overhead, uttering their shrill, sad cries; and everywhere are the scavengers and birds of prey: golden eagles and steppe eagles — the frozen body of one of which was found at 26,000 feet on the South Col of Everest in 1965 — griffon vultures, lammergeiers, ravens and kites. Kaulback observed that as soon as the kites were on the wing in the early morning they were immediately mobbed by troops of magpies, which would come rushing down from above the kites and strike their heads as they sailed along. These very large Tibetan pied magpies would perch in a row on the back of a yak while pecking straws out of its shaggy coat, or hopping about the roofs with sidling gait, intent on pilfering.

Chapter Seventeen

KIANG, CHIRU AND YAKS ON THE CHANG-TANG

The commonest mammals on the Tibetan sub-plateau are inevitably pikas, marmots, fat grey woolly hares ambling among the juniper bushes immune from human molestation, and the sandy-coloured foxes with their exceptionally thick, bushy, cold-thwarting brushes and large ears. Wolves, preying mainly on the antelope and gazelles, are also numerous. Though predominantly black or yellow in colour, they may be off-white, silver-grey or grey with yellow tints. But especially there are the wild asses, the graceful kiangs or kulans, the colour of the tall summer grasses in their more luxuriant summer pastures, though the colour of individuals varies from a light or dark rust-brown or reddish-grey to a rich golden brown, which contrasts with the white or pale fawn of chest, belly, flanks and legs. However, in bright sunlight these colours are subject to kaleidoscopic changes to pale sandy-yellow or golden chestnut or even deep black. Standing only 12 or 13 hands, a kiang resembles a pony rather than an ass, despite its heavy head, carried high, and rather long ears. Nevertheless it can weight up to 900 pounds, being massively built with short, muscular neck, broad chest to accommodate large lungs, particularly strong hind legs for acceleration, and small hoofs of the hardest horn. An erect stiff mane of black hair, 4 inches long, extends as a clearly defined, though narrow, dorsal stripe to the root of the tail, which ends in a tassel like a mule's.

Sven Hedin, that most indomitable of explorers, has described having a thousand kiang in view at one time:

> They formed dark lines, sometimes large, sometimes small, sometimes spots like a rosary. Some herds galloped off to a point about two hundred yards in front of the caravan, where they stood and gazed and then dispersed, springing away in graceful movements . . . Further down the plain, beyond a small cliff, were five herds . . . the nearest of which numbered 133 head. They came galloping almost up to us . . . Then they set off in wild flight one after another, their hoofs thundering over the ground, made a wide curve behind us, and vanished in a dense cloud of dust, the hard beat of their hoofs being still audible. A strong puff of

wind dispersed the cloud, and they came in sight again; they stood quaking with fear, and looked at us, pricked up their ears, dilated their nostrils, and sniffed the wind.

Although the kiang usually travel in single file, treading down paths a foot wide and clear of stones to and from good feeding grounds or water all over the sub-plateau and the Chang-Tang, more than one explorer has remarked on the cavalry-like manoeuvres performed by their herds when disturbed or alarmed, repeatedly shying at imaginary objects and raising clouds of dust. Waddell has recalled how he at first mistook such a herd for

> the wild horsemen of the Chang-Tang, as they came galloping along in a whirlwind of dust, then executed a perfect wheel-round, then extended out in line at regular intervals, and advanced again; and . . . reformed into close order and came to an instant halt. Several of them galloped towards us and stood looking at us . . . as near as 300 yards away, and a few trotted through the lines of our baggage mules.

No doubt these manoeuvres form a part of the kiangs' defence against wolves, though with a maximum speed of 36 — 40 mph (slightly faster than a wolf at full stretch), and the ability to maintain a steady 30 mph for 15 miles at a time, they must be almost immune from attack except in deep, soft snow. In the more southerly areas of the Chang-Tang, and also in the west over against the Karakoram, the snowfall is very much heavier and snowstorms of arctic severity may continue for days at a time. In those regions, according to Hedin, some of the herds of kiang are cut off by deep spring snow:

> They cannot run when the snow is deep, and after trying in vain to reach bare ground, they die of starvation and are frozen in the snow-drifts. Our three guides . . . assured me that the wild asses are frozen in an upright position, and often stand on all fours when the summer sun has thawed the snow. They had seen dead wild asses standing in herds as though they were alive.

Both Howard-Bury in 1891 and Hedin in the latter years of that century and the early 1900s described the kiang as 'swarming' over the Tibetan plateau and widely distributed in herds of from 10 to 150 where grass was plentiful, especially near lakes and freshwater springs. Since they are reputed not to be able to survive for longer than two or three days without water, they must presumably 'drink' snow during the winter when the

Tibetan plateaus are frozen solid. Howard-Bury encountered them at an altitude of nearly 17,000 feet, grazing in barley fields despite the stone pillars and strings erected to keep them and also the hares out of the fields. They are known to graze as high as 18,500 feet but seldom range below 15,000 feet in Tibet, in contrast to the kulons in Mongolia, which are very rarely found as high as 3,000 feet, and those in Dzungaria, whose grazings lie around 700 feet. One would suppose that in many localities in Tibet, and for much of the year, the high-altitude kiangs must find forage hard to obtain. Meinertzhagen, for instance, spotting a small herd grazing on a hillside in Ladakh at the end of May, subsequently marked out an area of 100 yards by 10 on which they had been feeding, and after systematically collecting every scrap of vegetation, secured seventeen withered blades of coarse grass and seven small alpine plants; but kiang, like zebra, are efficient grazers, and Waddell, when traversing the flank of Chumolari on the borders between Bhutan and Tibet, saw hundreds feeding over what was apparently a bare desert plain, but in fact browsing on scattered clumps of grass and weeds that were studded between the loose pebbles, sandy gravel and thistles with which the ground was thickly strewn. Since they are dependent on grass, varying in abundance at different altitudes and at different times of the year, they no doubt migrate seasonally from one locality to another.

Other races of wild asses are to be found in semi-desert regions of the Altai and Mongolia, Baluchistan, Pakistan, India and Iran, but, so far as I am aware, no naturalist has watched the Tibetan kiang. Herds of stallions and mares are said to winter together until the weather becomes less severe, when the adult stallions break away in small groups of from two to ten — Waddell found stallions several miles up in the mountains in April — leaving the mares, yearling foals and younger stallions to forage in tens and twenties until all come together again for the mating at the end of August or early in September, a few weeks after the mares have dropped their one foal, or sometimes two, on the highest available ground. Hedin describes thirty mares, guarded by a stallion, standing on a mound in a meadow near the shores of a lake at sunset in the middle of August:

> Now and again a mare left the group and made a circuit about her sisters, but the stallion ran after her immediately and forced her to return to the others. This game was frequently repeated, and it seemed to me that the mares were making sport of the stallion.

Encountering man and his motley caravans of ponies, mules, camels, yaks, dogs and sheep only infrequently, the herds of kiang are inquisitive and will follow a caravan for miles, repeatedly wheeling round it at a distance of one or two hundred yards. A stallion and three mares circled Hedin's camp all afternoon on one occasion, trotting round and round with short springy steps, heads held high, tails streaming out obliquely; and on another occasion a single kiang kept ahead of his caravan for nearly two hours:

> Sometimes he trotted, sometimes he galloped, with his little tail sticking straight out behind him, but always with his head proudly arched . . . Ever and anon he stopped and turned round and gazed at us, and uttered a curious sound . . . The nostrils are very much larger than a horse's. When a kiang sniffs and snorts, or utters his hoarse scream, intermediate between a horse's whinney and a donkey's bray, though shriller, his nostrils expand into two large apertures surrounded by taut sinewy muscles, and project almost straight out before him.'

Eric Shipton had a close encounter with a kiang in a valley at 12,000 feet in the Karakoram. He was walking through the meadows and groves of willows (containing hoopoes) when he saw some animal standing alone by the river. The shimmer caused by the hot sun made it difficult to distinguish what it was until, as it approached nearer, he realised that it was a kiang. It came up to within fifteen yards of him and stood swishing its tail and staring at him, and when he turned round to go on his way, followed him, stopping when he stopped and walking when he walked, but finally lagged behind as he neared camp.

North of the kiangs' grazings on the central plateau is Tibet's third environmental belt — the Chang-Tang or northern plain, averaging 500 miles in width and covering twice the area of the remainder of Tibet. This bleak and desolate wilderness, intersected by ranges of undulating hills, is nowhere lower than 14,000 feet and lies predominantly between 18,000 and 20,000 feet. For much of the year it can fairly be described as a montane desert and compared to the deserts of Arabia or Arizona, but more particularly to the semi-desert region between 13,000 and 17,000 feet around Lake Titicaca in the Andes. As Hingston noted, the Chang-Tang displays the typical desert wastes of bare rock and brown sands, rippled or salt covered or piled in crescent dunes; the same sparseness of vegetation, thorniness of what plants there are, and absence of trees and therefore of colour in the landscape; the same cloudless skies and glare from the naked soil, over which the air rises in shimmering waves or invests in a true mirage. With only a scanty rainfall the atmosphere is so dry that skin and fingernails split. The morning sun heats the plains, the warm air rises, and fierce west winds sweep down from the mountains, raising up whirling 'dust-devils' that career over the empty plain. Nevertheless, the Chang-Tang differs from a true desert in the absence of intense heat, though it experiences the extreme range of temperature, often 50° F between day and night, characteristic of deserts. In winter, temperatures fall as low as minus 50° F, but snow lies only in occasional drifts and there is no permanent snow below 19,000 feet. Actually the lowest temperature recorded by Hedin in the course of his various Asian travels was minus 39.6° F when he was at 16,000 feet in the Kun Lun mountains bordering the Chang-Tang to the north.

The few travellers' impressions of the Chang-Tang are graphic:

From the end of June until the middle of November the average altitude of our camps was over 16,000 feet, the lowest being 14,621 feet, and the highest 18,315 feet, while the highest pass crossed was 18,760. All the enormous stretch of country crossed in that time contained not a single tree, and only two species of shrub, and these rarely exceeded six inches in height. (Hamilton-Bower, 1891)

The traveller . . . drags along for more than two months in the wind and snow without seeing a single human being or a single tree between the plains of Eastern Turkestan and the first encampment of Tibetan shepherds 150 or 200 kilometres to the north of Llasa. (Henri, Prince d'Orleans, winter 1889-90)

It hailed and snowed all day long and an icy wind blew from every quarter. The landscape was enshrouded in thick mist . . . The neighbourhood of our camp was . . . lifeless except for the screaming of gulls on the lake. Of vegetation there was not a sign, except the grass which already showed its yellow autumn tinge. The wind howled; the hard-grained snow whistled around the tent. (Sven Hedin, September 10).

However, despite the low temperatures, the absence of water, and a growing season of only two or three months in damper depressions, stretches of the Chang-Tang provide excellent summer grazing of coarse grasses and herbaceous perennials with long, thick tap-roots for domestic stock and also for herds of wild yak, gazelles and antelope — as do the sandy, 17,000 feet steppes between the Kun Lun and the Takla Makan desert, though since the large numbers of antelope and yaks on those steppes are much troubled by the nostril-fly they graze near lakes only in the evening or at night, or during rain or hail storms when the flies are not on the wing, retreating by day to the sanctuary of the sand-dunes, where the yaks appear as black as coal against the yellow sand.

According to Herbert Tichy, these summer pastures of the Chang-Tang resemble alpine meadows, except that the flowers, instead of standing out singly against the carpet of grass, overlay the green with their brilliant colours:

> But it is as if one were transported to the Alps, so many old friends does one find: primrose, gentian, campanula, cinquefoil, forget-me-not, poppy — the golden poppy of Tibet — saxifrage, buttercup — all are there. In some places it is impossible to take a step without treading on a couple of edelweiss.

Edelweiss, indeed, flower as high as 17,500 feet, and W.G. Thorold, who accompanied Hamilton-Bower on his trans-Tibet expedition, collected 115 species of flowering plants, the highest at 19,000 feet.

> How could I ever have imagined that Tibet was a dreary waste, for ever wind-blown! [wrote Hanbury-Tracy.] Yellow-breasted larks rose tremulously in sky-aspiring flight, swifts wheeled and darted, tiny crescents in the thin crystal air; butterflies, black and yellow, white, or blue hovered . . . from scented shrub to scented shrub . . . Leisurely our ponies trod . . . over slopes massed with flowering scrub . . . and over grassland patched with kingcups, white and blue-mauve anemones, primulas, nine or ten inches high, with many-flowered head. There were asters, dwarf, almost flat to the ground . . . in the alleyways between the scrub were geraniums . . . and high up, where the grass grew threadbare and scant, the little pink and white heads of polygonum showed an inch or two from the ground. Where the earth was scrawny and baked . . . minature irises, blue, yellow, and purple, were oases of sudden colour . . .

The Chang-Tang is the last stronghold of the wild yak and of Tibet's peculiar species of antelope, the chiru. The latter is remarkable for the interior lateral sacs in its nostrils, which perhaps aid breathing by warming and moistening the cold dry air. Whatever their purpose, they give the chiru a swollen muzzle, which is distended when the rutting buck bellows a challenge. The chiru is also peculiar in that the inguinal gland on the inside of the thigh is large enough to contain a man's fist and secretes a musky yellow powder. Native Tibetans believe that, when the chiru is pursued, it fills the gland with air, thereby enabling it to run more swiftly.

Delicately built animals, 30 inches at the shoulder, the bucks carry very long, ringed horns diverging towards the tips and curving slightly forward. These graceful lyre-shaped horns jutting up above the plain, are the one feature that betrays the presence of the bucks, well camouflaged by their pale fawn or reddish-khaki and white colouring, though they moult into black and white in winter. As an adaptation to their harsh environment the chiru, when grazing in the wide valleys along the banks of glacial streams, in whose icy waters they stand for hours on warm days, make forms like hares — as do the goa — scooping out with their hind hoofs shallow trenches or hollows in the sand, in which they can couch, sheltered from the incessant wind. According to C.G. Rawling — who travelled over the Chang-Tang in the summer of 1903, and made another journey across southern Tibet the following year — the chiru when alarmed would often throw themselves into these holes; but although their bodies would be hidden, the bucks would, again, be revealed by their horns projecting above the level of the ground. This habit of form-making was later confirmed by Meinertzhagen in Ladakh where he saw every member of a herd lying in its own small scraping: 'Quite suddenly they all made off in different directions at a great pace, due to a biting fly coming among them . . . back they came and again lay down in their wind shelters.' No doubt scent from their unusually developed inguinal glands, and also from those in their hoofs is deposited in these 'forms'.

Rawling found the chiru to be the most widely distributed of all animals above 15,000 feet on the Chang-Tang, and to be numbered in tens of thousands, with does four times as numerous as bucks. At the end of July he had 15,000 or 20,000 in view at one time, when thousands upon thousands of does with young (born late June or early July) were migrating to new grass on the higher tablelands. As late as the 1920s Burrard could also report that Chiru were roaming in herds of many as 10,000 all over the Chang-Tang and as far south as the kiangs' plateau, though very rarely descending below 15,000 feet. During the rut, late in November, however, the herds are split up into harems of from six to twenty does which, according to Rawling, the buck guards as a red deer stag does his herd:

'No sooner was a buck's back turned than two or three bachelors would approach from opposite directions. Round the master would spring, and with blazing eyes, horns laid back, and the deep-toned roar of a carnivore, rush upon the most daring and chase him from the field. Woe betide the laggard, for the needle-pointed horns would be buried deep into the fugitive's quarters. There was no play about it, for blood was seen to flow freely on several occasions.'

Today chiru are, reportedly, seldom seen. However, Snellgrove describes a herd coming regularly to drink at a pool — the only water in the district — just below the monastery at Samling: first the bucks and then the does and young ones.

In the nineteenth century herds of wild yaks ranged from western Turkestan to China. Large herds, composed of cows, summer-born calves, heifers and young bulls, might reputedly number as many as 2,000 head, particularly in the spring when concentrated on new grass on easy valley slopes near water; but normally they appear to have run in small herds of up to 50, though never scattered about barren stretches like kiang and antelope, with adult bulls apart in groups of two to five until the autumn rut. If threatened by wolves or snow leopards, bulls and cows are said to form up, like musk-oxen, in protective 'squares' around the calves, when the bulls' sharp-pointed black horns, three feet long, must present a formidable defence.

Eventually, however, competition from summering herds of domestic yaks and cattle banished the wild yaks to sanctuaries as high as 20,000 feet in the mountains, where wiry grass and small shrubs supplied them with provender, the white crust of saline earth with minerals, snow with water to drink, and the icy streams flowing from glaciers with wallows. Although wild yak may still inhabit the Himalaya, the harsh plateau environment of Tibet and Kansu, and especially the Chang-Tang, has probably always provided these most arctic-alpine of animals, which might be termed alpine musk-oxen, with their ideal habitat; for if the behaviour of domestic yaks is any criterion their wild relatives would not thrive in any other environment. 'The heat of the summer sends the animal to what is termed the old ice, that is to the regions of eternal snow', wrote John Wood of the domestic yak, 'the calf being retained below as a pledge of the mother's returning, in which she never fails.' And Meinertzhagen has described how his pack-yaks were at their best in deep snow, boring their way through it with apparent enjoyment, even when belly deep, and eating chunks of it. Typically, when all were showing signs of distress after a climb of 4,000 feet, panting and grunting, with their huge tongues lolling out, on reaching the plateau, where they were faced by an icy blast, first one and then another, snorting with pleasure, commenced to frisk and buck like young goats, scattering their loads in all directions; and it was some time before they regained composure and resumed their monotonous two miles an hour, which is the maximum speed at which they can be driven uncomplainingly, though wild yaks trot or gallop for hours when alarmed, tails waving from side to side, over the roughest and steepest ground.

Despite their rigorous environment wild yaks grow to an immense size, with cows weighing more than 6 hundredweight and the massive bulls standing 5½ or 6 feet at the shoulder, between 10 and 18 hundredweight; but they, like the kiang, have large lungs that allow more blood to contact the limited supply of oxygen. They are also equipped with a superlative pelage of dense, soft and closely matted woolly underfur, which is moulted in great masses in the spring, when, though completely separated from the skin, it adheres in patches to the long, coarse, wavy guard-hair. The latter, which is brownish-black in the cows and jet-black, except for a patch of white or grey on the face and muzzle of adult bulls, is so long that it hangs in shaggy fringes from shoulders, flanks and thighs down the legs, growing to its greatest length along the side below the ribs. It sweeps the ground when the animal stands, forms a mattress on which it can lie on the frozen ground, and affords sufficient protection against even the Chang-Tang's temperature of -34°F. Moreover, when the yaks are feeding with their backs to the wind, as they like to do, their hindquarters are protected by their extraordinary large, thick and bushy tails, which, when they are angry or alarmed, are whisked violently — a gesture that alerts the whole herd. The tail, together with the long hair around the legs, acts as a wind-proof shield, while their heads, lowered when feeding, are sheltered by the hairy mass of their bodies and by their strong manes. Even when standing upright, a yak always carries its head close to the ground, with the neck inclined sharply down from the pronounced high hump of its shoulders; though when hunted and breaking into a clumsy, heavy jog-trot — which, however, gets it swiftly over the ground — the head is carried a little higher. To bear its great weight over the mainly rough and stony terrain, the hoofs are strong and so constructed that the two toes can be drawn very close together to increase traction when the animal is climbing slippery rocks or crossing steep moraines of loose stones. No doubt the pair of secondary hoofs also grip the ground in steep ascents.

A yak's tongue is thickly studded with extremely hard, sharp, horny barbs, directed backwards down the throat; and it is with its tongue, rather than its teeth and horny upper jaw, that it plucks up tufts of the tough, wiry grass too short to be cropped by any animal lacking this kind of tongue. It also curls the tongue around the foliage of creeping bushes, though it is reported to prefer mosses and lichens, with which its immense stomach may be crammed full in the late autumn. Although the herds of yaks can crop the lush, velvety, new growth of vegetation at the edge of the receding snow-line in the spring, one can agree with Hedin that it is remarkable that large cattle can develop such massive and muscular frames on the generally poor fodder of the Tibetan highlands, for once the spring flush has lost its sap the grass becomes so tough and bitter that caravan pack-animals will only eat it when driven to do so by extreme hunger, while during the long winter it is withered and dead. Nevertheless the yaks survive by scraping away the snow with their hoofs from buried vegetation and by moving into areas that have been exposed by avalanches, filing singly over the snow in each other's tracks. One doubts, however, whether they ever forage in the manner attributed to the domestic yak by John Wood:

> If the snow on the elevated flats lie too deep for him to crop the herbage, he rolls himself down the slopes and eats his way up again. When arrived at the top, he performs a second summerset, and completes his meal as he displaces another groove of snow in his second ascent.

Chapter Eighteen

THE NORTH-AMERICAN BIGHORNS

With the exception of the mouflons and urials on the Mediterranean islands, and the desert bighorns in the southern USA and Mexico, the world's wild sheep are confined exclusively to the highest mountains or montain plateaus, though this habitat extends across three continents north of the equator. James Clark has pointed out that as they spread across the continents so they diversified into numerous races, ranging from the 450 pounds giant argalis or snow sheep of north-east Siberia to the dwarf Cyprian urial weighing barely 80 pounds. There are pure white, thin-horned Dall's sheep and glossy black Stone's sheep, whose blackness is accentuated by white on the muzzle, white rump patch and belly, and a white trim down the back of each leg; there are long-haired, heavy-maned urials and short-haired desert bighorns; the latter have to adapt to summer temperatures of 125⁰ F, while on mountains far north of the arctic circle snow sheep in Kamchatka and Dall's sheep on the Brooks Range in the extreme north of Alaska have to survive the long dark winter nights when temperatures fall to minus 60⁰ F.

In an earlier chapter we assigned these various races of sheep to five groups; they can be further reduced to two species: *Ovis ammon* of Eurasia as far east as Mongolia and Shensi, and *Ovis canadensis* of north-east Siberia and western North America. The latter presumably migrated from Asia into North America by way of the Beringia Plain linking Anadyr to Alaska. This 'causeway' attained its maximum area during the last glacial era some 18,000 to 20,000 years ago and was finally submerged beneath the sea about 7000 BC to form the Bering Strait. In Utah the dung of mountain sheep has been radio-carbon-dated to 9000 to 10,000 BC. In their new American environment the not very heavily muscled, light-boned, rather long-legged Asiatic argalis developed into the short-legged, broad-chested, almost ibex-like bighorns with massive shoulders and haunches. The argalis' habitat of open, rolling mountains, foothills and plateaus did not require them to be especially proficient climbers and jumpers: whereas the predominantly rugged terrain, incorporating scree slopes, crags, cliffs, foraging ledges, alpine meadows and shrub-covered ravines colonised by them in North America, set a premium on these qualities.

The immigrants occupied an environmental niche tenanted in Asia by snow sheep and ibex, and thrived, for in 1697 an accumulation of more than 100,000 horns was discovered at an aboriginal village in Arizona. This had apparently been piled up by the members of an Indian tribe in the belief that evil spirits would be trapped in it, thereby preventing bad weather.

A North-American population of between 1½ and 2 million bighorns is considered reasonable for the early nineteenth century, and at the end of that century they were established on almost every mountain slope from the Brooks Range down through the Rockies to northern Mexico. When the first settlers arrived at that time in Idaho, for example, the bighorns were to be numbered in thousands, ranging in huge flocks over the central parts of that state. Today, their total population in Idaho can be reckoned in hundreds. Similarly, those in California's Sierra Nevada had been almost exterminated by the 1870s by a combination of hunting and competition with the vast numbers of domestic sheep, goats and cattle that were turned out in summer to graze the high craggy country: 'Immense bands of sheep had denuded every living green thing, save sage brush, and had actually trampled the soil into dust, even destroying the roots of the grass in great measure.' In Idaho this overgrazing resulted in nutritional deficiencies which rendered the bighorns vulnerable to the domestic sheep's scabies mite and also, if they were ranging on lime soil, to lungworm, since this parasitic worm passes a part of its life-cycle in a small mountain snail that requires lime for shell-building. Those bighorns ranging over granite country were usually free from this parasite, as were the Dall's sheep which had no contact with domestic stock. Furthermore, the fencing of domestic stock-ranges cut off the bighorns from access to their traditional grazing grounds and precluded any subsequent use of the routes to these, since each generation of bighorns learned the migratory paths between the mountain grasslands by following the older sheep, whose foot glands deposited scent trails, which also served to keep the members of a flock in contact during misty days and dark, winter nights. This barrier to their seasonal migrations further decreased the extent of the bighorns' grazing area. Moreover sage brush, colonising those areas which domestic stock had denuded of grass, attracted an explosive influx of mule deer into the remaining rough pastures of bighorn country.

However, in Alaska and the Yukon, where chain after chain of glittering snowy peaks and tumbling blue glaciers, sharply outlined against the bright blue sky, stretches away in the crystal-clear air 50 miles to the horizon, there are still herds of 150 Dall's sheep grazing the slopes of the high, wide valleys; and the Brooks and Alaskan ranges are estimated to hold 40,000 of these white sheep. The deer-like, strikingly white hair, rather than sheep's wool, of the Dall's sheep contrasts with the pale brown to near black fleeces of the larger Rocky-Mountain bighorns. The Dall's rams are also distinguished by their relatively slender, pale gold to deep bronze or amber horns, which sweep out and away from the head in a graceful flaring 50-inch curve and a wider spread than those of the bighorns; and since this horn conformation does not interfere with their vision, they do not rub away the tips as the bighorns do; nor are the rams as boisterous during the rut. Adolph Murie has described how he often climbed the numerous, intensely green ridges in the Mount McKinley national park in search of the rams among the population of some 3,000 Dall's sheep, which, because there was no hunting in the park, could in some cases be approached to within a few feet. There were always many rams and a few ewes and lambs on those high pastures, with their fragile, yellow arctic poppies, saxifrages, monks-hood and the white flowers of the mountain avens, and their typical mountain birds — wheatears, rosy finches, flashing black and white snow buntings and the inevitable golden eagle soaring over the peaks or sailing swift and low along the ridge-tops, hunting ground-squirrels. Golden eagles had their eyries in the cliffs of every mountain sheep range. The rams fed on the gentler, green slopes or on the knolls on the ridges, and rested on the terraced ledges, whose grey rocks broke the green here and there. Many were veterans of twelve years with long, gracefully curved, golden horns outlined against the sky.

In the southern parts of their range the smallest race of bighorns, though with relatively the longest horns, are untypically desert dwellers in the hot, barren canyons and ranges of California, Arizona, New Mexico and northern Mexico. Some live on lava plateaus miles from the mountains, sheltering from the sweltering noonday heat in underground caves and tunnels in the lava. Almost every cave and crevice throughout their haunts in Mexico is a foot deep in their dung: whereas during the winter they bed down in windswept places. In this unique environment they feed mainly on shrubs, fruits and the fleshy parts of saguaro and other cacti and prickly pear, drinking only every three or four days, but obtaining additional moisture by chewing the saguaro, despite its sharp spines and their soft tongues and upper palates.

These desert sheep usually stay in one district throughout the year, though they move locally to the vicinity of reliable water-holes in the summer. Similarly, in the Yukon, each group of the black Stone's sheep pass their entire lives on separate ranges a few square miles in area and mingle only to a limited extent with neighbouring groups in the border zone between their respective ranges. In Colorado, according to Clifford C Spencer, a third of the bighorns live at or above the timber-line, between 8,500 and 12,500 feet, throughout the year, except for a short period when heavy spring snow forces them down into the aspen-type country just below the timber-line; the remaining two-thirds spend the summer in the high country but go down a few miles to lower country for the rest of the year, migrating about the same time every year regardless of weather conditions. In British Columbia and Alberta, however, the Rocky-Mountain bighorns undertake long-distance migrations five times a year to different feeding grounds, which may be as much as 20 miles from the rutting place and likely to be the same year after year. The rams, which tend to move between ewe grounds, may indeed feed on as many as seven different hills during the course of the year.

According to Valerius Geist, who made a prolonged study of the northern sheep, both rams and ewes descend to their main wintering grounds late in September or early in October, 'after the crisp but woefully short Indian summer'. They do so *before* the first severe snowstorms, and for a few weeks feed on frozen herbaceous vegetation on the lower slopes, prior to the rams dispersing to their respective rutting places in late October and early November. By mid-December the sun shines for only two hours a day between the mountain peaks, and at the end of that month and in early January the rams, thin and exhausted after their matings, usually move to different winter ranges. Geist goes on to describes how periods of intense cold follow, when the silence of the clear, brightly lit nights is broken only by the great horned owl or the calls of timber wolves; but by March the snow is hard enough for the sheep to walk on its surface, distributing their weight over the hard crust by spreading their legs and placing hoofs and dew-claws simultaneously on the snow. This increased mobility enables them to extend the area of their feeding range; and later that month or in April the flocks of ewes and rams usually migrate to their respective spring grounds. However, these various winter and spring movements may involve no more than a change in altitude in order to reach a place where the snow is only moderately deep, or a shift to a locality at a similar altitude where constant winds have kept the ground clearer of snow. Finally, between May and early July, there is a traditional migration to the high-altitude summer ranges above the belt of flies and mosquitoes, though in the early spring and summer, when mineral salts in their feed are insufficient for building up their frames after the poor winter feeding and, in the case of the ewes, after lambing, the sheep crave for these minerals and for salt. To obtain these they follow the deep, narrow trails trodden out by their ancestors to salt-licks, and acquire other trace elements by eating decomposed rhyolite (rock) flavoured with sulphur and salt. Geist found that both bighorns and Stone's sheep were very easy to tame with offerings of rock-salt.

Ram and ewe groups usually occupy different summer ranges and, depending upon the precise locality in the Rockies and the timing of the snow-melt, the ewes may either give birth to lambs on the winter range and then undertake a late upward migration, or, if conditions consistently allow for an early upward movement, lambing will take place on the summer range. The ewes begin to breed when three years old, occasionally when two, lambing as a general rule late in March in the more southerly parts of their range and early in June in Alaska. When her time is upon her, the ewe makes for high, rugged, cliff country, where she will be secure from predators, and settles herself on a ledge or at the base of a crag, where she may remain for several days without feeding or watering. In an article in *Animals* magazine Andy Russell has described the birth of a Dall's lamb:

> The ewe was standing on a narrow ledge on the face of a high broken cliff. With few preliminaries she lay down in a little hollow in the 3-foot-wide ledge and gave birth. The whole procedure took only a few minutes. The lamb struggled to its feet and tottered precariously on the edge of nothing, while its mother licked it dry. Then. . . the ewe. . . set out along the ledge, with the lamb staggering along behind. . . When she reached a wider place, the ewe stopped and allowed the lamb to suckle. The warm milk had a magical effect for when they continued their journey, the lamb skipped and gambolled.

It has been said that a lamb may remain on its birth ledge for as long as a week, with the ewe suckling it every hour and always close at hand to protect it from golden eagles; but though the latter are reputed to attack lambs until they are six or eight weeks old, they have in fact never been seen to do so in regions as far apart as Alaska and Colorado, preying almost exclusively on ground-squirrels and ptarmiran. Moreover, lambs only two or three days old, and so small that they can walk erect beneath their mothers' bellies, precociously clamber up cliffs so precipitous that the ewes are scarcely able to find a foothold; and when only 2½ weeks old a lamb can cover 30 miles over rough country and streams in the company of a loose-knit flock of 25 or 60 other lambs and ewes.

The older naturalists believed that, in contrast to the desert bighorns, those of the Rockies and arctic regions subsisted almost entirely on the sweetest and most delicate mountain grasses herbs, though avoiding the too lush feeding in the valleys; but closer observation has shown that in some regions they rarely eat grass, preferring the leaves, twigs and fruit of shrubs. Thus in Colorado, sedges, grasses and herbs are supplemented by browse, and newly opened aspen and spruce buds are so attractive that the rams climb into the dwarf spruces at the upper limits of the forest in order to get to buds that they are unable to reach while standing on the ground. On the other hand Dall's sheep, while browsing the leaves and stems of the low willow bushes, feed mainly on reindeer moss, sphagnum, sedge, dryas and bearberry. Inhabiting a range some 3500 miles long, the forage of any particular group of bighorns obviously depends upon what is available in a particular region at a particular season of the year. In Canada their habitat is under snow for nearly half the year, but after the first autumn snowfalls large rams are able to crop off the seed-heads and the tops of grasses and herbs protruding above the shallow snow, and never attempt to brush the snow from the herbage when feeding on a mountain slope. Thus, by selecting the upper parts of plants, they obtain the maximum food value with a minimum of labour. Nor do they scrape for food in hard and crusty or wet and slushy snow, but paw in soft snow and, like ibex, search for terrain where forage is most easily obtained on ground that has been cleared of snow by winds, sunshine or avalanches, or move to localities which do not have a heavy snowfall. However, when temperatures fall and snow accumulates on the cold ground, they push the snow away with their muzzles to expose buried foliage, and when the snow's depth exceeds 6 inches paw out feeding craters. Facing up-slope a ram clears snow from a small area by digging with powerful strokes of one of his front legs, while at the same time spreading his hind legs, thus providing himself with a stable three-legged stance. Each stroke is directed to the rear at a slight angle away from the body, throwing the snow back and opening up its blanket. According to Geist a hungry bighorn must make as many as 1800 strokes per hour of feeding, and since the food it picks up during January, the coldest month, is usually insufficient to cover its expenditure of energy, the animal must burn up its reserves of fat.

By the end of the rut there is a foot of snow on the bighorns' winter ranges, with much more to fall — in Alaska 72 inches fell in six days in February 1932 — with the result that for two months or more all vegetation will be buried and the sheep must obtain all their food by digging through the snow. Geist could not conceive how Stone's sheep could survive were they not able to winter on slopes and ridges regularly cleared by the sudden violent, warm, chinook storms that howled in from the Pacific, for there were occasions after some snowstorms when the sheep could only stand belly-deep in the snow, imprisoned on their tiny wintering area until the next chinook; but the latter, tearing off clouds of snow from slopes, ridges and trees, and raising temperatures from minus 40° F to plus 40° F in a matter of hours, enabled the rams to congregate in small groups to feed on snow-covered 'islands' melted by the warm wind.

With subzero temperatures, the hours of daylight short, the forage desiccated, frozen and much less nutritious than when green, the rams, weakened by the rut, work two or three or more together to open food craters when the snow exceeds 18 inches in depth. Co-operating in this manner, it is essential, in order to eliminate any unnecessary expenditure of energy in fighting for dominance, that a working group consists of rams with the same social standing indicated by similar horn size. Rams with smaller horns are therefore driven viciously from the feeding area and eventually retreat to the cliff zone, where they work alone in an area that contains less vegetation but in which there is slightly less snow on the rocks, while the dominant group line up side by side and, facing up-slope, excavate immense feeding trenches.

Except for this co-operation when foraging in deep snow, there is no communal activity during the harsh conditions of midwinter and the rams tend to be more solitary than at other seasons. If possible they avoid travelling through deep snow but, when doing so, the leading ram halts frequently and waits for another to take over the labour of trail breaking. They feed mainly during the warmest part of the day, resting and ruminating until about eleven o'clock, by which time the sun has softened the crust on the deep snow, for, like ibex, they search out sunlit areas, and their feeding grounds lie in the warmer air well above the cold air masses in the valley bottoms. After foraging until dusk, they couch down for the night in their feeding areas or shelter in caves. However, during the frequent early winter storms there may be more extensive movement. Immediately after a storm, for example, Geist watched bighorns pawing feeding craters in the new, soft snow that covered the open slopes; but as soon as the sun and wind had cleared the snow from the steep slopes in the cliffs above, they moved up to feed on the exposed vegetation, only to come down again to their original craters in the meadows when the snow had melted away from these. This winter feeding schedule contrasts with that at other seasons, when the sheep forage from a little before daybreak until mid-morning, then rest at intervals for twenty minutes or an hour during the remainder of the day until dusk, when they bed down just under the crest of a ridge.

The rams' sexual urges begin to operate as early as the middle of August, when towards evening on one occasion Geist saw a group of dark-grey Stone's rams, with amber-coloured horns, racing, frolicing and bounding exuberantly through the cliffs, then 'freezing' suddenly and standing statue-like in a tight knot. However, the rams remain in clubs until the middle of October, and only then become interested in the ewes. By early November of the middle of that month the younger rams in particular, after milling around, striking, butting and riding one another for several days, are constantly chasing the as yet unreceptive ewes, being more aggressive than the older rams at this time. A ewe may be surrounded by as many as nine of these over-eager young rams, testing her with necks extended and curled noses lifted in the air. On her slightest movement they rush at her, and in order to secure some peace she may be obliged to crawl out to the end of a narrow rock or to hide under an overhanging ledge. Small flocks of ewes, accompanied by their previous year's lambs, may indeed move up to the high cliffs in order to escape the rams' attentions. But once the rut is fully under way the older and larger rams are the most aggressive and assume the dominant role in the mating activities. The younger ewes are the first to come into heat and are promptly cut out of the flock, though since only one or two ewes are normally on heat at the same time, the rams move from bunch to bunch in quest of those that are receptive, and a chase, starting with one ewe and one ram, often ends with as many as eleven rams in pursuit. Observers differ as to whether or not these bighorn rams establish harems, and the practice does not appear to be invariable. It may perhaps depend on the race or locality of the sheep in question, or of the degree of jealousy of a particular harem owner. Thus Geist, writing of Dall's and Stone's sheep, states that successful rams — those with large horns — collect bands of from four to seven ewes; but Spencer, writing of the Colorado bighorns, states that they do not assemble and guard harems, but move from flock to flock during the breeding season. Old rams would point their noses in the air, sniff the breeze for a while, and then deliberately start out across the hills and go to other flocks.

What is certain is that during the rut the rams eat very little and expend considerable energy in chasing the ewes and in fighting other rams for possession of them, and also in free-for-all scrimmages in which as many as fourteen rams may engage at one time, and which may continue all day long. But fighting tends to depend on the relative size of their massive horns, which serve as symbols of rank. Those of the bighorns, which are triangular in section and as much as 15 inches in circumference at the base, grow in a continuous tight curl. They may form a circle-and-a-half in old rams and reach a maximum length of up to 50 inches or more along the front curve, with a 30-inch spread between the tips of the horns. Between one and ten years of age the weight of a ram's horns increase twenty or thirty-fold, whereas its body weight only doubles. If a stranger joins a group of rams it is challenged only by those with horns of similar size, determined by two rams stretching out their necks and slightly turning their heads, so that the horns are displayed to the best advantage. The newcomer is ignored by rams whose horns are patently larger or smaller, and if it begins to fight with one with approximately similarly sized horns, then after the first clash the contestants 'freeze' for a minute or so and show each other their horns; but one hesitates to agree with Geist when he suggests that this enables them to compare the force of the blow with the size of the horns delivering it, or that the dominant rams' habit of 'displaying' their horns on meeting subordinates ensures that the latter are reminded of the blows that are associated with the greater horn size of their superiors.

Despite the avoidance of unnecessary fighting by this sizing-up of horns, the primary function of a ram's horns is to serve as a weapon. Combat between two rams may open with them standing side by side, though facing in opposite directions, and in some cases with either ram's head over the other's back. Then, with ferocious grunts and snorts, they strike sideways and upward at each other with a sharp hoof. These preliminaries may last for a few seconds or for as long as twenty minutes, before each walks away to a distance of 20 to 60 feet. Suddenly, as though at a signal, the two whirl around and charge at great speed, though sometimes, as we have seen, instead of completing the charge on all-fours, they may rear up on their hind legs and cover the last few yards in this posture, with rigid forelegs extended; but immediately prior to impact, heads are lowered, as they attempt to meet squarely, horn to horn. The tremendous crack of the heavy, hollow horns can be heard a mile away, and the collision causes a ripple or 'shockwave' to roll the entire length of each muscular body. For a few minutes the impact dazes the combatants. Then they back away and crash again. Such a duel may last for two hours, though at the end of it both are usually still on their feet and not infrequently walking side by side. Geist, indeed, observed two rams reeling in exhaustion, though not physically injured, after fighting for twenty-five hours. One may ask — how can any animal's skull withstand such a battering over so long a period from an instrument weighing 25 pounds in the case of a large bighorn ram or 18 pounds in that of a Stone's ram, impelled by a 250-pound body travelling at 30 mph? But, as in the case of the Asian argali sheep, the impact is absorbed by two inches of parietal bone between the horns and by a cushioning air-space in the sinuses. Moreover, the horns are very thick and heavy, particularly on the impact side, and spring from massive horn-cores that are hollow.

Horns may also be used in defence when one ram deliberately attacks another without the sizing-up preliminaries, perhaps jumping down on him from the top of a rock or racing at him raised on hind legs, with intent to leap and deliver what Geist has described as a combination of sledgehammer blow and karate chop; but in every such instance witnessed by Geist the defending ram took the blow skilfully on his horns.

The long-sighted and extremely wary bighorns, always receptive to the piercing whistles of marmots, are not significantly threatened by predators — other than man. Indeed the extermination of potential natural predators has not resulted in an increase in the numbers of sheep. Their high pastures put them beyond the range of most carnivores, and since they can travel at 30 mph for a quarter of a mile, and descend a 50-foot vertical cliff in a running series of 20-foot bounds aided by the suction-grip of the concave, sharp-edged under-hoof, they are too agile to be caught in steep terrain. James Clark watched a bighorn cross a face of rock on which its only footing was provided by the single inner toes of its cloven hoofs; and a forest ranger has described the technique of a band of fourteen bighorns at a height of about 12,000 feet in the Sierra Nevada:

In traversing comparatively gentle slopes, the animals ran in single file, but while negotiating cliffs and precipitous slopes they would invariably spread out, each animal selecting its own path to avoid falling rocks dislodged by its companions. Twice they were compelled to cross precipitous chutes or slides tilted at the dizzy angle of something like sixty degrees, imprisoned between vertical rock walls; the bottom of these chutes were covered with a loose decomposed granite devoid of any kind of footing. The Bighorns . . . here would leap down off the walls and race across the chutes at great speed, being carried across by sheer momentum amid a shower of flying talus. Only one . . . crossed at a time, while the others stood by . . . and the ones that crossed over waited until all the others had joined them before proceeding up the rocks.

Victor Cahalane also recalls startling a group of five Dall's rams, which after milling round while watching him for several minutes, suddenly turned and fled down a 50-degree slope in a tight bunch. As they raced at full-speed he fully expected one of them to stumble and the entire band to roll to the bottom of the gulch, a thousand feet below, in a flying pinwheel of broken legs and necks. Instead, the rams never faltered. Their white legs moved like blurred pistons as they sped on down to the very bottom and dashed up a steep slope opposite him. There they stopped and immediately began to graze.

Both bighorns and thinhorns are, however, sometimes intercepted by predators in narrow defiles or passes when migrating to and from summer grazing hills, and such is their preference for hard ground that they often follow the rocky or gravelly beds of streams instead of travelling more easily along their turf banks. Nevertheless, they proceed with caution and, according to Murie, Dall's sheep, before venturing to cross a stretch of low, intervening country between two hill-ranges, may spend an hour or even one or two days surveying the valley from a high point of vantage before ewes and rams move across together in a compact band. One June 14, for example, a band of some 64 ewes and rams undertook such a crossing, walking in single file through tall willows and scattered spruce woods. They halted frequently to look ahead and, just before reaching the first hills, fed for about 45 minutes on the flats at their base. When they emerged from the woods on to the open hills, they were considerably strung out as they galloped up the slopes in high spirits.

Sheep and grizzly bears may feed on the same mountainside, but it is a very rare event for a bear to attack one. In some localities wolverines and pumas may take toll during the winter, ambushing sheep among the cliffs when they are on lower ground; and one of the large northern lynxes will watch a band of sheep for several hours before moving to a rocky place, towards which the sheep are feeding, and leap down on to the back of one as it passes. Coyotes attack the bighorns only under the most favourable conditions, when the latter are grazing in the foothills or on open slopes; and wolves, though reported to prey heavily on Stone's sheep, do not usually persist very long in sheep hunts, preferring mountain caribou and moose. According to Charles Sheldon, wolves, like coyotes, hunt the bighorns on the smoother parts of their range: the rolling hills of the basins, the pastures on the divides between mountains, or sometimes the level bars of a glacial river. To detect the sheep in these locations the wolves follow the ridges, the lower mountain slopes and any flat terrain above the timber-line, always keeping above them and then driving them downhill towards the valleys and running at them from a distance before they can turn and climb above their pursuers; but never attempting to follow them uphill if they succeed in reaching a steep slope or a ridge of broken rock.

There are reports of bighorns dying from the effects of being 'quilled' in the face by irascible porcupines, but apart from the losses caused by man and his domestic stock, hard winters and heavy snowfalls are probably the main cause of mortality. Conditions of fresh snow falling on hard-packed snow late in the winter are particularly dangerous, causing broken legs and death because, as Geist has pointed out, at that time in the winter the snow melts a little every day and freezes hard at night, forming an impenetrable snowpack that may not only form an ice-crust on top but on the bottom as well. So far as the rams are concerned, once they have attained the status of dominance during the rut, with its exhausting schedule of fighting, chasing ewes and mating, they begin to age and die rapidly. According to Geist, mortality among this age-group is five or eight times as high as among the younger subordinate rams, and he noted that the horn growth of the rams that died before attaining to the average life-span of perhaps ten years was superior to that of those that had survived longer and reached an age at which their teeth were worn right down.

Chapter Nineteen

ROCKY-MOUNTAIN GOATS

The mountain sheep come into contact at one time or another with Rocky-Mountain goats, caribou, mule deer, wapiti and moose, pumas (*alias* mountain lions or cougars), black and grizzly bears, coyotes, wolves, wolverines, lynxes and snowshoe rabbits, and with a variety of species of ptarmigan and grouse; but of the thirteen kinds of mammals *permanently* resident in the alpine zone all except the goats are small. Bighorns, caribou, mule deer, moose, wapiti and grizzlies move up to this zone in the early summer to take advantage of high summer's protein-rich herbage and also the absence of the majority of biting flies; but they go down again in the autumn, unless the ridges and slopes remain more or less free of snow, when both bighorns and caribou may winter high.

In some localities, as Don Blood has pointed out, the caribou may undertake two altitudinal movements during the course of the year. Throughout the summer and early autumn they have grazed and browsed in the alpine meadows and upper fringes of the subalpine forests, prior to migrating down the mountainside in October and November when snow blankets the dwarf vegetation on the high tops; but later in the winter, deep, soft snow not only covers much of the vegetation in the valley bottoms but also renders it difficult for the caribou to move about in search of alternative feeding areas, and they are obliged to subsist on the hanging tree-lichens. The supplies of these are limited in the valleys; so when in January or February the snow has settled, the caribou take advantage of its compacted surface to climb out of the bottoms and up to the spruce and fir forests near the timber-line where these arboreal lichens are more abundant. There, standing on platforms of snow several feet high, they are able to browse lichens that would be high out of reach during the summer, and feed almost exclusively on these until April, when they move down again into the valley bottoms where the earliest ground vegetation is thrusting through the melting snow. They remain in the valleys until June, grazing mainly in meadows and open woodlands in those places where the snow has melted most rapidly, and only in that month begin to follow spring up the mountain slopes to the alpine pastures.

The mountain goats, being almost ignored by man the hunter, still inhabit their original range, which comprises rolling uplands over the entire montane country of broken cliffs and barrens above the timber-line from the Columbia River to the Yukon, and from east of the Rockies to the Pacific; but they are confined to the glaciated areas of the western mountains and have not colonised other apparently suitable regions such as the vast ranges of the Yukon and Alaska occupied by the Dall's and Stone's sheep, nor the Sierra Nevada south of the Columbia. They are most numerous on the high pastures of the eastern slopes of the Rockies, where up to a hundred habitually collect between June and August at favourite 'licks', galloping along the deep, worn trails, that radiate for miles over the surrounding hills, in order to be the firstcomers to one, and often passing for long distances through stands of timber which are not a part of their normal habitat. Some of these licks are mineral seeps trickling down the rock and depositing a 'rime' that the goats taste; others, according to Ian McTaggart Cowan, contain such elements as sodium, manganese, magnesium and copper, and are almost tasteless, but 85 per cent of them are composed of hard, white carbonate of lime which the goats must gouge out with their teeth. Nevertheless, large quantities of the latter are consumed by the mouth-frothing goats, and some of those licks located in the banks of cliffs have been gnawed out by so many generations of goats over the course of years that today's goats disappear within the deep cavities.

In the heavily timbered and more precipitous mountains nearer the Pacific the goats are thinly distributed, with each band concentrated around a limited area of high-altitude winter range on slopes that usually face south and west, from which strong winds blast away the snow, and on which there is a rapid spring melt. Although the goats have a wider choice of diet than any other American ungulate, including such varied vegetation as brush, mountain sorrel, sedge, huckleberry, mountain bramble, twinflower, Oregon grape, bunchberry, evergreen violet, rattlesnake plantain — to mention only a few — and also some that are poisonous to domestic stock, they seem able to subsist on very little forage. A herd will remain for a long period on a small patch of snowy ridge or slope where palatable plants have been exposed by the wind, and their staple food is the foliage of many kinds of alpine plants and creeping shrubs, together with mosses and lichens that they prise from the rocks with their lips. Being ill-equipped, with short stocky legs, to scrape for food in deep snow, but better able to withstand cold winds than the bighorns, they winter permanently, no matter how severe the weather, on high exposed ridges avoided by the sheep, sheltering at night on shallow beds of dry earth under overhanging ledges. Only in one locality — Mount Rainier (14,410 ft) in the Pacific north-west of the USA — where glare-ice kills off the vegetation, the goats are forced to descend to the valleys. More than 1000 inches of snow have been recorded on this mountain in a single year, and the annual average is 575 inches. They can perhaps survive on one limited area of range throughout the year because they do no herd together in large numbers. A band of mountain goats rarely comprises more than five to seven nannies and kids, and the billies are often solitary. The herds of twenty or thirty nannies reported by Geist to browse during the summer on dwarf alpines and grass on a single nursery slope would appear to be exceptional, as was his observation one spring day of as many as thirteen adults at play: bouncing, bucking and finally cartwheeling down a slope, spinning around horizontally in spirals.

To counter the intense cold of their exposed habitat, mountain goats are equipped with shaggy, white coats of long guard-hair, which extends as low as the knees and overlays a soft and very fine wool, three or four inches deep and comparable to that of an angora goat. They are further protected by an overall layer or, rather, pad of fat, a dense mat of stiff hair on the chest and a very thick hide, five-eighths of an inch thick on the flanks and rump of a large billy.

Like those other goat-antelopes — the chamois, goral and serow — the muscular Rocky-Mountain goat is also suitably adapted to travel over the rugged country it inhabits. It is a more specialised rock climber than the mountain sheep, and better suited to ice-covered cliffs and deep snow, ploughing steadily through the latter instead of labouring through it in a series of bounds as sheep do. It goes where sheep do not normally venture, 'walking, easily, effortlessly, and without hurrying', according to Cowan, 'along shifting trails across sliding scree slopes, and seeming deliberately to follow imperceptible paths on breathtaking crags.' Although a goat's torso appears to form an awkward rectangle when viewed from the side, it is actually rather narrow across the shoulders, and this conformation allows the animal to negotiate with ease the thinnest trail across a mountain face. Moreover, the small black hoofs (triangular in section with short points) are soled with what has been described as a unique non-skid device in the form of a concave, spongy pad protruding from the centre, which clings like rubber to steep surfaces, and the two segments of the hoof have sharp rims which can spread almost at right-angles, adjust at different levels and squeeze like pincers. This hoof structure, combined with the gripping power of the 'dew-claws', is no doubt of crucial assistance when a goat is making a particularly hazardous descent over a smooth rock face, and the very short foreleg enables a climbing goat to hook its hoof over a projecting rock and pull itself up. Nevertheless, these goats are cautious in their movements, seldom taking a step until assured of their next foothold; and when obliged to turn round on a narrow ledge, but unable to do so on all four feet, rear up on their hind legs, with front hoofs set against the cliff wall, and reverse direction carefully. Geist observed that goats and sheep react in a different manner to slipping on crags. Sheep, losing a foothold, jump away and land on another foothold below: goats spread their legs apart, flatten themselves against the rock face and claw for footholds as they slide down. According to Cowan, old goats become stiff in the joints. Although, given time, they can climb almost any steep incline, a down slope affects their knee joints and, confronted with a steep descent, an aged goat will sit on one hip and slide gradually down to the bottom. This habit appears to be confirmed by the fact that the hide of an old goat is frequently thicker over one hip than over the other.

Both billies and nannies are armed with slightly curved black horns, 9 to 12 inches long and as sharp as stilettos, These deadly weapons are very rarely employed in combat with other goats. If so used, the lateral jabs at an adversary's flanks produce terrible injuries, despite the thickened hide, resulting in peritonitis and in some instances the death of both combatants, though goats are difficult to kill and bleed very little. Since the skull is thin and fragile, the horns function as weapons only and not, as in the case of the bighorn, as a defensive instrument with which to catch an opponent's blows. A goat relies for defence on evasive action and on the tough, dermal shield over the buttocks, where the majority of stabs are received. Equipped with such lethal weapons, fighting between goats tends to be replaced by a ritualistic display in which the high shoulder mane, beard, head and horn size are the features establishing dominance of one billy over another. This display is also employed by a rutting billy if a nanny is unreceptive. His prolonged courtship is in any case tentative in the early stages, and it is the nanny who is the more aggressive. Indeed, according to Geist, he prostrates himself and crawls on his belly to her. However, he becomes progressively bolder as the November rut approaches, thrashing shrubs with his horns or rubbing them against rocks, depositing an oily secretion from the large glands behind the base of the horns, and eventually becomes dominant over her, though only for a couple of weeks. Geist has suggested that the more aggressive a female the more successful she will be in chasing away billies after she has been served, and thus prevent them from eating up the limited supplies of poor feed on her range, and depriving her of essential food to nourish the unborn kid and subsequently provide milk for it. He has also drawn attention to a curious consequence of an animal being equipped with exceptionally sharp horns — namely, that the kids, once their horns have begun to grow, must not fight in play because of the risk of injury or death. The possession of sharp horns has therefore resulted in very protective and aggressive nannies, who maintain constant watch over their kids and chase away yearlings and two-year-olds immediately there is any aggressive inter-play among the young animals; and the kids' unique ear-splitting distress-calls cause anxious mothers to come running up hastily.

Although the kids — born from late April to June — are able to skip about within half an hour of birth, their mother hides them away for the first few days, returning to suckle them every couple of hours, until they are ready to join up with other families on the summer nursery slopes. But the rate of reproduction is slow, since kids may be produced only in alternate years; moreover both young and adults are subject to a heavy mortality from parasites and disease and are particularly at risk to avalanches. Predation is not such an important factor, for the goats are almost immune from attack by any predators except lynxes and pumas on the rocky ramparts they make use of as escape routes, though they become more vulnerable to wolves, coyotes, wolverines and bears when grazing on open slopes or at the 'licks' in the valleys or when descending to pass through wooded country from one mountain range to another. But these hazards, combined with the harsh environment of their mountain habitat, keep their overall population low.

Although ranging from sea-level to 17,000 feet, pumas are most numerously distributed in dry, semi-open montane forest in the most rugged and inaccessible terrain from the far north through tropical forest, to Patagonia. Mountain pumas are much larger than those in the lowlands, with males six to nine feet in length (one-third of which is tail) and up to 250 pounds in weight, compared with the five feet and 100 pounds of the latter. They hunt mainly above the timber-line for bighorns, mule deer and marmots, caching the remains of large kills, which remain fresh for weeks in the low temperatures prevailing at high altitudes. The size of their hunting territories depends upon the numbers of available prey, and varies in the Rockies from 25 square miles for a male to from 5 to 20 square miles for a female, though a male's territory usually overlaps those of several females. However, some wandering males do not occupy territories and if one enters another's range, the two avoid each other by the use of warning-off scent marks and scratches.

Chapter Twenty
MOUNTAIN GRIZZLIES

The alpine zone of goats and sheep is invaded early in the summer by an inhabitant of the subalpine forest and avalanche slopes, exploring upwards in search of food — that large brown bear, the grizzly. Bears vary greatly in colouring and the grizzly is no exception, for though its pelage is typically silver-tipped, it may be almost golden or black or off-white, and William H. Wright, writing seventy years ago, described some grizzlies as being as white as the mountain goats. Nevertheless, the relatively small grizzlies of the Rockies, the mighty hump-shouldered 'silver-tips' of Alaska's west coast and the barren-ground grizzlies of the Yukon and the North-West Territories are all brown bears; and all are omnivorous, including in their fare such varied items as spawning salmon, carrion, marmots, pikas and ground-squirrels (dug out of their burrows), grass and tubers. The tundras and steep hills of the Yukon, for example, almost devoid of vegetation except for wind-dwarfed alders and low clumps of sedge, but the broad gravel-bars that break up the rivers into mazes carry a dense growth of pea-vine, and this the grizzlies shovel aside to lay bare the tuberous roots. Enormous quantities of berries are also eaten in the summer and autumn, and these the bears obtain by straddling bushes and small trees and forcing them over, or by hooking down the branches with their paws, half breaking them. In August 90 per cent of a Yukon grizzly's food may consist of berries, especially those of the thornless soap-berry, so called by the Indians because of the bright red froth produced when the berries are crushed.

The considerable wastage of berries falling from the bears' half-open mouths attracts numbers of ground-squirrels, chipmunks and mice. Grubbing for rodents, whether mice, voles, pikas, marmots or ground-squirrels must take up a considerable part of a grizzly's feeding time, since the rodents' burrows and runways are usually among rocks or under the roots of large trees, or in similarly inconvenient retreats for bears, and many burrows prove to be unoccupied. Even if they are occupied, the fact that they have several entrances makes it possible for the owner to dart out of one and watch the short-sighted bear digging at another entrance a few feet away. Mounds pushed up by spotted ground-squirrels engage a grizzly for hours at a time, as it excavates one after another and grabs and bolts the squirrels. Enos A. Mills watched a grizzly digging energetically for what was probably a woodchuck in an extensive scree:

> Several slabs of rock were hurled out of the hole and tossed down the mountain-side. Stones were thrown right and left . . . After a short time only his shoulders showed above the scattered rock slide as he stood erect. Then he began piling the stones upon the edge of the deepening hole. The slope was steep and the stones had to be placed with care to prevent their tumbling back. After lifting into place one huge slab, he stood and looked at it for an instant and then slightly changed its position. On top of this stone he piled another large one, eyed it closely, shook it to see if it was solid, and finally shifted it a trifle.

A favourite hunting ground of a mountain grizzly is a steep slope inhabited by colonies of hoary marmots, despite the fact that the bear has great difficulty in digging them out of the crevices that render them inaccessible to wolves. After pressing its nose down to the scree to pinpoint its prey, the grizzly, huffing and puffing, flings the rocks aside to expose the marmots. A grizzly's stength and huge claws, five or six inches long, enable it to dig faster and deeper than the short-clawed black bear, and the quantity of soil it throws up in the course of its operations is hardly credible, since it may entail the excavation of holes 8 — 10 feet deep and 12 — 15 feet long. Two hours' digging, producing only a single pika, may involve shifting a mass of earth weighing tons and the piling up of stones round the edges of the hole. Grass slopes, from which hibernating ground-squirrels have been rooted out, may be pitted with colossal holes, as if scooped out with a bulldozer.

Grizzlies are particularly common in the Dall's sheep country, where he-bears range over a territory of about 100 square miles and the she-bears over about 25 square miles. The 2,000-mile stretch of mountains from Idaho to the Brooks Range, together with that separate string of frigid summits known as the MacKenzie Mountains, form the largest remaining grizzly territory in America, and is inhabited by what must be the hardiest brown bears on Earth. As Frank Dufresne has pointed out, most of the tall country through which they roam is free of ice and snow for no more than three or four months of the year; the mercury drops to 70° F below zero in the winter; and the grizzly, like the hoary marmots, spends two-thirds of its life hibernating in its den under tons of drifted snow.

In the southern Rockies, in Colorado, some grizzlies den-up at the timber-line as high as 12,000 feet, but in the central Rockies they do so in the upper part of the subalpine forest of dense spruce and hemlock between

6,000 and 9,000 feet. There, since natural shelters are not used, they usually excavate dens 10 or 12 feet deep between the wide-spreading roots of trees, which may form the ceiling of the den, or under stumps or logs, though some bears dig into the side of a hill. Access to the den may be by a long tunnel or may be directly into the sleeping chamber, which is usually furnished with a bedding of spruce or fir boughs. According to Don Blood, dens usually open on to north and east slopes, where deeper snow and the accumulation of drifts improves the insulation of the den and less frequent snow-melt precludes the likelihood of the den becoming wet. The date of the beginning of hibernation can vary by as much as a month, depending upon the availability of food in the autumn rather than on weather conditions, but permanent occupation is normally taken up during November; and this very often coincides with a storm, possibly because the bear is aware that its tracks to the den will be covered with snowfall.

Cubs are born in the dens about the beginning of February, but not until the she-bear is between 4½ and 8½ years old, when her first litter will consist of only one or two cubs, though subsequently as many as four. Thus the grizzly has one of the lowest reproductive rate of any land mammal, but because of the she-bear's maternal care and the precocity of the cubs, the mortality rate is low. Since grizzlies produce cubs only every two or three years, she-bears and yearlings hibernate in the same den and emerge in March or two or three months later in the far north.

According to Wright, he-bears break out between one and three weeks earlier than she-bears with cubs, but nearly all of each age-class do so about the same time in any one locality. What particular conditions are responsible for this mass emergence? Wright observed in the Selkirks that,

> They den so high up among the peaks, that when they emerge there are from four to six (and in some cases even ten) feet of snow still lying over the country like a great white blanket. Only on the slides, which have been swept by tremendous avalanches that usually come down in March, is the ground clear. Yet on one of our trips in this region we saw where thirteen grizzlies came down the mountain side in a single night . . . the animals, in coming out, had broken through some five feet of snow . . . it is, therefore, not the melting snow that arouses them.

According to Mills, but contrary to most other observers, grizzlies emerge from hibernation with plenty of fat on them because while in their dens the walls of their stomachs contract, almost completely closing the interior. During hibernation their claws have grown long, and the hard, cracked skin on the soles of their feet has been shed, with the result that their feet are soft and tender when they break out in the spring. For the first few days after doing so they feed sparingly — as they had done before denning-up — and they remain in the vicinity of the den for several weeks until the deep, wet snow has melted sufficiently for them to travel easily.

Chapter Twenty-One

THE DOOMED CONDORS

There was a time when those great vultures, the Californian condors, soared over the western mountains of North America.

Only a poet can portray the condors' world. Peter Matthiessen has done so in his book *The Cloud Forest*:

> The world is as it was long, long ago, its life breathing quietly beneath the sun. Great rolling brown ridges mount, one upon another, to the westward horizon . . . Jutting cliffs form the eastern face . . . falling steeply from the distant high plateaus . . . As the sun rises, so, often, do the birds, forsaking the early morning hunt with the dying of the dew and circling upward into oblivion of blue too bright to contemplate. But the great condor, sulking on some remote ledge in the fastnesses of its preserve, fails to appear. One by one its small relatives — buteos, eagles, small falcons, turkey vultures — vanish, blacks specks which trick the eye, then are no more. Midday comes, and the songbirds sit stone still in the bush. There is sun, heavy silence, a pervasive scent of parched vegetation, a lizard materialised on a rock . . . The condor, appearing, does not break the silence. There are two. They crest the horizon to the westward, several miles away . . . They roll down across the dry ravines . . . coming on swiftly, unswerving . . . Sweeping forward, a scant hundred feet above the brush, they descend the grade of ridges, one bird four wing-spreads behind the other, and the definitive broad band of white at the wing's shoulder glints powerfully now in the hard light. They pass the ridge's summit at eye level, implacably, and in that moment the naked orange of the head is bright. Then, as swiftly as they had come, they glide away, broad-backed as they sink across the canyon, alone in a world of gray-green brush, brown mountain, ocher cliffs, blue sky. The birds do not circle at the canyon, but forge straight on, dark silhouettes against the dark plateaus in the far distance, as if, striking eastward on some ancient errand, they meant to return across the continent.

The Californian condors had already vacated the greater part of their exten-

147

sive North-American range before the first white men reached the West, and today their entire population of apparently less than 30 individuals has been confined by persecution to the Los Padros national forest in a relatively small area of south-central California. We do not know what climacteric was responsible for the original contraction of their range, but maintaining a viable population must have always presented problems. In the first place, it is unlikely that they breed until they are ten years old, though adult plumage is assumed in the sixth year. In the second place, they normally breed only every other year, though it is possible that they may do so every year when carrion, their exclusive food, is plentiful. And in the third place, the single young bird is dependent upon its parents until its second summer, because it is five months old before its flight-feathers develop sufficiently for it to fly more than a few feet, and ten months old before it can fly well enough to go in quest of its own carrion. The intervening period is passed in or near the nest, which is sited in such places as the sandy or detrital floor of a cave, in a pothole in the face of a cliff, behind boulders on a steep slope or, exceptionally, in a hole in a giant redwood (sequoia), between 1500 and 6,000 feet up in the hills. Today, the reproductive potential of the Californian condors is the lowest of any North-American bird, for, with few pairs breeding in recent years, the entire population probably produces not more than one, or two, young each year. That their race continues to survive can perhaps be attributed mainly to their longevity, since captive birds have lived for nearly 50 years, and also to their ability to adapt to an environment in which the temperature threshold fluctuates from below freezing to considerably above 100° F.

Another species of condor, the Andean condor, with a slightly longer wing-span than the 9½ feet of the Californian birds, ranges down the full length of the Andes from Colombia south into Tierra del Fuego, soaring effortlessly over the ridges and high plateaus for hours at a time with hardly a single beat of their immense wings, though the widely spaced and notched primaries, constantly adjusting like sensitive fingers to the air currents, and the spread tail-feathers, produces a steady hissing or musical whistling. Each soaring circle is completed in 13 to 17 seconds, and then, having reached their ceiling at 15,000 feet — or 18,000 feet above thunderstorms — they set off on a series of 8 or 10-mile glides at a mile a minute. These might carry them as far as 125 miles in their search for the carcase of mule, steer or deer, above which they will soar for an hour or so before the first bird ventures to alight near it, and is followed by others, though not all will feed at one time. But condors, like lammergeiers, cannot soar if suitable air currents are lacking. On calm days they are hard put to it to gain sufficient height to cross a ridge and can do no more than flap for

9. Marmot or Prairie Dog

10. Chamois

11. (Left) Raven at nest with young
12. (Below) Female Ptarmigan incubating eggs
13. (Right) Rocky Mountain Sheep — Ram feeding
14. (Bottom right) Bar-headed Goose

15. Dotterel

16. Grizzly Bear — Mother
and 2 year-old cub

17. Mountain Gorilla

18. Rock Thrush

19. Apollo Butterfly

several hundred yards before alighting, and then repeat this process. In foggy weather they may be confined to their roosts for days at a time. Even in good weather they spend at least 15 hours a day in the vicinity of the latter, preening, sunbathing with outspread wings, and bathing in pools; with the non-breeding members of the colony roosting in loose groups of up to twenty on rocks or trees scattered over an area of two or three miles.

The destruction of the high montane forests of Colombia has resulted in a severe decline in the Andean condor population, although they continue to nest in caves and the entrance shafts to old mines high up the cliffs of the hinterland. In Peru their search for food also takes them to the coastal desert and islands. From the high sierras they sweep and glide in long lines down over the arid valleys to the coast; but there large numbers are shot when they raid the guano-bird colonies for eggs and young:

In the heart of the colony stood a condor, with a small circle of abandoned and rifled nests round about. [wrote R.C. Murphy on the island of Asia]. When this pilferer had been shot and picked up by the feet, the albumen and mostly *unbroken* yolks of a round dozen of fresh eggs slid out of its gullet. Scarcely any pieces of shell were visible in this rich meal, the supposition being that the condors eat the contents of the eggs through their trough-shaped tongues.

Unlike the California condors, which have never been recorded attacking live prey, the Andean condors in addition to scavenging for carrion, dead fish, porpoises and sea-lions near the fishing villages, also prey to some extent on diving petrels, which they extract from their burrows.

Chapter Twenty Two

THE ANDEAN CLOUD-FOREST AND PUNA

'Never had I seen mountains like these, and I was crushed by the grandeur — speechless with the overpowering wonder of it', wrote Colonel P.H. Fawcett, that seeker after Eldorado, on first setting eyes on the Andean cordilleras, which include Aconcagua, at 22,835 feet the highest mountain in the Americas, and more than a dozen other peaks towering to above 20,000 feet. Yet the parallel ranges of the cordilleras are no more than 100 miles wide in places and exceed 200 miles only in Bolivia where, in the southwest of that country, they reach their greatest breadth of 500 miles.

Tony Morrison — a contemporary naturalist, to whose books and articles we are indebted for numerous accounts of Andean wildlife and terrain — has described how the cordilleras' wildernesses of snow, ice and the fire of more than forty volcanoes include every kind of landscape and climatic conditions, from perpetual cloud cover and merciless sun to warm, moist air and air so thin that breathing is painful, and from lethally cold high deserts to the dripping jungles of the low foothills fringing the Amazon basin, with its marvellously luxuriant vegetation and superabundance of indigenous birds and insects.

There, on the eastern slopes of the Andes, the cloud-forest extends from the subtropical zone, commencing at 4,000 feet, to the upper limits of the temperate zone at between 9,500 and 12,000 feet. This is the retreat of the splendid, golden, helmet-crested cock-of-the-rock, nesting close to bouldery streams and cliffs and 'hypnotising' the females by standing motionless in front of them for minutes at a time in courts that they have cleared on the forest floor. Providing that it has not been heavily cleared, the cloud-forest is also the habitat of the gorgeous quetzal, no larger than a pigeon, undulating through the trees like an emerald and ruby meteor. Visibility is very poor in the forest when rain-clouds settle on the trees, and even on sunny days no more than five per cent of the sun's rays penetrate to the forest floor. The vivid, luminous, shimmering green of the quetzal's plumage blends with the wet, pale green and grey foliage, and the deep crimson of its breast and underparts are hidden. Moreover, when not

150

nesting, the bird either sits motionless on a branch for long periods or is concealed in the high upper-third of the canopy, where there is dew and rain to drink and insects and fruit to feed on. When nesting, the male is sitting tight inside the old nest-hole of a woodpecker maybe 60 feet above the ground, since its beak and claws are not strong enough to dig into living wood, and its two tail plumes are bent up and over its head in order to curve out of the hole. The widespread burning and felling of forest in South America must put the quetzals at grave risk, not only because of the overall loss of habitat but because of the local destruction of dead and dying trees suitable for nest-holes.

The rain-forest is the habitat of one race of the only South American bear — the curiously marked black or brownish spectacled bear, whose yellow or white facial markings vary incongruously from one individual to another, irrespective of age or sex. This bear feeds mainly on nuts and fruit and various kinds of palms, up which it may either climb 80 or 100 feet in order to bring down the fruit stalk, or break down the young trees and, tearing open the green stem, eat the unopened leaves in the interior. It ventures out of the rain-forest only occasionally, either to go down to the tropical savannas and scrublands of the Andean foothills to feed on the green maize-cobs in the valley bottoms or, if ravenous, climb above 10,000 feet to the grasslands of the temperate zone and kill a young llama or deer. Yet, by contrast, another race of spectacled bears inhabits the excessively parched mountainous region of northern Peru, where rain falls only rarely, where animal life is limited, and where the sparse vegetation consists mainly of cacti and small thorn-bushes and a few scattered thickets of trees in canyons or on higher slopes. However, in this near-desert the bears search for food under the midday tropic sun, especially for the *chapote*: a pear-shaped fruit with a hard outer shell enclosing numerous seeds. Their habitat can be compared to that of black bears on the arid plateaus of rock and scrub in Baluchistan.

But we are concerned primarily with the High Andes lying between the upper limits of the temperate zone and the lower levels of the permanent snow at 15,000 or 17,500 feet. There, the cold grass steppe of the *puna* can be likened to the arctic tundra, with strong winds, no rain for nine months of the year and intense cold at night; though, unlike the dry Peruvian puna or altiplano, the northern *paramos* of Venezuela, Colombia and Ecuador are damp with a very high humidity and a drifting wet fog or penetrating drizzle which is liable to turn to snow. Spectacled bears sometimes visit these northern paramos, as do mountain tapirs which, protectively clad with a long, woolly, black pelt, feed on grasses growing in the deep, black soil, though in other parts of their range their food consists of ferns and bamboo shoots. Nevertheless, although agriculture ceases at the upper limits of the temperate zone, shepherds and their families live permanently above 17,000 feet in southern Peru at a higher altitude than the Sherpas in the Himalayas.

Flowering plants are sparse on the thin stony soil around 12,000 feet on the puna. Clumps of the coarse *ichú* grasses of the Incas, growing in close tufts up to three feet tall and a foot in diameter, give a characteristic yellow colouring to the landscape here and there, for their needle-like outer leaves remain on the plant long after they are dead, providing shelter for the young leaves growing in the centre. The dwarf, sage-like *tola* shrub between one and two feet high, spreads over thousands of square miles, tightly packed on sandy soil but more openly spaced on rocky ground. Its tough, slow-growing bushes of small, dull, greyish-green leaves provide the main shelter against the frequent 40 or 50 mph winds for the vicuna and for several species of birds, such as Darwin's rhea — whose huge, three-toed tracks often mingle with and dwarf those of the vicuna — but especially the ornate tinamous. Both these ground-nesting species — the male rhea incubates the eggs of half a dozen females laid in one nest — have been able to survive on the puna because their chicks can withstand sub-zero temperatures that would prove lethal to those of most ground-nesters. The mottled grey plumage of the male tinamou may also be advantageous in camouflaging it from such predators as foxes and wild cats.

The strangest plant of the puna and also in the most arid places in the high cold zone, thriving indeed where the permanent snow-line is highest at 17,500 feet in southern Peru, is the moss-like *llareta* or *yareta*, a curiously compacted relative of the parsley. Along the high Puna de Atacama in Chile, where night temperatures fall below minus 22°F, only lichens, the tola bushes and the yareta can withstand the extreme cold. The yareta's cushion-shaped clumps, clinging to the ground and covering the rocks like an exotic green fungus, are composed of thousands of tiny rosettes of bright green leaves which, being fleshy, retain moisture, and are speckled with minute yellow flowers only two millimetres in diameter; beneath the densely packed rosettes is a hard brown fibrous mass that has accumulated after many years' growth. Like many other plants adapted to a barren cold environment, both tola and yareta are highly resinous — gloubules of resin ooze out between the yareta's rosettes — and provide good fuel. To quote from a nineteenth-century book on 'wonderful' plants: 'It is obvious that the yareta was brought into the world solely for the use of the Indians, who are bereft of any other fuel in these inhospitable areas.' Today, according to Morrison and other travellers, both plants are being exploited on a massive scale by commercial interests in a treeless region in which anything that grows can be burnt; and this exploitation has already resulted in the arid semi-desert being replaced in some areas by barren zones devoid of life except for a few scorpions and mountain viscachas.

The only tall growth on the windy mountainsides of the puna, where other plants are low and compact, are the slow-growing, cactus-like *puyas*. The main part of these giant bromeliads of the pineapple family consists of an enormous spiky green globe of leathery, strap-like, four-foot-long leaves, which are knife-edged and barbed with sharp fish-hook thorns. When the oldest leaves shrivel and die they hang parallel to the supporting trunk, which is scaly and two feet thick. But after perhaps 100 years of growth the puya suddenly, within a period of only three months, thrusts up from the leaf cluster, a cylindrical flowering spike 12 inches thick and 15 or 20 feet high, with as many as 8,000 pale, greenish-yellow inflorescences growing on stubby branches wound in a spiral round its centre. The puya has therefore one of the most gigantic flower-spikes of any plant of Earth.

On the northern páramos the puya has its counterpart in the espeletia which, because of its monk-like appearance when encountered in fog, is known as the *frailéjone* or tall friar. Its soft, lanceolate leaves form tight rosettes; as the stem grows it carries the rosette of accumulated leaves higher and higher; new leaves appear and the old ones dry out one by one and die, forming, as they hang down, a succession of densely overlapping sheaths one above the other around and protecting the trunk. Ultimately, when the plant has reached its full stature of from 10 to 35 feet, its trunk is surmounted by an enormous rosette of long, leathery leaves, whose dense covering of silky hairs gives them a silky lustre. Morrison has described how when the espeletias bloom, stems bearing pale-yellow flowers, each composed of dozens of florets, protrude nearly a foot from the centre of the crowning rosette; and both leaves and flowers are visited, up to an altitude of 15,500 feet, by a species of hummingbird, *Oxypogon*, in search of insects.

Solitary flowering puyas are as conspicuous as trees on the bleak, open puna and, viewed from a distance, resemble serrated fences of unequally spaced, dark-green posts. Morrison found that they attracted a variety of birds that would otherwise have made use of cliffs or rocks, affording favourite roosts for such birds as bare-faced doves, and nesting places for turtle doves and small passerines, notably the black-winged spinetail, which builds a nest almost two feet high in clumps of puyas at the bottoms of gulleys; but he also noted that the puyas could be mortuaries, containing the shrivelled corpses of small birds that had dashed into the spiky leaf-globes when pursued by variable-hawks, and had subsequently been unable to extricate themselves from the maze of thorns. The carcasses of various small mammals that hawks had caught on the puna were also to be found in the puyas.

The majority of birds on the high puna are small and therefore able to shelter in low vegetation among the rocks or in burrows, with rock flickers (relatives of the North-American flickers) nesting in tunnels and hunting in troops for worms, larvae and insects; and white-winged Inca finches roosting in dormitories of 200 or more, huddled together against the cold and damp under rocks or in glacial declivities above 16,000 feet. A few large species, however, such as the Andean geese (relatives of the Magellan geese inhabiting the plains and shores of Patagonia) breed as high as the snow-line. Among the birds frequenting the puyas are hummingbirds, which are a remarkable feature of the puna up to a height of 16,000 feet, since they survive nights of snow or hard frost in exposed sites and become active as the morning sun warms them up. A number of Andean peaks are each inhabited by its own particular species of hummingbird. Eric Shipton watched one species drawing nectar from a cactus flower during a snowstorm when he was climbing to 16,000 feet on Cotopaxi in Ecuador; and another species exists as high as 20,000 feet on Mount Chimborazo in Ecuador. The puya representatives include the giant hummingbird, nine inches long, and two kinds of hillstars, or *Oreotrochilus,* which are the commonest Andean hummingbirds. Morrison describes them as 'two-inch darts of brilliant green' visiting one flower after another; but because of the rarity of flowers in the High Andes they in fact feed almost exclusively on insects. Some hillstars nest in clumps of puyas, but despite their wide distribution on the high plateaus, they tend to shun the cold open puna in favour of those slopes where sunshine prevails, or gulleys with bushy vegetation. To withstand the freezing nights, one species of hillstar roosts in its nest in a crevice or old mine-shaft or deep within a cave. In this shelter its body temperature falls sharply and the bird becomes temporarily inert.

This ability to pass into a temporary state of torpidity has obvious advantages in the Andes, where night temperatures can be subzero even in sheltered places. However, Jean Dorst estimated that 75 per cent of nesting hillstars select the east face of a rocky cliff in order to take advantage of the sun's heat as soon as day breaks; and the remaining 25 per cent build their nests in shrubs at the base of cliffs. Their elaborate nests, composed of fern fronds, vegetable fibres, tufted fruits, feathers, wool and cobwebs, also afford excellent protection against the cold; and this is increased by their spaciousness, since they may be 4 inches deep and 5 inches wide, in contrast to the minute and fragile nests, providing scarcely enough room for the female and young, fashioned by hummingbirds in warmer habitats.

As an additional adaptation to environment, hillstars incubate their eggs for 20-21 days, compared to the 11-14 days of tropical species, and the nestlings take 30-38 days to fledge instead of 20 days.

Other adaptations by Andean hummingbirds are provided by the tiny *Metallura tyrainthina,* whose soft feathering, repelling the humidity of the Venezuelan páramo, contrasts with the rigid feathering of the hillstars on the cold puna and of the firecrowns hovering like large bees about the red flowers of the weigelia bushes in the southern beech forests of Tierra del Fuego. The latter are, however, reported to lapse into a temporary state of torpor during very cold weather in that bleak habitat. This is also the incongruous home of reddish-green austral parakeets flying with raucous cries over the glaciers, though Eric Shipton found wrens to be much the commonest birds in the beech forests.

Chapter Twenty Three
ANIMALS OF THE HIGH ANDES

Although the hostile environment on the high tops of the puna restricts the available forage, animal life is not as sparse as might be supposed, even if not comparable to that on the eastern slopes of the Andes, where the type of vegetation is directly related to altitude, and the number of species of both birds and mammals increases dramatically in the lower, warmer zones. As Frank M. Chapman pointed out many years ago, a diagrammatic representation of the plant zones on the 20,000 feet volcano of Chimborazo might have been made by an ornithologist, so closely does the distribution of birds conform to that of plants. On the other hand, by contrast with the faunal poverty of the western slopes and deserts of Peru and Chile, the puna could be described as almost richly endowed both in species and numbers. There are a few arthropods, notably the altiplano scorpions, which are hardy enough to move about at night, despite the fact that the ground temperature is then well below 32°F; a species of toad exists as high as 15,600 feet; and tiny lizards are active once the sun is up. The iguana lizard, which ranges up to 16,000 feet on the Peruvian altiplano, feeding on leaves, buds and insects, raises its body temperature by taking maximum advantage of the sun's heat, which is intense for a few hours. We are indebted to Tony Morrison for his observations on this lizard, which, after sheltering in its burrow during the night, pokes out its nose and tests the air as soon as the sun appears. The latter's slight early-morning heat is sufficient to warm the blood vessels of the lizard's sinuses, and from there warmed blood begins to circulate round the rest of its body. Eventually, when sufficiently warmed, it crawls out of its burrow on to a mass of perhaps black, decaying vegetation that will absorb the sun's heat quickly, and stretches out to bask in the sun. Its spread-eagled posture, increasing the surface-area of its body, enables it to benefit from the heat of both the sun and the vegetation beneath it, with the result that when the air temperature is only around freezing, that of the basking lizard may be as high as 85°F; but Morrison found that even when the lizard's body temperature was only 35°F it was still able to move about sluggishly, though other reptiles would have remained torpid in such a condition.

156

Small rodents can survive very low temperatures, and in the semi-desert of the Peruvian altiplano an American naturalist, Oliver P. Pearson, recorded no fewer than sixteen species of mice, vole-mice and rats. These included what is possibly the only mammal living exclusively on the puna — the brown, speckled with white, puna mouse, 6 inches long including its 2-inch tail. Though apparently unknown until 1939 this mouse exists in vast numbers between 14,250 and 16,500 feet. Insulated by long, loose fur, it shelters at night in burrows 30-50 feet long and a foot below clumps of grass among the rocks, emerging from numerous exits during the day to feed almost entirely on two rank-smelling plants: one a herb, the other a dwarf, fleshy-leaved tola shrub. Both, oddly enough, are also eaten by the mountain viscachas. The puna mice cut up stems of these plants into 12-inch lengths, which they manipulate into caches of several dozen under the rocks; like most inhabitants of the puna, however, they produce young during the rainy season when food is plentiful.

Another small rodent, the chinchilla, which in the Andes replaces the pikas and marmots of the Rockies and the mountains of the Old World, may breed higher than the pika, since it does so at 20,000 feet, and today indeed does not do so below 14,000 feet, though its altitudinal range formerly extended down to sea-level. Ten inches long, with a furry tail (usually held in a tight curl), large eyes, exceptionally large ears, long whiskers and tiny feet, the texture of its incomparably fine, soft bluish-grey fur is so dense — lice and fleas are unable to exist in it — that the chinchilla can withstand the lowest night temperatures; for though basking in the sun morning and evening, it feeds mainly at night on coarse grasses and herbs, and obtains drinking water from these. As an additional adaptation to its bleak environment the young are born fully furred, though the parents squat on either side of them if it is very cold, and can run within a few hours of birth. But ironically the beautiful fur that has made it possible for the chinchilla to survive has also been the direct cause of its destruction — one of its three races may indeed be extinct — and the restriction of the survivors to the altiplano of northern Chile, which includes part of the almost totally sterile Atacama Desert, possibly the most arid region on Earth, since there are parts of it in which no rain has ever been recorded. As long ago as 1593 Sir Richard Hawkins (son of the slaver, Sir John Hawkins) noted that:

> Amongst others, they have little beastes like unto a squirrell, but that he is gray; his skinne is the most delicate, soft, and curious furre that I have seene, and of much estimation (as is of reason) in the Peru; few of them come into Spaine, because difficult to come by: *for that the princes and nobles laie waite for them.* They call this beast chinchilla, and of them

they have great abundance.

By the nineteenth century chinchilla fur — so lightweight that 150 pelts were needed to make a full-length coat — had become extremely popular, and the London auction rooms of the Hudson's Bay Company, which began dealing in it in 1842, were selling more than 200,000 pelts per annum; by 1899 half a million pelts were being exported from South America, and in 1905 a quarter of a million were traded in the Chile mart alone. As Morrison has commented, it is incredible that so numerous a small mammal could have been hunted to the verge of extinction in such hostile country as the semi-desert wildernesses of the Andean altiplanos. Yet this has been brought about by Indian trappers employing smoke and their weasel-like grisons to drive the chinchillas out of their burrows into nets.

Fortunately for the mountain viscachas — close relatives of the chinchilla and the most noticeable and abundant small mammals of the Andes between 2,700 and 17,000 feet from Peru to 52 degrees south in Patagonia — their luxuriously soft, silky fur has no market value, though they are hunted by the Indians and have been known to the Spaniards since 1533; for though the dense, fluffy coat protects them against the cold, it is moulted in small random patches because there is never a long enough period of warm weather to shed it all at one time, and the sparse guard-hairs allow the fur to wet easily. According to Pearson, such a catastrophe proves fatal if the viscachas cannot dry themselves quickly in the sun: so during rain or hail or snowstorms they retreat to the shelter of their burrows; nor do they come out to feed if the ground is covered by several inches of snow.

The twenty-one races of mountain viscachas are only distant relatives of the large 15-pound viscachas of the Argentinian pampas, and being but fifteen inches long and 2½ to 3½ pounds in weight are about the size of rabbits. With their long ears and pearl-grey fur, grizzled with black on the back, they somewhat resemble the latter, though when bounding recklessly in 6-foot hops up a rocky slope, with uniquely upturned bushy tails, 10 inches long, streaming behind, they look more like squirrels or monkeys or even wallabies.

The viscachas live in colonies, and Pearson, who appears to have made the only detailed study of them (in southern Peru), recorded thirty colonies, containing 780 individuals, in one area of 28 square miles. Typically a colony consists of a dozen or two dozen members, though it may comprise as few as four or as many as 70 or 80. They are remarkably peaceful, engaging in no action more militant than an occasional sparring with front feet or noses, the latter of which are generously equipped with a sweeping moustache of coarse black vibrissae. However, each family of from two to five members — the female produces only one young in each of the annual two or three litters — has its own burrow sited a few feet from that of the next family and also its own sunning place on a rock outcrop on a grassy slope. Since the viscachas' claws are very short, suitable only for scratching up edible roots and stems and not for excavating the burrows in which they shelter from the cold nights, these are merely crevices among the piles of boulders or shallow holes dug out by generations of viscachas in the loose gravel or soil under the screes. In either case the entrances are too narrow to admit their main predator, the large, long-legged, jackal-like Andean fox or wolf, which also preys on guinea-pigs and hunts day and night among the viscacha colonies, investigating one hole after another; but the viscachas are virtually uncatchable on the screes, as they bound from rock to rock *en route* to their burrows, and will detour almost any distance to avoid crossing an extensive stretch of open ground.

Their typical habitat is arid montane country, whose sparse vegetation is broken up by patches of rock and sand. So much is this environment to their liking that they have, as we have seen, colonised the barren zones created by the despoliation of the yareta. The type of vegetation seems unimportant, though lichens are always present, together with a few scattered tŏla bushes. Ichú grass is dominant near some colonies but almost absent at others, and the blue-grey spiny-grass and the great round clumps of the inedible yareta are dominant among the boulders near high-altitude colonies. The one essential is rock with deep crevices and narrow, stony tunnels in which to litter and rear their young. Next in importance to rocks is water. Colonies are rarely more than 50 yards over open ground from water, though as viscachas are not often to be seen actually drinking, the main attraction of water is perhaps the ribbon of succulent green vegetation in its arid surroundings. Pearson noted that the most-favoured screes were often those on the steep sides of bowls or cirques, where truck-sized blocks had plunged from the towering cliffs to form a Herculean scree. The viscachas would come down from the screes to feed in the centre of a bowl, where a seep of water or ice might be indicated by a green carpet of *Distichia*, whose firm, moss-like carpet more than 100 feet wide, completely covered most moist places, tumbling out of the cirques like green glaciers. He watched one colony of 200 viscachas feeding on the *Distichia* in a cirque, despite the fact that the leaves and stems of the mats were so tightly packed that a man could walk across them, as across a pile carpet, without crushing them; and despite the fact that the viscachas had difficulty in cropping more than a quarter of an inch off the greenery, whose compactness both retained moisture and repelled frost.

Unlike the plains viscachas and the chinchillas, the mountain viscachas are diurnal and Pearson has described how, after awakening at sun-up, they hop to some favourite place on top of a boulder or cliff, and cuddle up in families for hours, sitting up on their haunches like rabbits, or stretched out on their sides, to bask in the life-giving sun, soaking up its heat, with eyes half-closed in contentment. Nevertheless, they remain fully alert and extremely wary, for at the slightest sight or sound of danger one will utter a series of very high-pitched mournful whistles, like those of a marmot, at which warning all of its fellows 'freeze' or climb the rocks for a better view, only diving for their burrows if man or dog approaches too closely. A hawk is proclaimed by a shorter alarm-call, and other animals, such as leaf-eared mice and vicunas respond to the viscachas' warnings and rush to cover on hearing them, though the viscachas ignore a vicuna's warning *hee-haw*.

Herds of vicuna graze everywhere among the viscacha colonies except on the actual rocks, and the two species meet at the edge of the screes on those occasions when the viscachas venture their maximum distance of 75 yards into open ground to feed on grass and the tola. It could be argued that without the advantage of their communal warning system the viscachas would not have sufficient time to feed, for it is only after their long, early-morning period of warming up that they begin to do so; though then, as if to make up for the lost hours, they nibble feverishly for the remainder of the morning at almost every species of plant, including the spiniest and rankest-smelling. After another interlude for sun-bathing, they feed again in the late afternoon or evening until after sunset. Moreover, each blade of grass is eaten singly, and, since a captive animal provided with barley grains by Pearson took 12 seconds to consume each grain, he estimated that a wild viscacha would have to feed for three and a half hours in order to obtain its daily requirement.

Of the larger mammals only foxes, the mink-sized grisons, a big black skunk with broad white markings on the head, and the vicuna are common on the puna. Pumas, though encountered as high as 17,000 feet, are infrequent wanderers — as well they might be, since the blood of cats does not possess the special properties of that of vicunas and viscachas, enabling them to live permanently at high altitudes. Pumas are, however, widespread though declining in Patagonia, killing numbers of sheep in the winter, and are the chief predator on the Andean deer. Little is known about the latter, the huemul or guemal and its close relative, the taruca or Peruvian guemal of the high northern paramos, whereas the huemul are confined to the southern Andes, with Patagonia as their headquarters, and are known to range from sea-level to 16,500 feet. Both are about the size of chamois and have small, spiky antlers. Pearson found them living during the summer in small groups, comprising a stag and two or three hinds and calves, among grassy hills studded with rock outcrops and caves between 11,500 and 14,000 feet on the Peruvian altiplano; but they herd together in the early winter when they move down from the incessant hurricane-strength blizzards of the Patagonian mountains into the forested foothills of southern beech. Eric Shipton was told that they were to be found in most Patagonian forests but were so shy that they were seldom seen; and this was certainly his experience (and also Roger Perry's in southern Chile), for though he often came across their tracks he never saw them, with the exception of a single, untypical occasion. Then, on hearing a slight noise behind him, he looked round to see two huemul gazing at him less than four yards away: 'I rose slowly to my feet ..... but not only did they hold their ground, they showed not the slightest alarm. I advanced until I was about two yards from them; still there was no reaction ..... after a few minutes they seemed to grow bored with me, and ..... started to nibble at the grass.'

There remain to be considered the cameloids — vicuna, guanaco, llama and alpaca — though the vicunas are sufficiently distinct from the other three to form a separate genus. They are also the smallest, standing between 28 and 35 inches at the shoulder, compared to the llama-like guanaco's 43 inches. Their more or less uniform red-brown, pale-fawn or golden pelage, set off by a fringe of long, white hairs hanging from the chest, contrasts with the dark-brown upper parts and white belly of the guanaco, and they also lack the latter's black face. In size and actions the vicuna has been compared with the pronghorn antelope of the North-American plains, but since it does not have horns and has a long neck and rather large feet it more resembles a small, hump-less camel.

Llamas and alpacas have not been known in the wild state for centuries, and though their probable ancestor the guanaco graze as high as the vegetational limit at 17,000 feet on the peaks of Chile and Argentina, the latter are essentially grassland and shrub animals, and their hoofs are adapted to a terrain of clay rather than to rock climbing. They have always been most numerous on the pampas of southern Argentina, though prior to widespread persecution after the Spanish Conquest, their range included mid-Peru, parts of Bolivia and the length of Chile south to the Patagonian pampas and Tierra del Fuego. It is on record that Darwin saw guanaco in herds of 500 or more on the Patagonian pampas, but they are now heavily slaughtered for their hides, with the result that the largest groups of bachelors number no more than from a dozen to fifty, and breeding harems of females average from four to ten. These the male collects into a territory of between 20 and 100 acres, which he patrols, uttering a sharp bleat at any sign of danger. Darwin's large herds on the pampas were presumably composed of non-breeding guanaco, concentrated on richer grasslands than any available to the vicuna, which thrive only above 12,000 feet on the short grasslands of the cold, semi-desert puna, moving up closer to the snow-line in summer.

On the puna three-quarters of the annual rainfall occurs in the summer, often as snow or hail, and the passing phase of abundant vegetation fades rapidly with the increasingly arid approach of winter and the barren dryness of spring. In parts of Bolivia, indeed, some herds of vicuna, crowded out by large numbers of domesticated alpaca, range over ground that is frozen for most of the day, and on which the vegetation is so sparse that for several months of the year it does no more than give a green tinge to the soil. However, zero temperatures are rare on the puna, and it could be argued that in comparison with many grazing animals in North America, vicunas need withstand neither extreme cold, extreme heat, nor extreme variations in air temperatures. Nevertheless, they must make use of most of the hours of daylight in foraging over the sandy puna for rosette plants and scattered tufts of perennial grasses — their principal food — and cropping shoots of the soaking mats of *Distichia*. As Carl B. Koford has noted, although much of the puna over which the vicunas feed appears, when viewed from a distance, to be destitute of vegetation, on closer inspection it is found to be sprinkled with rosette plants, few larger than a pocket-watch and about five to the square yard. In order to obtain maximum nutrition from this poor feed the vicuna possesses special cells in the rumen, and also peculiar lower incisors which, like those of rodents, have open roots and continue growing throughout the animal's lifetime. The vicuna drink every two days, though on sunny mornings, according to Pearson, they frequently wade into the deeper icy water of a stream and stand or kneel in it for several minutes before emerging to couch in the sun while their fur dries off.

With such poor forage it is essential that every grazing area be strictly limited to the number of vicuna it can support, and this requirement has resulted in an unusual pattern of social behaviour. Koford has illustrated this in his ecological monograph on the vicuna:

While scanning the bleak rolling grasslands of the puna a traveller may be startled by a prolonged screech. The cry attracts his gaze to a racing troop of fifty gazelle-like mammals, bright cinnamon in colour — vicunas! As they gallop up a barren slope he sees that a single large vicuna pursues them closely. The pursuer charges at one straggler, then another, as if to nip their heels. But suddenly the aggressor halts, stands tall with slender neck and short tail erect, stares at a line of llamas in the distance, and whistles a high trill. Then it gallops away to join a band of several vicunas, some obviously young, which graze close by. And these it follows as they file uphill, away from the approaching llamas and the sombre Indian who trudges behind them.

The barefoot herdsman tells the traveller that the small retreating band is a family of vicunas, females and young, protected from the rear by their leader, an adult male, and that the large fleeing troop consists entirely of males.

Three main constituents are involved in the vicunas' social pattern. The first is the family band of from five to fifteen females, plus a few juveniles, collected around a single male in an all-the-year-round feeding territory, preferably situated near a river, in which the band grazes in isolation from other groups. The territory averages about 30 acres but varies in size, depending upon the pasturage available, from 20 to 250 acres on the most barren land. Its boundaries are apparently demarcated by the male with heaps of dung, though, like other cameloids, all the remaining members of the band deposit their dung in the same place, forming a mound as much as 8 feet in diameter and 12 inches high in the middle. According to Koford, there are many barren hills on which the only greenery visible at a distance are the brilliant green circles marking the sites of these communal dung-heaps. Although the male makes no active attempt to prevent any of his harem from leaving his territory, he defends it for months or even years, whether or not it contains any females, chasing away intruding males.

The second constituent is the bachelor troop of from 20 to more than 100 one or two-years-olds, plus a few adults that are probably aged or crippled, though the components of the troop may change several times a day as a result of agglomeration and attacks by territorial males. The third constituent is that of solitary, unmated males, which attempt to establish territories and attract females, warning off other solitary males by standing stiffly upright with ears and tails erect on their high mound. Vicunas rarely fight, and if they do so, mainly by neck biting. Anger is indicated by spitting, which is in fact a quick, forceful expulsion of air, only incidentally spraying saliva and fragments of masticated food. Angelo West states that when the lambs or *crias* in the family band are between eight and twelve months old, they are chased away by the male, their father, and even attacked if they attempt to remain in his territory. Their eviction has the effect of forcing the female crias to search for other males that will accept them in their territories, though the male crias can join the bands of bachelors, which graze on the even poorer pastures along the fringes of the family territory.

Vicunas, like other cameloids, usually rut in the late summer, with the result that the one, or two, lambs are born ten or eleven months later, every other year, at that season when the vegetation is most abundant on the puna. In West's experience the lambs are always born in the morning, because if they were dropped during the afternoon storms of rain, hail or snow, they would be unable to dry off and would die during the cold nights. Even so, only half those born survive the high degree of exposure (in a ratio of two females to three males), though as a counter to this high mortality rate, those that live are reported by some observers to be weaned within six months of birth and to be mature when a year old, in contrast to guanaco lambs which, in a generally less harsh environment, may not mature until two or three years old. Nor do the vicunas suffer from excessive natural predation. The smaller wild cats are little more numerous than pumas, and foxes, though common, are apparently not attracted by vicuna lambs. It is possible that condors may occasionally attack lambs that have strayed from their mothers, and Koford saw females driving condors away from their lambs, even when as many as fourteen condors were gathered around one lamb. However, for protection against any predator, both vicunas and guanacos rely upon their fleetness of foot, and Morrison has described how, with ears forced down and neck reaching forward so that the body is streamlined like a greyhound on the track, a vicuna, when chased by an automobile can maintain a speed of 30 mph for several miles at a stretch, enabled to do so in the thin atmosphere at 15,000 feet by an enlarged heart and lungs and an exceptionally high level of oxygen-carrying, red corpuscles in the blood.

In the pre-Columbian era hundreds of thousands of vicuna ranged over the puna and altiplano between 12,000 and 16,000 feet, and the Inca kings practiced conservation, rounding up the herds in each district at three to five year intervals, though never domesticating them. According to Garcilaso de la Vega's late sixteenth-century *Royal Commentaries of the Yncas*, these round-ups took place after the breeding season, when 20,000 or 30,000 Indians would take part in *chacos* or drives that resembled the *tainchels* of the Scottish Highlanders: split up into 'two parties, one going to the right, the other to the left, and forming a great circle of 20 or 30 leagues (60 to 90 miles) in circumference'. In the course of these chacos 20,000 or 40,000 head of game might be taken, including 'lions, bears, many foxes, and wild cats', and the 'hunters recorded the number of animals that had been killed, as well as the vermin and the game, to know the number of head that had been killed and that remained alive; so as to be able to tell whether the game had increased at the next hunt.' At the conclusion of a chaco the guanacos and vicuna were sorted into those that were to be butchered for their flesh and those, the majority, including the finest specimens of both sexes, that were to be sheared for their precious wool and liberated.

But after the Spanish Conquest there was no control over hunting, and possibly as many as 80,000 vicuna were slaughtered every year during the sixteenth century. As late as 1926 the Peruvians were still exporting the wool of some 6,000 vicunas, and by 1968 the total stock surviving throughout the Andes was only 10,000. These were almost entirely confined to an area in southern Peru and northern Bolivia between 11,000 and 15,000 feet; but in the meantime a National Vicuna Reserve had been established in 1965 in Peru with a stock of 1,700 head, and this proved so successful that by 1977 the Reserve's stock had increased to 30,000 and the total Andean population to some 60,000.

Chapter Twenty-Four

BIRDS OF THE HIGH ANDEAN LAKES AND RIVERS

In southern Bolivia and northern Chile, to the south of Lake Titicaca, the puna gives way to one of the most remarkable landscapes on Earth, which has been graphically described by both Peter Matthiessen and Tony Morrison. At altitudes of between 12,000 and 17,000 feet the altiplano's treeless, semi-desert plateaus have a moonscape bleakness comparable to that of the Chang-Tang, but strewn with cracked pumice, ash and windrows of rocks thrown up by volcanic activity. Moreover, thousands of square miles are covered by vast flats of salt and borax on which nothing grows. Although these *salares* may have a little water on them in the summer months, they are dry throughout the extremely cold winter, and temperatures can fluctuate in 24 hours from minus 10° F during the night to 90° F among the rocks at midday.

The fauna of the salares is as remarkable as the environment. In 1886 an expedition into the snow-capped mountains beyond the Atacama Desert discovered three different species of flamingoes, including the previously unknown James's flamingo, breeding above 14,000 feet on salt lakes and lagoons — shallow sheets of water encircled by stretches of bare mud with a glinting crust of crystallised salt. Although the presence of these high-altitude flamingo colonies has always been known to the hungry Indians, who hunt the adult birds with bolas and raid their nests on an ever-increasing scale for eggs, it was not until 1956 that these colonies were rediscovered by zoologists on the highest lakes between Chile and Bolivia, where thousands of the James's flamingo were nesting on the Laguna Colorado. Lying at 14,200 feet, this has been variously, though always dramatically described as a shallow lake, stained brick-red or cherry-pink with the flamingoes' algae food. A mile wide and apparently fluctuating between 3 miles and 10 miles in length, it is flanked by black basalt rocks on one side and by purple volcanic cones, with red and yellow interiors, on the other. Beaches of grey gravel slope down to its shores of black mud, and masses of salt crystals mingle with ice and feathers on its waters.

Readers of an earlier book of mine, *Life at the Sea's Frontiers*, will be aware of the propensity of flamingoes for breeding in the most extraor-

166

dinary habitats, and the three South American species appear to be almost restricted to these salty lagunas in the highest and most arid areas of the central Andes. There are indeed no confirmed sightings of the small James's flamingo and larger Andean flamingo below 7,500 feet.

The fauna of Lake Titicaca, lying at more than 12,000 feet, is also of great interest since it is the largest body of water at this altitude in the world, and is backed by a continuous range of 20,000-foot peaks, whose white glaciers and ice-fields are sharply defined against the clear, blue Andean sky. Morrison has described how, during the winter from May to August, the sky is almost perpetually cloudless, but in spring storms may suddenly sweep across the lake and shroud the mountains in rain, freezing hail or snow.

Despite its altitude the lake's waters, 800 feet or more deep, never freeze, remaining at a more or less constant temperature of between 50° F and 55° F throughout the year; and this is also the case with smaller lakes situated as high as 16,000 feet. However, the dry Andean climate, coupled with the low temperatures prevailing in the hinterland, has resulted in Lake Titicaca's two amphibians adapting to a permanently aquatic existence. One, the quele — a large frog, 16 to 24 inches long and unable to support its own weight out of water — lives in the lake at depths of more than 6 feet, enabled to do so by large, interior body cavities that increase the area available for the absorption of oxygen from the water. The other, a huge toad, whose lake population has been estimated at one billion, has eyes resembling those of a fish and well-developed webs on its feet. Thus equipped, it is known to be able to exist at the remarkable depth of 400 feet.

In sheltered bays, where the water is not more than 15 feet deep, large areas of dense thickets of bulrushes or *totora* provide the main cover for the lake's birds — teal, pintail and the Andean geese that graze on the boggy ground in the vicinity of the lake or high up in the mountains near glaciers; cormorants, *serranita* gulls (which closely resemble those on the high lakes of Tibet), and various grebes, including a flightless species, whose crude paddling 'flight' is unable to lift it from the water, and two unusual coots.

The giant coot, which is an inhabitant of freshwater lakes only, up to an altitude of 16,000 feet, is rare and extremely localised. The size of a small goose and weighing about seven pounds, this coal-black coot has a small, bright-lemon and white frontal shield above the red beak, dark-red legs and vivid coral-red feet. Breeding twice a year in August and again in late November or December, it is notable for its nest, 3 or 4 feet in diameter, which it builds (and adds to year after year) on floating rafts of aquatic vegetation 10 or 12 feet across and strong enough to support a man. So steep are the sides of the nest cavity that it is almost impossible to see the eggs unless one is standing on the raft.

The smaller horned coot is also very rare and localised in the 10,000 to 14,000 feet zone, and the largest known colony contains only about thirty pairs. This coot is distinguished by a peculiar muscular appendage over the beak which might be described as a trunk or proboscis, and which assists it in holding water-weed when dragging this with its beak through the water during nest-building operations. Yet the giant coot, which drags material to the nest in a similar manner, lacks this appendage. Unlike the latter, the horned coot anchors its bulky nest, about 13 in feet diameter, on a conical mound of stones, weighing up to one pound a piece, that the pair carry in their beaks from the shore to add to the pile built up over the years from the lake bottom to a height of 2 or 3 feet just below the surface.

The permanence of these small colonies of rare, high-altitude birds is always at risk. When, for example, large-mouthed bass were introduced by anglers to lake Titicaca in 1960, they altered the ecological balance by prey-ing on the fish, frogs and crabs (and also on ducklings and young grebes), thereby diminishing the food available to the grebes and reducing their numbers from about 200 in 1960 to 100 in 1965, though conservation has now restored them to their 1960 level.

The mountain torrents and rapids down the length of the Andes, from tropical Venezuela to sub-antarctic Tierra del Fuego, have also been col-onised by scattered populations of half a dozen races of a specialised duck, the torrent duck. According to Paul A. Johnsgard, the female is rust-red below, dove-grey above, and has a conspicuous, carmine beak. When swimming, the reddish underparts are mostly below water, and only the brilliantly coloured beak enables one to see the bird in the swirling waters. Similarly, the larger grey and white male is easily lost to view in the water, particularly if the bird is swimming so low that only its black and white striped head is exposed.

Although the major part of the torrent-duck population is concentrated between 5,000 and 10,000 feet, their range extends from as low as 600 feet above sea-level in Chile to as high as 18,000 feet in Peru. Like the harlequin ducks of arctic and subarctic regions, the torrent ducks have been able to occupy an ecological niche for which almost no other ducks are equipped, since few are sufficiently skilful at swimming and diving in the rushing waters of rapids and under waterfalls to obtain adequate supplies of food in such conditions. In either case their presence in these turbulent waters is influenced by the specialised food available.

The cold, well-aerated water of the torrent ducks' habitat is probably the dominant factor determining their altitudinal range, because it is rich in aquatic insect life, especially the young caddisfly and stonefly, the latter of which live mostly on rocks and stones washed by the oxygenated waters of mountain and hill streams. However, their special food requirements limit the length of suitable territory on any given stretch of river. Thus on one river a single pair of ducks may be in possession of a reach several miles long, while on another two or three pairs may be in close proximity on a mile of tumbling water, with each pair restricted to a short length of streamway, because there are extensive spans of unproductive smooth water above and below the waterfalls or rapids at either end of the rough water.

The torrent ducks are admirably adapted to cope with the swiftest and most tumultuous waters. Their small bodies are elongated and torpedo-shaped, and their very large webbed feet enable them to swim strongly against powerful currents. In this they are assisted by their long stiff tails which, according to Morrison, apparently serve not only as rudders but as hydrofoils to deflect the pressure of the current. They can remain stationary beneath the water of a raging torrent or swim rapidly upstream close to the bottom and reappear on the steep side of the next rock. To escape danger, they will swim over waterfalls several feet high and, after vanishing in the spray below, crawl back into rocky recesses behind the falls and remain hidden for half an hour or more behind the veil of water. Large rounded midstream boulders are an essential feature of their habitat, for on these they can rest between foraging dives — as do their constant associates, the white-capped dippers; and from them, as Johnsgard has described, leap into the white water, and disappear from sight for ten seconds or longer, while probing rock crevices for food with their long, thin beaks, which are flexible and indiarubber-like and have soft tips. Then they suddenly emerge near the place at which they had dived and scramble back up the slippery side of the boulder, aided by the stiffened tail-feathers, which they press down against the rock, as woodpeckers do against tree trunks, and possibly also making use of the claws at their wing-joints.

Also essential are riverside cliffs, often vertical, in which they can nest in crevices or in ringed kingfishers' old burrows, which may be 8 feet long and from 6 to 60 feet above the level of the river. Hatching after about six weeks, the ducklings bounce and tumble down the cliffs, and, though weighing little more than an ounce, are able to navigate the rapids, appearing to walk, run or 'crawl' over the surface of the water, with one webbed foot striking swiftly after the other. They can also clamber up the midstream boulders, since their tails and feet are exceptionally well developed and wholly out of proportion to their body size. On a Peruvian river Morrison was able to watch the daily life of a pair of torrent ducks and their four ducklings — they do not usually have more than three — from the time that the latter were leaving the nest and taking to the water; and during his month's observation not a single duckling was lost, despite the strong current. He describes how, at any sign of movement on the steep bank above the river the drake would utter a piercing warning whistle that could be heard above the roar of the rapids, and the duck would dive, heading up-stream, while the ducklings would stop paddling and allow themselves to be swept down-stream. Since the gradient was very steep, the family was instantly separated by 50 to 100 yards, before the ducklings came to rest under overhanging rocks or behind tiny waterfalls. In the meantime the drake kept watch from a rock under the bank, and once the danger had passed, the duck followed the ducklings down-stream and slowly collected them together again, guided to their hiding places by their high-pitched, whistling calls.

BIBLIOGRAPHY

Ali, S. 1949. *Indian Hill Birds.*
Allen, R. 'The Future of the Alps'. *Animals.*
Andrews, R. C. 1932. *The New Conquest of Central Asia.*
Animals Editors. 1972. 'The Snow Leopard in Pakistan'.
   Animals 14,(6), 256–9.
Ashmole, P. 1968. 'Condors in Peru'. *Animals 2,*(4),159–60.

Baillie-Grohman, W. A. 1896. *Sport in the Alps.*
Balfour, J. H. 1848. 'Notes of a botanical excursion . . . to the mountains
   of Braemar . . . and Ben Lawers'. *Edin. Philos. J.*45, 122.
Bate, M. 1968. 'The extermination of the Vicuna'. *Animals 2,*(2),85–9.
Beer, Sir G. De. 1955. *Alps and Elephants. Hannibal's March.*
Beuchner, H. K. 1960. 'The bighorn sheep in the United States'. *Wildl.
   Monogr.* no.4.
Bille, R. P. 1975. *Guinness Guide to Mountain Animals.*
Blood, D. Hall, T. W. and Baumgarten, S. 1976. *Rocky Mountain
   Wildlife.*
Bolton, M. 1976. *Ethiopian Wildlands.*
Bonham, P. F. 1970. 'Studies of less familiar birds, 157: Chough and
   Alpine Chough'. *British Birds 63*:28–32.
Bonington, C. 1971. *Annapurna South Face.*
Bower, H. 1894. *Diary of a journey across Tibet.*
Brown, D. 1972. *Alaska.*
Brown, L. 1964. 'I search for the Walia'. *Animals 4,*(1),3–5.
_____. 1965. *Africa: A Natural History.*
_____. 1965. *Ethiopian Episode.*
_____. 1969. 'Ethiopia's elusive Nyala'. *Animals 10,*(8),340–1.
_____ and Amadon, D. 1968. *Eagles, Hawks and Falcons of the World.*
   2 vols.
Burrard, G. 1925. *Big Game Hunting in the Himalayas and Tibet.*

Cahalane, V. H. 1947. *Mammals of North America.*

Carr, H. R. C. 1948. *The Mountains of Snowdonia.*

Carruthers, D. 1949. *Beyond the Caspian.*

Chapman, A. 1893. *Wild Spain.*

_____. 1928. *Retrospect.*

_____ and Buck, W. J. 1910. *Unexplored Spain.*

Chapman, F. *Bird Life of the Andes.*

Clark, J. L. 1929. *Trails of the Hunted.*

_____. 1969. *The Great Arc of the Wild Sheep.*

Clark, R. W. 1976. *Men, Myths and Mountains.*

Coombs, F. 1976. *The Crows: A study of the Corvids of Europe.*

Corbet, G. A. 1966. *The Terrestial Mammals of Western Europe.*

_____ and Southern, H. S. 1977. *The Handbook of British Mammals.*

Cowan, I. M. 1965. 'Canada's Mountain Goat'. *Animals 6,*(12),318–23.

Curzon, G. M. 1896. *The Pamirs and the Source of the Oxus.*

Delacour, J. 1977. *Pheasants of the World.*

Demidoff, E. 1898. *Hunting Trips in the Caucasus.*

_____. 1900. *After Wild Sheep in the Altai and Mongolia.*

Dorst, J. 1967. *South America and Central America.*

Dufresne, F. 1963. *No Room for Bears.*

Dyrenfurth, N. G. 1955. *To the Third Pole.*

Dyson, J. L. 1963. *The World of Ice.*

Ferguson-Lees, I. J. 1958. 'Chough and Alpine Chough'. *British Birds 51,*99–103.

Fleming, R. J. 1976. *The Birds of Nepal.*

Flux, J. E. C. 1970. 'Life History of the Mountain Hare in north-east Scotland'. *J. Zool. Lond. 161,*75–123.

Geist, V. 1971. *Mountain Sheep: A study in Behaviour and Evolution.*

_____. 1977. *Mountain Sheep and Man.*

George, G. St. 1974. *Soviet Deserts and Mountains.*

Gibbons, R. 1975. 'Life in the high Hindu Kush'. *Wildlife 17,*(9),388–92.

Goodspeed, T. H. 1961. *Plant Hunters in the Andes.*

Goodwin, D. 1976. *Crows of the World.*

Gordon, S. 1915. *Hill Birds of Scotland.*

_____. 1925. *The Cairngorm Hills of Scotland.*

_____. 1943. *A Highland Year.*

Graf, J. 1968. *Animal Life in Europe.*

Griffiths, D. E. 1975. 'On the alpine slopes of the Rockies'. *Animals 17,*(11),498–502.

Grinnel, J. and Storer, T. I. 1924. *Animal Life in the Yosemite.*

Hallet, J. P. 1968. *Animal Kitabu.*
Hamilton, W. J. 1939. *American Mammals.*
Hanbury-Tracy, J. 1938. *Black River of Tibet.*
Hanney, P. W. 1975. *Rodents.*
Harrer, H. 1970. *Seven Years in Tibet.*
Hayden, H. and Cosson, C. 1927. *Sport and Travel in the Highlands of Tibet.*
Hedin, S. 1898. *Through Asia 1893-7.*
_____. 1903. *Central Asia and Tibet.*
_____. 1910. *Trans-Himalaya.*
Heuvelmans, B. 1970. *On the Track of Unknown animals.*
Hewson. R. 1962. 'Food and feeding habits of the Mountain Hare'. *Proc. Zool. Lond. 139,*415–26.
Hill, W. C. O. 1961. 'The Abominable Snowman'. *Oryx 6,*86–98.
Hillary, Sir E. and Doig, D. 1963. *High in the Thin Cold Air.*
Hindley, G. 1971. *The Roof of the World.*
Hingston, R. W. G. 1925. 'Animal life at high altitudes'. *Geographical Journal* 185–98.
Holyoak, D. 1972. 'Behaviour and ecology of the Chough and Alphine Chough'. *Bird Study 19,*215–27.
Howard-Bury, C. K. 1922. *Mount Everest, the Reconnaissance, 1921.*

Izzard, R. 1954. *The Innocent on Everest.*
_____. 1955. *The Abominable Snowman Adventure.*

Jerome, J. 1979. *On Mountains.*
Johnsard, P.A. 1972.'Torrent Ducks of the Andes'. *Animals, 12,*(2),80–3.
Johnson, T. 1908. *The Itinerary of a Botanist.*

Kaulback, R. 1932. *Tibetan Trek.*
_____. 1938. *Salween.*
Keel, J. A. 1958. *Jadoo.*
Kinloch, A. A. 1876. *Large Game Shooting in Tibet and the North-West.*
Koford, C. B. 1957. 'The Vicuna and the Puna'. *Ecological Monographs 27,*153–219.

Lee, S. 1829. *The Travels of Ibn Batuta.*
Ley, W. 1955. *Salamanders and Other Wonders.*
Long, T. 1971. *Mountain Animals.*

174

Longstaff, T. 1950. *This my Journey.*
Lovari, S. 1977. 'The Abruzzo Chamois'. *Oryx 14,*(1),47–50.

MacKinnon, J. and A. 1974. *Animals of Asia.*
Mallinson, J. 1978. *The Shadow of Extinction.*
Mani, M. S. 1962. *Introduction to High Altitude Entomology.*
Marshall, R. 1956. *Alaska Wilderness.*
Matthiessen, P. 1962. *The Cloud Forest.*
_____. 1979. *The Snow Leopard.*
McGowan, D. 1936. *Animals of the Canadian Rockies.*
McNeely, T. A.; Cronin, E. W. and Emery, H. B. 1973. 'The Yeti — not a Snowman'. *Oryx 12,*(1),65–73.
Meinerthzhagen, R. 1927. 'Ladakh, with special reference to its natural history'. *Geog. J. 70,*129–63.
Mills, A. E. 1919. *The Grizzly.*
Montagu, I. 1964. 'The Wild Man of the Gobi'. *Animals 27,*(10),85–6.
Morgan, J. K. 1972. 'Bighorns, Biologists and People'. *Animals* 14,1,18–26.
Morris, P. A. and Malcolm, J. R. 1977. 'The Simien Fox in the Bale mountains'. *Oryx 14,*(2),151–60.
Morrison, T. 1968. 'Three Flamingoes of the High Andes'. *Animals 11,*(7),305–9.
Mountfort, G. 1969. *The Vanishing Jungle.*
Murie, A. 1963. *A Naturalist in Alaska.*

Napier, J. 1972. *Big Foot: The Yeti . . . in Myth and Reality.*
Nathan, M. 1973. 'The social life of the Geladas'. *Animals* May,208–14.
Nebresky-Wojkowitz, R von. 1956. *Where the Gods are Mountains. Three Years Among the People of the Himalayas.*
Nethersole-Thompson, D. 1966. *The Snow Bunting.*
_____. 1973. *The Dotterel.*
_____ and Watson, A. 1974. *The Cairngorms.*
Nicol, C. 1972. *From the Roof of Africa.*
Nicolson, N. 1975. *The Himalayas.*
Noel, J. B. L. 1927. *Through Tibet to Everest.*
Noyce, W. 1954. *South Col.*

Omond, R. T. 1905. 'Zoological notes from the Log Book of the Ben Nevis Observatory'. *Ann. Scot. Nat. Hist. 55,* 129–41.

Pearson, O. P. 1948. 'Life history of the Mountain Viscachas in Peru'.

Journ. Mammal. 29, 345–74.

Peissel, M. 1968. *Mustang, a Lost Tibetan Kingdom*.

Perry, R. 1964. *The World of the Tiger*.

———. 1969. *The World of the Giant Panda*.

———. 1970. *Bears*.

———. 1976. *Life in Forest and Jungle*.

———. 1977. *Life in Desert and Plain*.

———. 1978. *Wildlife in Britain and Ireland*.

———. 1979. *Highland Wildlife*.

Petrocz, R. G. 1970. 'Winter among the Bighorns'. *Animals 12*,(11),520–3.

Pfeffer, P. 1968. *Asia: A Natural History*.

Prater, S. 1965. *The Book of Indian Animals*.

Proctor, D. 1971. *Hannibal's March in History*.

Przewalski, N. 1875. *Mongolia*.

Raven, J. and Walters, M. 1956. *Mountain Flowers*.

Rawicz, S. 1956. *The Long Walk*.

Rawling, C. 1905. *The Great Plateau*.

Roberts, T. S. 1977. *The Mammals of Pakistan*.

Rothschild, M. 1956. 'Diurnal movements of the Mountain Chough'. International Ornithological Congress II: 1954,611–17.

Russell, A. 1964. 'White sheep of the Arctic'. *Animals 4*,(4),90–3.

Sage, B. L. 1973. *Alaska and its Wildlife*.

Sanderson, I. T. 1961. *Abominable Snowman: Legend Come to Life*.

Schaller, G. B. 1971. 'A Naturalist in South Asia'. New York Zool. Soc. *Bull.* spring.

———. 1973. 'On the behaviour of Blue Sheep'. *Journ. of the Bombay Nat. Hist. Soc. 69*,(3),523–37.

———. 1973. 'Observations on Himalayan Tahr'. *Journ. of the Bombay Nat. Hist. Soc. 70*,(1), 1–24.

———. 1976. 'Mountain Mammals in Pakistan'. *Oryx 13*,(4),351–6.

———. 1977. *Mountain Monarchs*.

——— and Mirza, Z. B. 1971. 'On the behaviour of Kashmir Markhor'. *Mammalia 35*,(4),548–67.

Sheldon, C. 1911. *The Wilderness of the Upper Yukon*.

Sheldon, W. G. 1975. *The Wilderness Home of the Giant Panda*.

Shipton, E. E. 1936. *Nanda Devi*.

———. 1938. *Blank on the Map*.

———. 1951. *The Mount Everest Reconnaissance*.

———. 1963. *Land of Tempest : Travels in Patagonia 1958-62*.

———. 1969. *That Untravelled World*.

———. n.d. *Mountains of Tartary*.

Snellgrove, D. 1961. *Himalayan Pilgrimage*.

Spencer, C. C. 1943. 'Notes on life history of Rocky Mountain bighorn sheep'. *Mammal. 24*,(1)I–II;9.

Stockley, C. H. 1936. *Stalking in the Himalayas*.

Stonor, C. 1955. *The Sherpa and the Snowman*.

Styles, S. 1955. *The Moated Mountain*.

Sumner. L. and Dixon, T. S. 1953. *Birds and Mammals of the Sierra Nevada*.

Swan, L. W. 1961. 'The ecology of the high Himalayas'. *Sci. Amer. 205*,(4), 68–78.

Synge, P.M. 1937. *The Mountains of the Moon*.

Tassi, F. and Florio, P. L. 1970. 'The Chamois of the Abruzzo'. *Animals 13*,(1),14–16.

Tchernine, O. 1961. *The Snowman and Company*.

———. 1970. *The Yeti*.

———. 1974. 'The Yeti–Some of the evidence'. *Oryx*, November,553–5.

Tichy, H. 1954. *Cho Oyu–By favour of the Gods*.

Tilman, H.W. 1949. *Two Mountains and a River*.

———. 1952. *Nepal Himalaya*.

———. *Mount Everest*, 1938–48.

Todd, F. S. 1975. 'The tenacious Thunder Bird'. *Wildlife 17*,(1),8–13.

Tombazi, A. 1925. *Account of Photographic Expedition to the Southern Glaciers of Kachenjunga*.

Tyler, S. 1975. 'The Simien Fox'. *Wildlife 17*,(II),564–5.

Vaurie, C. 1972. *Tibet and its Birds*.

Vlcek, E. 1959. 'Old literary evidence for the existence of the Snowman in Tibet and Mongolia'. *Man. 59*, 133–4.

Waddell, L.A. 1899. *Among the Himalayas*.

———. 1905. *Llasa and its Mysteries*.

Waltermire, R. G. 1977. 'Bale'. *Wildlife 13*, (11), 498–503.

Watson, A. 1965. 'A population study of Ptarmigan in Scotland'. *J. Anim. Ecol. 34*, 135–72.

——— and Hewson, r. 1973. 'Population densities of Mountain Hares on western Scottish and Irish moors and on Scottish hills'. *J. Zool. Lond. 170*, 15–19.

West, A. 1974. 'The Vicuna recovers with the help of the Alpaca'. *Wildlife*

16,(9),388–95.

Whistler, H. 1949. *Popular Handbook of Indian Birds.*

White, F. B. 1879. 'The mountain lepidoptera of Britain'. *Scott, Nat.5,* 97–105;149–60.

Wilmore, S. B. 1977. *Crows, Jays, Ravens.*

Wood, J. 1872. *Journey to the Source of the Oxus.*

Yalden. W. B. 1972. 'Giant mole-rats in Ethiopia'. *Animals,* June,278–9.

Young, S. P. and Goldman, E. A. 1946. *The Puma.*

INDEX